RENEWALS 458-4574
DATE DUE

Small Firms, Global Markets

Small Firms, Global Markets

Competitive Challenges in the New Economy

Edited by

Jerry Haar

and

Jörg Meyer-Stamer

Selection and editorial matter © Jerry Haar and Jörg Meyer-Stamer 2008
Chapters © their authors 2008

All rights reserved. No reproduction, copy or transmission of this publication may be made without written permission.

No paragraph of this publication may be reproduced, copied or transmitted save with written permission or in accordance with the provisions of the Copyright, Designs and Patents Act 1988, or under the terms of any licence permitting limited copying issued by the Copyright Licensing Agency, 90 Tottenham Court Road, London W1T 4LP.

Any person who does any unauthorised act in relation to this publication may be liable to criminal prosecution and civil claims for damages.

The authors have asserted their rights to be identified as the authors of this work in accordance with the Copyright, Designs and Patents Act 1988.

First published in 2008 by
PALGRAVE MACMILLAN
Houndmills, Basingstoke, Hampshire RG21 6XS and
175 Fifth Avenue, New York, N.Y. 10010
Companies and representatives throughout the world

PALGRAVE MACMILLAN is the global academic imprint of the Palgrave Macmillan division of St. Martin's Press, LLC and of Palgrave Macmillan Ltd. Macmillan® is a registered trademark in the United States, United Kingdom and other countries. Palgrave is a registered trademark in the European Union and other countries.

ISBN-13: 978–0–230–00192–3 hardback
ISBN-10: 0–230–00192–0 hardback

This book is printed on paper suitable for recycling and made from fully managed and sustained forest sources. Logging, pulping and manufacturing processes are expected to conform to the environmental regulations of the country of origin.

A catalogue record for this book is available from the British Library.

A catalog record for this book is available from the Library of Congress.

10 9 8 7 6 5 4 3 2 1
17 16 15 14 13 12 11 10 09 08

Printed and bound in Great Britain by
CPI Antony Rowe, Chippenham and Eastbourne

Library
University of Texas
at San Antonio

Contents

List of Figures vii

Preface x

Notes on Contributors xiii

Part I Generic Issues

Introduction: The Environment of Small-enterprise Competitiveness 3
Jörg Meyer-Stamer and Jerry Haar

1 Local Development, Global Value Chains and Latecomer Development 18
   Peter Knorringa and Jörg Meyer-Stamer

2 Issues in Financing Small Enterprises 38
   Deborah L. Riner

3 The Unsuspected Player: Small Firms in Business with Low-income Sectors 63
   Patricia Márquez and Ezequiel Reficco

4 Innovation and Entrepreneurship among Born Global Enterprises 86
   Maija Renko and Jerry Haar

Part II Country Case Studies

5 Competitive Business Practices in Developing Economies: The Case of Small and Medium-size (SMEs) Companies in Mexico 105
   Jaime Alonso Gómez

6 Italian SMEs and Industrial Districts on the Move: Where are they Going? 131
   Anna Carabelli, Giovanna Hirsch and Roberta Rabellotti

7 Globalization and Spain's SMEs 166
   Guillermo Cardoza and Gastón Fornes

8 Unravelling Informal Entrepreneurship: Small-firm
   Clusters and Economic Ungovernance in Nigeria   192
   Kate Meagher

9 Indian Small Firms under Globalization:
   Has Policy Helped?   214
   Keshab Das

Conclusion: Between a Rock and a Hard Place:
The Harsh Reality of SMEs in the New Global Economy   236
   Jerry Haar and Jörg Meyer-Stamer

Index   243

List of Figures

I.1	Ratio of opportunity to necessity TEA by country (GDP per capita, US$)	5
I.2	Entrepreneurship rates (business owners per workforce) in six OECD countries	10
2.1	Assets held abroad by Mexicans in foreign bank accounts, 1990–2005	45
2.2	Companies citing suppliers as their principal financing source, by size of firm	47
2.3	Companies using bank credit: percentage borrowing for working capital	48
2.4	Reasons for not using bank credit: percentage citing high interest rates	49
3.1	Average ROE of leading micro-lending SMEs in Latin America (2002–4)	69
3.2	Delinquency among the most representative MFIs in 2004 (% overdue of loans)	69
4.1	Innovative and entrepreneurial characteristics of born global firms	96
5.1	SMEs in Mexico	106
5.2	Companies by number of employees and sector	107
5.3	Composition of companies by size and sector (per cent)	107
5.4	Number of SMEs, by sector and size	108
5.5	Companies in Mexico	109
5.6	SMEs: type of investment (percentage of companies that invested resources by concept)	111
5.7	Problems in Mexican SMEs	112
5.8	Mexican SMEs' main challenges	113
5.9	SME fund: main results, 2000–4	115
5.10	Programme inventory (by government institution)	116
5.11	Support programme inventory	117
5.12	Remittances: historical data, Mexico	126
6.1	The manufacturing sector by employment size classes in selected EU countries (percentage of each class over total manufacturing employment), 2002	134

6.2	Industrial districts: main indicators, 2001	137
6.3	Industrial districts: sectors of specialization (per cent)	138
6.4	Italian manufacturing export shares in world export by sector (1997–2004) (per cent)	142
6.5	IDs identified by ISTAT: 1991 and 2001 Industrial Censuses	144
7.1	Economic indicators in selected European countries, 2005	168
7.2	Exports, imports and trade surplus/deficit (in millions of euros)	168
7.3	SMEs' nominal and sectorial evolution in Spain, 1995–2003	169
7.4	Birth and death rates by sector (Spain and the EU in per cent, 2001–2)	170
7.5	Number of SMEs by volume of income (in millions of euros, 1 January 2003)	171
7.6	Perceived benefits of innovation by SMEs, 2003	172
7.7	Percentage of income invested in R&D in Spanish SMEs	172
7.8	SMEs' exports as a percentage of their income, 2003	174
7.9	Exporting companies per number of employees	174
7.10	Perceived opportunities of cooperation by SMEs, 2003	175
8.1	Socio-cultural and gender composition of enterprise heads	199
8.2	Occupational specialization and education (percent of enterprise heads)	200
8.3	Firm size and types of labor used	201
8.4	Supply Networks	203
9.1	Definitional investment ceilings criteria for SSI India, 1980–2006	217
9.2	Distribution of units in the SSI and tiny sector, 2001–02	218
9.3	Aspects of growth of SSI in India, 1990–2005	219
9.4	Rate of growth of SSI exports in India, 1990–2004	220
9.5	Export of major product groups from the Indian SSI sector, 1988–2003 (Value in Rs million)	221
9.6	Bank credit to SSI and tiny sector (Rs Million)	224

9.7	Status of infrastructure for SSI in Indian states	226
9.8	Sickness in small-scale industries, 1991–2004	228
9.9	Reserved items put on OGL	230
9.10	Units and workers in unorganized manufacturing, 1984–2001 (in million)	233

Preface

The currents of globalization will widen, deepen and intensify, impacting private enterprises both large and small, in both developed and developing nations. In fact, the distinction between developed and developing countries is becoming insignificant as far as economic policy challenges are concerned. Policy-makers in Mexico, Nigeria and Europe are similarly concerned about the impact of competition from East Asia. Businesses in North and South alike are concerned about concentration processes in the retail sector and the increasing power of retailers and other global buyers.

Smaller firms are the most vulnerable and are under enormous pressure to adapt in order to survive and compete. This holds true for both developed and developing countries. The plight of SMEs in developing countries has often been analysed. However, the process of globalization means that SMEs in developed countries are increasingly struggling to remain viable. With new regulations like Basel II, access to financing becomes more difficult. With the consolidation of global value chains, long-time suppliers are relegated to the third or fourth tier. WTO regulations make it more difficult for governments in industrialized countries to protect and pamper their SMEs; things are even more difficult for European SMEs due to EU subsidy controls. For developing countries, thanks to the WTO, the sharply focused infant-industry protection and industrial policy that was behind the rapid emergence of South Korea and Taiwan is not an option for today's latecomer countries. To quite a considerable extent, firms are left to their own devices.

However, adapting (a firm-based process) is insufficient. Changes in the external environment (state, local, institutional) must occur as well. Both developing and developed countries are trying to devise innovative approaches to business promotion and the creation of an enabling environment. Old-style interventions like industrial policy, top-down regional policy, trade protection and massive subsidy schemes have been phased out or are facing their demise. Both at national and local levels, governments are experimenting with new approaches. Being creative and innovative in the creation of SME promotion that is WTO-compliant is one of the key challenges governments in industrialized and developing countries are facing. The effectiveness in addressing this challenge is one of the main factors that shapes the long-term growth prospects of any country.

Concurrent with economic liberalization, a worldwide phenomenon, is the continuous expansion of political federalism. Central governments are divesting more and more governance and economic development responsibilities to state and local entities. As sub-regional economic promotion gains in importance, increasing attention will be focused on local industrial districts, or clusters, the value chains to which they are linked, and the small firms that compose the vast majority of enterprises within these locations. Cluster promotion, addressing market failure at the local level, and local economic development in general are widely used approaches both in developed and in developing countries.

In examining the forces and factors that shape the global competitive environment for small firms, and identifying representative case examples from around the world on successful and unsuccessful responses to competition, this volume addresses academic, policy and business practice issues vis-à-vis small-enterprise survival. The guiding questions are:

- What exactly are the challenges that small firms (for example, SMEs) are facing today? Has the 'second industrial divide' actually taken place, or is Chandler's view of the world more relevant than ever? Did the 'new competition' evolve in the way it was expected 15 years ago? And what about the 'new economy', for example, the impact of much more efficient means of communication and the collection and distribution of information – to what extent does it change the rules of the game both for territories and for different types of firms?
- What exactly are the challenges that policy-makers are facing today? Between local production systems and global value chains, what is the respective role of local, regional and national governments, as well as regional integration structures and international organizations? To what extent do public sectors manage to distribute different policy roles to different layers of government? How are territorial economies coping with the different governance challenges?

The volume is organized in two parts. The first part addresses generic questions, the second part presents country case studies. All contributions have specifically been written for publication in this volume.

We would like to thank our authors who toiled arduously, generously contributing their time and effort to bring this volume to fruition. We also thank the College of Business Administration at Florida International

University and the Columbia Program on International Investment and its director, Dr Karl Sauvant, for their assistance in this project. Deanna Salpietra of the Knight Ridder Center for Excellence in Management in FIU's College of Business Administration provided invaluable research and editing assistance, Professor Timothy Shaw of the University of London, editor of the Palgrave Macmillan series in International Political Economy, and Virginia Thorp of Palgrave Macmillan was very responsive and helpful throughout the process of manuscript submission through final acceptance.

Notes on Contributors

Anna Carabelli is Professor of Economics at Università degli Studi del Piemonte Orientale, Italy. She graduated from Bocconi University in Milan and received her Ph.D. at the University of Cambridge. Her research interests have been mainly in the field of economic methodology, epistemology, history of modern economic thought, with particular reference to Keynes and Hayek. She is the author of *On Keynes's Method* (Macmillan 1988) and of articles on Keynes's probability and uncertainty and on the comparison between Keynes and Hayek's views on expectations. Recently Dr. Carabelli also has been involved in the coordination of a research project on the financial structure and the financing of innovation.

Guillermo Cardoza, is a professor at the Instituto de Empresa Business School in Madrid and founding Director of the Euro-Latin America Center. From 1996 to 1999, Dr. Cardoza was Research Fellow at the Kennedy School of Government at Harvard University, where he undertook research on the management of innovation and competitiveness. He studied at Sorbonne Nouvelle University in Paris, where he obtained a Ph.D. in Business Economics as well as masters degrees in Latin American Studies, International Relations and Business Administration. He previously worked as an engineer for 3M Corporation. Dr. Cardoza has published articles in specialized journals and is currently doing research on innovation systems, internationalization strategies and comparative economic development. He also offers executive training programs in innovation to multinational firms.

Keshab Das is an associate professor at the Gujarat Institute of Development Research, Ahmedabad. A winner of the VKRV Rao Prize in Social Sciences (Economics) for the year 2004, he holds an M.Phil. in applied economics and a Ph.D. in economics from the Jawaharlal Nehru University, New Delhi, through the Centre for Development Studies, Trivandrum. Dr. Das has been a visiting fellow at the Institute of Development Studies, Brighton, U.K.; the Maison des Sciences de l'Homme (MSH), Paris; and Visiting Research Fellow at the Institute of Developing Economies, Chiba, Japan. He has published more than sixty research papers, and his books include *The Growth and Transformation of Small Firms in India* (Oxford University Press, 2001) and *Indian Industrial Clusters* (Ashgate, 2005).

Gastón Fornes joined the University of Bristol (UK) in 2004. He received a Ph.D. in management from the University of Bath (UK), a MBA from Universidad Adolfo Ibáñez (Chile), and his first degree in management from Universidad Nacional de Cuyo (Argentina). Before starting his doctoral studies, Dr. Fornes worked in industry for ten years in the U.S., Argentina, and Chile. His teaching centers on management in developing countries and foreign direct investment and its impact in the development process. His main research interest is management in emerging markets, especially foreign exchange exposure in these markets and the internationalization of companies from emerging countries. Dr. Fornes is currently doing research on the internationalization of Chinese companies vis-à-vis Latin America.

Jaime Alonso Gómez is a professor in the graduate school of business at Tec de Monterrey where be teaches strategy and international business. He has been a researcher and consultant for companies and institutions in the Americas, Europe, Asia and Africa. Dr. Gómez obtained his doctorate at the Wharton School of the University of Pennsylvania. Dr. Gómez serves on many boards and holds directorships in organizations, think tanks and institutions around the world. In 2005, Dr. Gómez was named 'Dean of the Year' by the Academy of International Business. Dr. Gómez is the first dean from Latin America and Spain in being recognized with this award.

Jerry Haar is a professor of Management and International Business and Associate Dean of International affairs and projects in the College of Business Administration at Florida International University. Dr. Haar is also a research fellow of the Columbia Program on International Investment. He has held visiting appointments at Wharton, Harvard, Oxford and Stanford, and was also a research associate at Columbia University and a Fulbright Scholar at the Fundação Getúlio Vargas in Brazil. Dr. Haar served as Director of Washington Programs for the Council of the Americas, a New York-based business association of over 175 corporations comprising a majority of U.S. private investment in Latin America. He holds a masters degree from Johns Hopkins University, Ph.D. from Columbia and completed an advanced management programme at Harvard. He has written 13 books and numerous articles, and has consulted for multinational firms, small businesses and public and multilateral organizations.

Giovanna Hirsch is currently researcher at AISLo (Italian Association for Local Development Studies). She holds an undergraduate degree in political science from the University of Turin, masters in political economy from the University of London and a Ph.D. in development studies from the University of Florence with a thesis on industrial cluster development and internal migration in China. She has been research fellow at the Universitià degli Studi del Piemonte Orientale. Her academic interests concern industrial clusters, SMEs and local development in developed and developing countries. The principal geographic foci of her work on economic development has been China, India and Italy.

Peter Knorringa is an associate professor in local and regional development at the Institute of Social Studies, a graduate school of social science based in The Hague. He has worked on value chain analysis and the role of global buyers; small enterprise development, clustering and local economic development; the role of trust, social capital, and networks in industrialization. His present research focuses on how to strengthen localised developmental impacts of fair trade, ethical trade and corporate social responsibility. Most of his research and project work has been in India and Vietnam, and some shorter research or advisory work in Indonesia, Ethiopia, South Africa and Siberia. He holds a Ph.D. from the Free University of Amsterdam.

Patricia Márquez is a professor at IESA's Center for Leadership and Organizations in Caracas, Venezuela. She leads IESA's participation in the Social Enterprise Knowledge Network (SEKN) and currently coordinates SEKN's research project 'Market-Based Poverty Reduction in Iberoamerica' (2005–2008). She was the Cisneros Visiting Scholar at the David Rockefeller Center for Latin American Studies (DRCLAS) and Visiting Professor at Harvard Business School for the academic year 2005–2006. Her teaching is in the area of corporate social responsibility; social enterprise; organizational behaviour and leadership. Professor Márquez received her B.A. in mathematics from Bowdoin College and her Ph.D. in socio-cultural anthropology from the University of California, Berkeley.

Kate Meagher is a British Academy Postdoctoral Fellow at the African Studies Centre, University of Oxford. She was a lecturer in rural sociology at Ahmadu Bello University in Zaria, Nigeria from 1991–1997, and completed a Ph.D. in Sociology at the University of Oxford in 2004. Her doctoral research, focusing on social networks and economic governance in informal manufacturing clusters, will soon be published as 'Identity Economics: Social Networks and the Informal Economy in Africa'. Dr. Meagher has published extensively on various aspects of the informal economy in Africa, including regional and global smuggling networks, the urban informal economy, rural non-farm activities, informal currency markets and theoretical work on social networks and informal economic governance. Her current research interests include collective organization in the informal economy, and the impact of informal economic networks on political process.

Jörg Meyer-Stamer is an academic and consultant. From 1998 to 2001 he was a project director at the Institute for Development and Peace, University of Duisburg, Germany, working on structural policy, competitiveness and sustainability in the state of North Rhine-Westphalia. Formerly, he was a fellow at the German Development Institute working on technology, industrial competitiveness, and economic and political development in Brazil. He is a founding partner in mesopartner, a consultancy firm specializing in local and regional economic development (www.mesopartner.com). He is the creator of the Participatory Appraisal of Competitive Advantage (PACA) method to kick-start or audit LED initiatives (www.paca-online.de). He has nublished numerous monographs and articles, many of which are available at http://www.meyer-stamer.de/profile.html. He holds a Ph.D. in political science from the University of Hamburg.

Roberta Rabellotti is a professor in the economics department at the University of Piemonte Orientale. She received her M.S. in development economics at the University of Oxford and a Ph.D. from the Institute of Development Studies, University of Sussex. Her areas of interest are industrial policies, small business promotion, international trade policies, industrial districts and clusters and sectoral industrial studies in developed and developing countries. Dr. Rabellotti has working experience with several international organizations such as the European Union, Inter-American Development Bank and United Nations. Author of over a dozen articles on global value chains, she is the co- editor with Carlo Pietrobelli of the book *Upgrading to Compete: Global Value Chains, Clusters, and SMEs in Latin America*.

Ezequiel Reficco is a senior researcher at Harvard Business School and a member of its Social Enterprise Initiative. His research focuses on the interplay between the strategies and social responsibility initiatives of corporations. He joined HBS as a researcher in 2001 and then joined its faculty during 2002–2004 as a post-doctoral fellow. He is currently based at the Harvard Business School Latin America Research Center, in Buenos Aires, Argentina. He has co-authored two books and has published in numerous popular and scholarly journals in the U.S., Europe and Latin America, such as the *Stanford Social Innovation Review* and *Harvard Business Review América Latina*.

Maija Renko is an assistant professor of business administration at the University of Illinois, Chicago. She holds a degree of D.Sc. in economics and business administration from the Turku School of Economics.

Previously Dr. Renko was a visiting assistant professor at Florida International University in Miami where she educated students in entrepreneurial thinking, business planning and strategic management. Her research aims at predicting and explaining the success and failure of high potential, technology-based start-up ventures. She has published numerous articles and book chapters on the management of technology and innovation, entrepreneurship and marketing. Dr. Renko's special interest is in understanding the success factors of new ventures in the field of biotechnology.

Deborah Riner holds a Ph.D. from Princeton University. She is the chief economist at the American Chamber of Commerce of Mexico. Prior to joining AmCham in 1990, Deborah was a vice president of Bankers Trust Company of New York. She speaks regularly to business and professional groups in Mexico and the U.S. The recipient of fellowships from the Brookings Institution, the Organization of American States and the Social Science Research Council, amongst others, Deborah has been a guest scholar at the Overseas Development Council, the Royal Institute of International Affairs, Universidad Católica de Chile. and Cedes in Buenos Aires.

Part I
Generic Issues

Introduction: The Environment of Small-enterprise Competitiveness

Jörg Meyer-Stamer and Jerry Haar

For quite some time, small and medium-sized enterprises (SMEs) were everybody's darling. Their importance for economic development was unchallenged. Their potential in establishing an international presence was, *inter alia*, documented by Germany's 'hidden champions' and by the small companies from Italy's industrial districts. A widespread perception saw SMEs as the main source of jobs, while big corporations were consolidating, outsourcing and downsizing all the time. Entrepreneurship – the launch of owner-managed small businesses – appeared as the main source of structural change, but also as an important vehicle for upward social mobility.

At the same time, there was wide agreement that SMEs suffered from a number of systemic disadvantages, such as a limited ability to invest in R&D and more difficult access to finance, and that they therefore merited specific benefits and targeted support. Some countries introduced special tax regimes for micro and small companies. In other countries, they enjoyed special status in terms of social security contributions or were exempt from laws that established intra-company trade union rights. There is hardly any country that does not have a variety of SME promotion programmes and institutions; for instance, the OECD's periodic reports on SMEs and SME promotion in its member countries give a good overview of the variety of programmes and activities (OECD, 2005). For the 2000–6 programming period of its structural funds, the Commission of the EU introduced SME support as one of the priorities. Likewise, SME promotion consistently is an element of national development policies in developing countries and in the foreign aid those countries receive.

But the benign view of SMEs has not remained undisputed. In recent years, research at the World Bank has questioned the impact of SMEs on growth and poverty alleviation. Beck, Demirgüc-Kunt and Levine(2003), using a sample of 76 countries, found a strong association between the importance of SMEs and GDP per capita growth. However, while a large SME sector is a characteristic of successful economies, the data in their study fail to support the hypothesis that SMEs exert a causal impact on growth. The researchers also found no evidence that SMEs reduce poverty.

Recent research on the link between entrepreneurship and growth came to a similarly disturbing conclusion. Stel, Carree and Thurik (2004) analysed whether the acclaimed impact of the total entrepreneurial activity (TEA) rate on economic growth stands the test of adding competing variables. They found that there is an impact but not a simple linear one of the TEA rate on GDP growth. Stel and his team found significant non-linear effect: the TEA rate has a negative effect for the relatively poor countries, while it has a positive effect for the relatively rich countries. The results show that entrepreneurship matters. However, the effect of entrepreneurial activity on growth is not straightforward.[1]

At country level, Italy has the highest share of SMEs in employment among the major industrialized countries. Many of them form part of 'industrial districts' – highly specialized local agglomerations of firms. Since the 1980s, a body of literature emerged that pointed to the potential of agglomerated SMEs to become internationally competitive (Piore and Sabel, 1984; Becattini, 1990). More recently, though, the strong role of SMEs has been linked to the weak performance of the Italian economy since the late 1990s (*The Economist*, 2005). Critics of the Italian model point at the low productivity growth and the relatively low R&D/GNP ratio, both of which can be causally linked to the strong presence of SMEs in the Italian economy.

How can one make sense of these findings? Is the main conclusion that Chandler was right, and that the 'flexible specialization' model suggested as an alternative to a Chandlerian way of organizing an economy by authors like Piore and Sabel (1984) and Best (1990) has not passed the test of time? Before hastening to derive conclusions, one should consider a number of points.

Voluntary vs involuntary entrepreneurship

Individuals do not necessarily start a business because they have a brilliant business idea. Frequently, individuals become self-employed or start a micro or small business because there is no alternative. The view put forward by Soto (1989) that the world of micro-enterprises is a hotbed of entrepreneurship is not necessarily wrong, but it is definitely

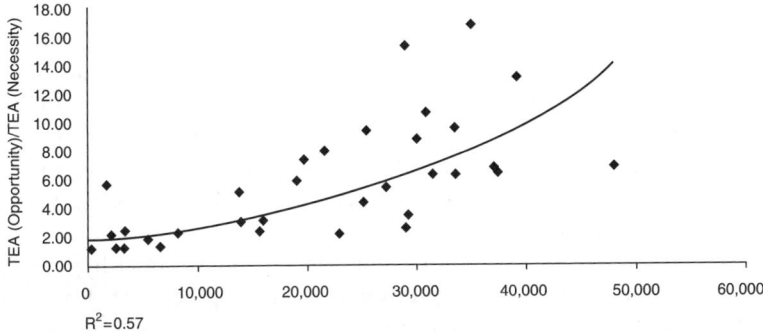

Figure I.1 Ratio of opportunity to necessity TEA by country (GDP per capita, US$)

only part of the story. The *Global Entrepreneurship Monitor* (Acs et al., 2005) has taken this issue up by distinguishing between 'opportunity' and 'necessity' entrepreneurs.

The curve that indicates the correlation between per capita GNP and the prevalence of opportunity entrepreneurship does not slope quite as steeply as one might expect. In other words, it is not only in developing countries that individuals start their own business because there is no alternative source of income. 'Informal sectors' that are not defined formally, in terms of registration, but qualitatively, by precarious work conditions and limited competitiveness, have also evolved in advanced industrialized countries.

There is also another important starting point for 'necessity entrepreneurship'. Both in developed and in developing countries one of the drivers of involuntary 'necessity' entrepreneurship is outsourcing. Not only large corporations but also SMEs themselves opt for outsourcing to reduce their fixed costs and to reduce the cost of labour, especially by saving on the social security contributions and levies that they have to pay on top of the net wage. From this angle, the issue is not one of growth and SMEs vs large companies, but rather growing shareholder value plus decreasing employment in large companies linked with increasing involvement of SMEs as subcontractors.

Limits to growth

A point that has been increasingly emphasized by agencies like the World Bank is the persistence of unfavourable business environments in many developing countries, despite lengthy efforts to 'structural adjustment'. The structural adjustment approach of the 1980s and 1990s tended to look at macroeconomic factors while neglecting microeconomic issues, such as the functioning of markets. The simple truth is, though, that from the perspective of an SME owner, macroeconomic reform has not been particularly successful. From the perspective of a business person, many of the adjustment processes that have taken place over recent years simply appear as a sequence of shocks and random changes in the rules of the game.

In a country like Brazil, the last major macroeconomic shock happened in 1999 (abandoning a managed exchange rate approach, leading to a massive devaluation), or perhaps in 2003 (another massive devaluation due to political uncertainty). It is difficult to say when severe macroeconomic turbulence started – when annual inflation increased above 50 per cent in the early 1960s? Or when the first oil shock ended the short-lived 'economic miracle' in 1974? Or the beginning of the debt crisis in 1982? In any case, a business owner who has been in business for 30 years has spent most of her life in a hyper-turbulent, unpredictable environment, and a few years of relative stability do not change the attitude that one had better brace oneself for the next crisis. Staying small, limiting the growth of one's business and thus the exposure to external shocks, is a perfectly rational approach.

Thus, in many developing countries the high share of SMEs is not correlated with growth because a significant number of those SMEs prefer to stay small since pursuing a growth strategy would involve major, unmanageable risks. Stabilization policies only reinforce the perception of instability as they involve fundamental changes in the rules of the game, thus one must expect a long time lag before SME owners manifest trust in a new environment of macroeconomic stability and embark on expansion projects.

Where do large corporations come from?

There is no natural trajectory from small to medium to large enterprise. Large corporations, and also many medium-sized enterprises, start out that way and remain that way for a variety or reasons (for example, mergers and acquisitions, leveraged buy-outs, management buy-outs). Compared to the total number of entries, the growth of a micro enterprise into a corporate behemoth, Microsoft-style, is a rare occurrence. The vast majority of SMEs stay in the SME world through their entire life cycle. This can be due to a variety of reasons, from the fact that for specific activities small size is the optimal size, to limited access to funding for ambitious expansion, to a lifestyle decision of the business owner, to the fact that the business owner is not particularly competent. And it is not only lifestyle decisions of business owners that can have an impact on economic performance. When the McKinsey Global Institute (1997) finds that the food industry in European countries is significantly less productive than its US counterpart, this is to some extent explained by lifestyle decisions of consumers, for instance a preference for bakery products that are produced and sold in a neighbourhood business, which usually is an SME.

Why look at SMEs?

Thus, there are numerous reasons why the tenuous link between entrepreneurship, presence of SMEs and growth of an economy should not come as a surprise. However, it would be unwise to conclude from this statistical observation that SMEs should be left to their own devices. SME promotion per se may cause neither growth nor poverty alleviation, yet at the same time there is not a single high-income economy without a competitive SME sector. The SME sector must not be glorified, and it is unwise to limit business promotion activities to SMEs. Nevertheless, it is essential that the variety of market failures that stand in the way of the SME sector are addressed. The question is not so much *whether* to promote SMEs but rather *how* to do it.

SME promotion in developing countries

In this respect, the practice in developing countries has been confronted with a fundamental critique and a new set of recipes. In the course of the 1990s, a body of literature on SMEs in developing countries has evolved that had little connection to academic research. The Committee of Donor Agencies for Small Enterprise Development, set up by a number of bilateral (for example, USAID, GTZ) and multilateral (World Bank, ILO) donor agencies, assessed the track record of decades of SME promotion activities, and the results were sobering (Donor Committee, 1998; see also http://www.bdsknowledge.org/). Not only had many projects not achieved their objectives, they had often done more harm than good. Usually a significant number of private service providers that catered to SMEs existed in developing countries. Donor interventions often failed to take this into account, frequently setting up or supporting government-run SME support organizations that were not particularly effective but still created unfair competition for private service providers, which consequently battled to survive. The conceptual conclusion from this was the 'BDS approach'. BDS stands for 'business development services', and the main tenet of the approach was this: instead of distorting the market for business services, developmental interventions ought to build and strengthen service markets.

The BDS approach has shaped donor interventions in developing countries since the late 1990s. It has been disseminated through the Springfield Centre's annual BDS summer course and the ILO's annual BDS conference. However, the 2005 ILO conference reader stated the following:

> BDS market development terminology is fading in favor of vocabulary that explains how market development can help the poor benefit from economic growth. What was understood as BDS markets are increasingly called business service markets, commercially viable solutions, or support markets.

What happened? Basically, there were two processes at work. First, the BDS approach as it had emerged from the Donor Committee's work, suffered from serious flaws so that practitioners in the field battled to implement the approach according to the rule book. Altenburg and Stamm (2004) argue that the BDS principles are too market optimistic, underestimating the degree of market failure, and neglect the political dimension of service provision. They point out that many services are effectively public goods, and that even services that might be private goods barriers to entry for potential providers can be significant. Moreover, politicians prefer highly visible interventions to silently functioning markets, therefore they will tend not to be excited about the BDS approach. Caniels and Romijn (2005) argue that effective services are the outcome of a lengthy interactive learning process between provider and customer, whereas the BDS approach encouraged standardized 'off-the-shelf' services that were supposed to become commercially viable in a very short period of time. The BDS approach thus missed the key point related to the D in BDS, for example, the emergence of services that have a significant developmental impact rather than addressing everyday routines in customer firms.

Second, though, the core message of the BDS approach has spread into the wider field of private sector development. The core message is that developmental interventions must try to build markets and make markets work better, rather than crowding out markets through government interventions (Ferrand, Gibson and Scott, 2004). This approach is even more optimistic regarding the potentials of markets and, just like the BDS approach, it is informed by marketing thinking rather than a sound conceptualization of markets and market failure on the basis of microeconomic theory. Just like the BDS approach, it ignores the crucial distinction between necessity- and opportunity-driven entrepreneurship. The deeper insight, which donors hesitate to acknowledge, is that there are small and medium-sized businesses that must be the object of economic policy considerations, while there is a huge number of micro and small enterprises that exist because of the lack of alternative income opportunities and that ultimately are a response to the absence of effective social policy. Lumping all sorts of micro, small and medium-sized businesses together and addressing them under headers such as 'promoting competitiveness' does not do justice to the diverse realities that underlie the SME sector and the diversified policy responses that are needed.

SME evolution and promotion in industrialized countries

The research quoted above questions the widely held perception that SMEs are a source of growth and prosperity in developing countries. However, the same research indicates that in industrialized countries SMEs are causally linked to growth. In fact, the pattern of SME evolution in industrialized countries has changed profoundly since the 1970s and 1980s. Until that period the relative importance of SMEs decreased. It is noteworthy that most industrialized countries have seen the tide turn from 20 to 30 years ago. Figure I.2 illustrates this phenomenon with reference to some European countries.

What exactly has caused this change in the evolutionary pattern is the object of discussions among researchers. One of the determining factors is, in all likelihood, technology. In many industrial sectors, technological change has lowered the minimum efficient scale for production. New industrial and service sectors have evolved and, thanks to the 'innovator's dilemma' (Christensen, 2003), established corporations are often slow to pick up radical innovation that ultimately generates new sectors, leaving the door wide open for new entrants.

Despite the revitalization of SMEs, the life of an SME in an OECD country is not an easy one. Since SMEs are perceived as important creators of jobs, governments in all countries and at all levels are busy promoting them in one way or another (OECD, 2005).

SME promotion activities are to a large extent designed by government officials; however, they are not exclusively designed against the background

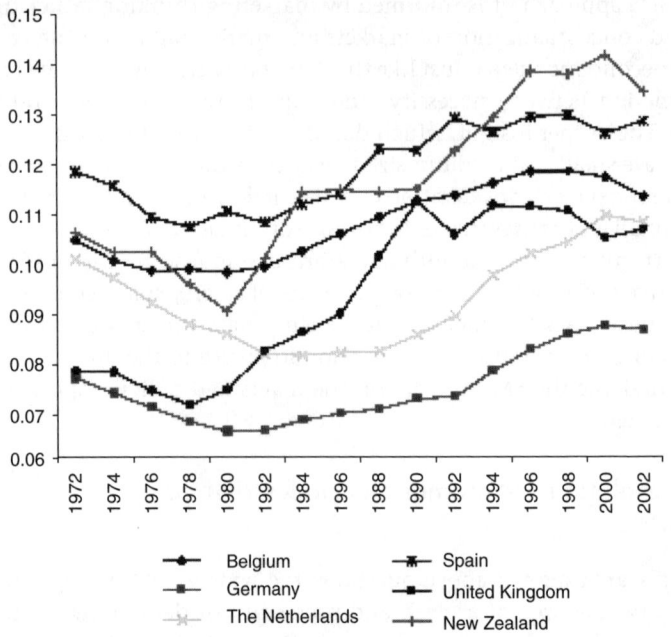

Figure I.2 Entrepreneurship rates (business owners per workforce) in six OECD countries

of the main bottlenecks indicated by SME owners. In an EU survey that was conducted in 2005, SMEs were asked: 'Which of the following would best assure the development of your company?' 31 per cent of respondents opted for 'social and fiscal regulations more suited to your sector of activity' (Eurobarometer, 2005). And indeed many governments have introduced policies to reduce the burden of red tape on companies. German government at national, state and local level were among them. Nevertheless, a study found that between 1994 and 2003 the cost of interacting with the public sector had increased by 75 per cent for small companies and by 130 per cent for medium-sized enterprises (Kayser *et al.*, 2004).

A distant second response in the Eurobarometer survey was 'better qualified people available in the market' (16 per cent), a complaint that also refers to what in most countries is a function of government. In other words, almost 50 per cent of respondents found that the growth of their business was constrained by dysfunctionalities in core government functions.

Governmental SME promotion agencies, on the other hand, tend to promote those issues that scored much lower, such as 'easy access to means of financing' (14 per cent) or 'an advice and support service for the development of your company' (6 per cent). Many governments have created a wide variety of organizations to provide all sorts of financial support (from grants to cheap credit to collateral to venture capital) and real services to SMEs. It is not unusual to find that there are actually so many organizations and promotion programmes that another burden is created for SMEs. Already entangled in red tape, they are now expected to enter a dense jungle of promotion activities. One of the 'dirty little secrets' of SME promotion organizations is that their outreach is quite limited. England's SME-focused business support services reach 10 per cent of SMEs (Caniels and Romijn, 2005), and that is actually a much higher share than that of organizations in other countries (which for obvious reasons prefer not to publish such data).

Globalization and the changing competitive environment for SMEs

Even those SMEs that in principle are entrepreneurial and capable of competing in highly selective markets are facing growing challenges, in particular if they serve more than local markets. National and international markets are transformed through the effects of the economic globalization process. Corporate internationalization through foreign direct investment (FDI) has happened for centuries, mostly driven by an interest to gain access to raw materials or markets. Since the 1960s, another motive has become relevant, namely the search for cheap labour. Many multinational companies relocated labour-intensive but not skill-intensive parts of their production process to countries with low labour costs. This process not only involved huge corporate behemoths but also many medium-sized companies.

The internationalization of companies is only one of the drivers of globalization, though. Another one, increasingly important, is the evolution of global value chains that are mostly organized by lead firms in industrialized countries. The evolution of national and global value chains has been one of the most important transformation processes in the world economy in the past three decades. Often retailers are the lead firms. Prominent examples are Tesco and Metro in groceries, Ikea in furniture and Hennes + Mauritz in fashion. In other industries, for instance in vehicle manufacturing, the manufacturers themselves rule the value chain. In other industries, companies that specialize in design and branding yet don't have their own factories have evolved, one of the most famous cases being Nike.

The evolution and increasing diversity of internationalization patterns has a variety of implications for SMEs. To begin with, a disproportionate share of FDI continues to go to China, contributing to the rise of that nation as the 'workshop of the world'. Companies everywhere, and in particular SMEs that so far have survived in niches and local markets, are under a constant threat that their customers confront them with the 'China price' – a threat to switch to Chinese suppliers unless the suppliers significantly reduce their price.

Related to the above, there has been a consolidation of supplier networks, such as those in the motor vehicle. Some suppliers, typically medium – to large companies, were encouraged to follow their customers to production locations all over the globe. Other erstwhile first-tier suppliers, typically SMEs, were relegated to second, third or fourth tiers, with severe consequences for their growth and upgrading options (Humphrey, 2000).

Another pattern is the increasing internationalization of services, most visibly, but not limited to, information technology (and here not restricted to software development in India). If the Indian experience is any indication, the main beneficiaries appear to have been large companies, both on the customer and the provider side.

Finally, there is the increasing relevance of product and process standards in international supply and subcontracting relationships, a trend that raises the barriers for SMEs' entry into international supplier networks and value chains.

For SMEs, especially for those in developing countries, the evolution of global value chains is not necessarily a blessing. The barriers to entry tend to rise, since lead firms are extremely demanding. Before even being considered as a supplier, a company must have a solid track record in business and quality, and it must comply with a variety of standards; obtaining them involves a lengthy and costly process. Being part of a value chain makes business more stable and predictable, but also more nerve-wracking since buyers constantly demand lower prices. To some extent, the emergence of relatively clearly structured global value chains may make the structure of the world market more transparent. The unvarnished truth, however, is that the world market is still an extremely complex and complicated animal, which can hurt SMEs badly if they don't thoroughly understand the rules of the game. For SMEs in developing countries, especially those who have little experience in international markets, the barriers to entry are high and increasing.

SMEs in industrialized countries may be familiar with the rules of the game, but they certainly do not like them. SMEs in a globalized market continue to find themselves between a rock and a hard place.

An overview of the chapters

In presenting the competitive challenges before small firms in the new economy – the theme of this book – the editors have organized the volume in two parts: one examines generic issues on the topic, and the other provides several case studies.

The first chapter addresses the critical context of small firms and their relationship to global market challenges – namely, local industrial development and its nexus to global value chains. Peter Knorringa and Jörg Meyer-Stamer point out that industrial policy disappeared in the 1980s and 1990s and was replaced by a new pressure on local governments, resulting in an increase in government-driven local economic development (LED) efforts. They argue that, although these efforts have been reinforced by recent value chain promotion, they must be complemented with strategic national initiatives if they are to be successful.

While efforts to develop and support clusters, strengthen value chains and promote sound governance are indispensable to small-firm competitiveness, these initiatives will not produce expected results without access to financing for SMEs. Deborah Riner examines issues in financing small enterprises – firms that share the common problem of access to capital regardless of where they are located. Her chapter summarizes SME literature on the subject and uses the case of Mexico to discuss the institutional constraints on SME financing – ones that apply to all developing countries, not just Mexico. She points out that the sources of financing that are most appropriate for SMEs depend on the institutional and economic context in which the firms do business. That context is different in developed countries and developing countries and between the developing countries themselves.

Although small firms are often constrained by their size in competing with larger enterprises, they do possess advantages in serving the large and growing low income sectors (LIS). Patricia Márquez and Ezequiel Reficco assert that SMEs are ideally positioned to work with LIS because of their mission centrality, proximity and flexibility and innovation. They discuss they ways in which SMEs can help to integrate LIS into the value chain as customers, suppliers and partners and allow LIS to become engines of value creation through access to the economy and transfer of skills.

If small and medium-size enterprises are to succeed in the global economy, public sector policies, financial accessibility, and niche strategies (for example, targeting low income sectors) will weigh heavily in the competitiveness equation but will be insufficient without the key forces of innovation and entrepreneurship. Focusing on SMEs in Finland's software sector, Maija Renko and Jerry Haar examine innovativeness and entrepreneurial orientation of young, small firms that internationalize at an early stage and their relationship to competitiveness. They identify four characteristics that are essential for the success of internationally oriented, innovative and entrepreneurial SMEs: people, markets, technology and networks.

Global case studies of Mexico, Italy, Spain, Nigeria and India illustrate how some of the generic issues and related subjects discussed in the first part of the book play out at the country level. Jaime Alonzo Gómez describes the current state and future prospects of Mexican SMEs – enterprises that comprise 99 per cent of total businesses in the country yet only 10 per cent of exports. He assesses that SMEs lack management know-how, technology, access to finance, human capital, customer service and innovation that are necessary for them to grow. SMEs lack an export orientation, logistics infrastructure, relationships with universities and research centres necessary for international expansion. The government has developed industrial policies and programmes to help create, develop and consolidate SMEs, but more macro and regulatory reforms are needed, according to Gómez.

Focusing on Europe, Anna Carabelli, Giovanna Hirsch and Roberta Rabellotti investigate Italian SMEs and industrial districts and convey intriguing findings. Italy has suffered from the structural changes experienced by the Europe Union. Since the late 1990s, the Italian economy has experienced a slow-down in economic growth, mainly due to the decline in labour productivity. The decline has been in particular in the 'Made in Italy' manufacturing sector, which is dominated by small firms and the traditional sector. The three authors address manufacturing systems and the predominance of SMEs and their organization in industrial districts, specialization in the so-called traditional sectors and the international pattern of specialization. The second section then presents a review of the recent and more interesting studies analysing the main changes that are occurring in industrial districts: the shift in production specialization, the international strategies of firms and districts, their innovation capacity and the emergence of new forms of enterprise organization.

The Spanish economy has been gaining importance in the world stage and its companies are continuously improving their competitiveness. In the last ten years, Spain has become a net exporter of capital and was in the first group of countries launching the Euro. Guillermo Cardoza and Gastón Fornés, in examining globalization and Spain's SMEs, argue that in spite of all this, Spanish productivity is 20 per cent lower than that in the EU due to the low level of development of the country's innovation system. This deficiency is caused by low corporate investments in R&D+I, weak links between universities, businesses and public entities, and the low level of human resources. Cardoza and Fornés give an overview of the Spanish economy along with a description of the SME sector (99 per cent of companies are SMEs) in Spain and the challenges that these companies face in global markets. The chapter also describes important policies and incentives available for promoting the development of SMEs in Spain, with particular attention on cluster formation, the industrialization of regions and the roles of business associations, universities and business schools in the consolidation of companies.

Informality in the SME sector in Nigeria is the focus of intensive examination by Kate Meagher. She notes that small enterprise clusters are viewed to promote competitive small-firm development and create economic governance in which inter-firm networks coordinate economic behaviour. Clustered firms rely on the strength of social ties, which allow them to out-compete large formal sectors, especially during times of economic upheaval, unstable markets and weak states. Clusters have led to economic growth all over the developing world except in Africa, due to the lack of networks, trust and social ties and the existing networks being the wrong kind – relying on risk minimization rather than productivity enhancement. The widely held view is that African clusters lack embeddedness; and this chapter reviews the history and development of African clusters – three Nigerian clusters, in particular – to understand why they are not as successful.

Finally, turning to India, Keshab Das argues that small Indian firms have the potential to contribute to the economic progress of the country. India has a history of small-firm development policy that has aimed to generate employment and reduce regional disparities in growth. However, Das asserts that the employment issue needs attention as post-reform small-firm policies have not given it much importance. Indian small enterprises must deal with roadblocks such as poor credit availability, low levels of technology and inadequate or absent basic infrastructure – physical and economic.

Small firms face daunting challenges in confronting the direct and indirect impacts of globalization. Clusters, value chains and governance are being reassessed and reshaped due to this trend. And each country and sub-region, down to the municipal level, is experiencing changes – some by choice, some by necessity – as they strive to not only preserve but expand growth, development, employment, competitiveness and overall economic well-being. The following chapters delve into the dynamics of small-firm competitiveness in global markets and, it is hoped, provide illumination of the policy options and strategic choices facing the SME sector worldwide.

Note

1. Note that 'relatively poor countries' in this case refers to countries like Argentina, China, Hungary, India, Mexico, Poland and Thailand.

References

Acs, Zoltan J., Arenius, Pia, Hay, Michael and Minniti, Maria (2005), *Global Entrepreneurship Monitor. 2004 Executive Report*, Babson College, London Business School, London.

Altenburg, Tilman and Stamm, Andreas (2004), *Towards a More Effective Provision of Business Services*, German Development Institute, Bonn.

Audretsch, David and Thurik, Roy (2004), *A Model of the Entrepreneurial Economy*, Max Planck Institute for Research into Economic Systems, Jena.

Becattini, G. (1990), 'The Marshallian Industrial District as a Socio-economic Notion', in F. Pyke, G. Becattini and W. Sengenberger, *Industrial Districts and Inter-firm Co-operation in Italy*, International Institute for Labour Studies, S., Should this 'S' be retained? Geneva.

Beck, Thorsten, Demirgüç-Kunt, Asli and Levine, Ross (2003), 'Small and Medium Enterprises, Growth, and Poverty: Cross-country evidence' Research Working Paper 3178, World Bank, Washington, DC.

Best, Michael H. (1990), *The New Competition. Institutions of Industrial Restructuring*, Polity Press, Cambridge.

Caniels, Marjolein and Romijn, Henny (2005), 'What Works, and Why, in Business Services Provision for SMEs: Insights from Evolutionary Theory', Working Paper 05.03, Centre for Innovation Studies Eindhoven.

Christensen, Clayton M. (2003), *The Innovator's Dilemma*, Harper Business, New York.

Donor Committee (1998), *Business Development Services for SMEs: Preliminary Guidelines for Donor-Funded Interventions. Summary of the Report to the Donor Committee for Small Enterprise Development*, Secretariat c/o PSD, World Bank, Washington, DC.

Eurobarometer (2005). SME Access to Finance, European Commission, Brussels.

Ferrand, David, Gibson, Alan and Scott, Hugh (2004), *Making Markets Work for the Poor. An Objective and an Approach for Governments and Development Agencies*, Commark Trust, Woodmead.

Humphrey, John (2000), 'Assembler-supplier Relations in the Auto Industry: Gobalisation and National Development', *Competition and Change*, 4(3), pp. 245–71.

Kayser, Gunter, Clemens, Reinhard, Schorn, Michael and Wolter, Hans-Jürgen (2004), *Bürokratiekosten kleiner und mittlerer Unternehmen*. Gabler, Wiesbaden.

McKinsey Global Institute (1997), *Removing Barriers to Growth in France and Germany*. Washington, D.C.

OECD (2005), *SME and Entrepreneurship Outlook*, Organisation for Economic Co-operation and Development, Paris.

Piore, Michael J. and Sabel, Charles F. (1984), *The Second Industrial Divide. Possibilities for Prosperity*, Basic Books, New York.

Soto, Hernando de (1989), *The Other Path: The Invisible Revolution in the Third World*, Harper-Row, New York.

Stel, André van, Carree, Martin and Thurik, Roy (2004), *The Effect of Entrepreneurship on National Economic Growth: An Analysis using the GEM Database*, Max Planck Institute for Research into Economic Systems, Jena.

The Economist, (2005), 'Addio, dolce vita'. A Survey of Italy, 26 November.

1
Local Development, Global Value Chains and Latecomer Development

Peter Knorringa and Jörg Meyer-Stamer

Introduction

In the course of the 1990s, the focus of productive sector development changed along two axes. There was a shift from promoting big companies and big development projects to emphasizing small and medium-sized enterprises (SMEs), and there was a shift from national-level development initiatives to localized activities. The clearest indication of these shifts is the demise of industrial policy. Thirty years ago there was little doubt that government had to play a crucial role in sectoral development, including industrial development, both in industrialized and in latecomer countries. Fundamental critiques of industrial policy were fringe phenomena. Much more common was criticism because of too little industrial policy; the political opposition would snipe at government for what appeared as inactivity that led to lost opportunities for wealth creation.

In the course of the 1980s and especially the 1990s, the picture changed completely. Industrial policy became a dirty word. Government intervention in industry was frowned upon. While in the 1980s Japan was still admired for the success of its industrial policy guidance in areas like microelectronics, since the 1990s selective government interventions, never mind guidance, were widely perceived as something that necessarily creates distortions and thus welfare losses (World Bank, 1993; Pack and Saggi, 2006). The focus of policy interventions shifted from discretionary interventions to efforts to create a more enabling environment for competitiveness through liberalization, deregulation and an effort to cut red tape (World Bank, 2004). Effectively, national governments both in industrialized and developing countries have gradually pulled out of active industrial development policies (and in developing countries also out of active agricultural development policies).

This has created both an opportunity and a necessity for regional and local governments, such as provinces/states, districts and municipalities. The necessity was due to the fact that structural change in many locations led to job losses, and that the pressure to create jobs was felt almost everywhere. Local politicians who wanted to be elected or re-elected could not ignore this issue. They could not stand at the sidelines and wait for markets to work their miracle – maybe. They needed to be seen as doing something here and now to create jobs. In many developing countries, the pressure on regional and local decision-makers was reinforced by decentralization processes, which effectively delegated many responsibilities to provincial and local governments. In some countries, like South Africa and Bolivia, economic development policy nowadays is a statutory task of local government. Thus, there has been a strong pressure on provincial and local politicians to launch economic development initiatives. The result has been a massive increase in government-driven local economic development (LED) efforts all over the world.

More recently, LED efforts have been complemented and sometimes reinforced by value chain promotion initiatives, both at a regional and at a national and international level. Practical experience and research showed that national and international markets are by no means an atomized world of infinite numbers of suppliers and customers (Rauch, 1999). Many market segments are governed by a small number of very powerful players, such as big retailers (Gereffi, Humphrey and Sturgeon, 2005). Entering the market often means moving onto the radar screen of the buyers of those retailers. Thus, policy-makers realized that promotional activities must not only strengthen the supply capability but also make an active effort to establish links with the gatekeepers to relevant markets.

In this article we will argue that a focus of economic development policy on LED and value chain development suffers from intrinsic limitations in terms of the outcome that can be expected. While it improves the environment for business and can thus be expected to have a tangible effect on growth and welfare, it will only induce an incremental change in terms of economic growth and improved standard of living. In particular, an economic development policy that focuses primarily on territorial initiatives will do nothing to change the position of developing countries in the global economic hierarchy. Countries like South Korea, Taiwan, Malaysia and Chile would never have emerged as newly industrializing countries if they had limited themselves to territorial development activities and value chain initiatives. LED and value chain development are important approaches, but they need to be complemented with strategic national initiatives if developing countries want to move out of a dependent integration into global value chains (GVCs).

Local economic development

Before having a closer look at value chains, we will examine local economic development (LED). We start with the upside, that is, the potential of localized development efforts. We then investigate the downside – the limits and dilemmas involved in LED.

The upside of LED

One variety of local economic development in particular has attracted a huge amount of interest over the past 20 years, namely cluster development. Industrial clusters were rediscovered in the 1980s (Piore and Sabel, 1984; Becattini, 1990; Porter, 1990). Most striking was the case of Italy, where growth in industrial output and exports was to a significant extent sustained by highly specialized and competitive clusters of SMEs. Italian 'industrial districts' were not only agglomerations of small companies that happened to be co-located. Industrial districts tended to display a long history of collective efforts to build a location-specific competitive advantage. They seemed to represent an alternative trajectory in industrial evolution. There was the Chandlerian model of huge corporations, and there were industrial districts that consisted of SMEs who competed quite successfully with huge corporations. The competitiveness of these clusters was based on a combination of intense local rivalry, effective collective action, relatively low transactions costs, due to relational contracting, and intense learning – by interacting.

The phenomenon of SME-based clusters that compete successfully in the world market is not limited to Italy and its specific economic, political and cultural features. For instance, we found that the ceramic tile cluster in Castellón de la Plana, Spain, is even more competitive, and displays even stronger collective action at the local level, than its counterpart in Sassuolo, Italy (Meyer-Stamer, Maggi and Seibel, 2004). The Castellón cluster had a more effective industry association and, thanks to effective interaction between private sector and provincial government, a stronger capability in skills development and applied research.

Generally, successful clusters have been observed in numerous industrialized and a number of developing countries (Linde, 2002). However, the feature that is highlighted in the case study on Italy in this volume also holds true for other countries: a disproportionate number of SME-based clusters specialize in consumer non-durables. Clusters are very effective in overcoming some of the obstacles to growth that stand in the way of SMEs, for instance, underinvestment in skills development. But they face limitations when it comes to creating capital- and/or technology-intensive industries.

Cluster promotion has become one of the most widely used LED approaches since the 1990s. Yet cluster promotion is only one of the elements of local economic development. In industrialized countries, where LED has been practiced for decades, it has evolved from a narrow focus at the development of real estate and locational marketing for investment promotion purposes to encompass a wide range of generic and targeted activities.

Regarding generic LED activities, a main focus since the 1990s was the local enabling environment, that is, an effort to remove unnecessary or outdated regulations and to speed up registration and permit processes. There have also been efforts to address market failure, such as coordination externalities and asymmetrical information, something that in particular benefits business start-ups and SMEs. Local fairs, networking events, or efforts to mobilize investment capital for start-ups are typical tools used in this respect.

Regarding targeted activities, there were not only cluster initiatives but also all sorts of other interventions, such as the creation of high-tech incubators or efforts to strengthen the links between local research centres and higher education institutions and private businesses in order to create a knowledge-based local competitive advantage. Whereas large corporations tend to have a routine of leveraging knowledge and innovation for competitive advantage, SMEs tend to behave more erratically, and local policy-makers are thus keen to encourage a more consistent behaviour among SMEs regarding the use of knowledge for innovation. To the extent that knowledge generation is based on localized processes, LED initiatives can make an important contribution to improved SME competitiveness.

The downside of LED

What is the overall track record of LED in promoting growth and prosperity in general and in supporting SMEs in particular? Even in places where LED has been implemented for decades it is hard to find an answer. Dynamic local economies are usually the result of the interaction between market forces, entrepreneurship and chance, and occasionally the outcome of national government's planning and development efforts.

Success stories of genuine business-focused LED are few and far between, while stories of disappointments abound (Meyer-Stamer, 2003: 2ff).

Some success stories refer to generic LED, which is increasingly conceptualized as an effort to improve the effectiveness and efficiency of public sector service delivery to private businesses. An often quoted example is the US city Indianapolis, which in the 1990s, under mayor Stephen Goldsmith, tried to turn itself into an 'entrepreneurial city' by, *inter alia*, systematically eliminating outdated or unnecessary regulations.

Targeted LED is frequently a response to decline of old industries or to low growth in peripheral regions, and it is intrinsically difficult to measure its impact (Bachtler and Wren, 2006: 147). Looking at the specific case of cluster development, it is interesting to note that even its strongest proponents emphasize the long time horizon needed to see an impact (Andersson *et al.*, 2004: 77ff). In fact, there is relatively little evidence of an impact of cluster initiatives, and research found that government interventions have only a very small effect on the evolution of clusters (Enright, 2000). Successful cluster initiatives are usually driven by the private sector (Sölvell, Lindqvist and Ketels, 2003) rather than the public servants who populate conferences that target 'cluster practitioners'.

How about the prospects of LED making a significant difference to the growth performance of not-so-dynamic regions in industrialized and transformation countries, and to all sorts of locations in latecomer countries? We tend to argue that the currently dominating approaches to LED are intrinsically limited in their potential to make a significant impact on development, that is, they are unlikely to lead to a leap in growth and prosperity. In the following four subsections, we will outline key reasons why LED's impact is limited. Our argument refers primarily to transformation and developing countries, though some of the points apply to industrialized countries as well.

Planning instead of doing LED

Most developing and transformation countries were governed in a highly centralized way until recently. LED is a new concept and task in these countries. The introduction of LED into developing and transformation countries is strongly influenced by foreign donor organizations. Institutions like the World Bank, UN Habitat and USAID promote an approach to LED that is primarily informed by urban planning concepts and methodologies. It has a strong bias for planning, and it is based on extensive stakeholder mobilization and consultation, such as comprehensive workshopping. This is an approach that dooms LED (Cunningham and Meyer-Stamer, 2005):

- The planning approach to LED confuses strategy with strategic planning. It is crucial for actors in a given location to have a clear understanding of the strategic positioning of the location, and to implement projects that strengthen this strategic position, and such projects should be based on sound planning methods. Yet a multi-year strategic plan that guides the overall development effort is likely to be quickly outdated in any location that tries to compete in a constantly changing global economy.
- The planning approach fails to acknowledge the difference between urban development and LED regarding the underlying governance pattern. Postmodern urban development, with its strong emphasis on citizen participation, flourishes 'in the shadow of hierarchy', in other words, there is a strong incentive for citizens (including corporate citizens) to participate since otherwise local government might come up with a less-than-ideal spatial plan, zoning regulations, etc. In LED, on the other hand, there is no shadow of hierarchy since local government cannot credibly threaten with the formulation and implementation of something like an LED regulation.
- The planning approach is not informed by the reality of business, especially SMEs. Its engagement approach puts a heavy burden onto SMEs, which do not have time for endless stakeholder meetings and workshops. Effectively, it creates an incentive for local SMEs not to participate at all.
- The planning approach does not even pay lip service to concepts such as competitive advantage, and it fails to conceptualize the need to address market failure at a local level as a main reason to justify LED.

Evidence from Latin America, where many locations and regions went through strategic planning exercises during the 1990s, gives little support to the notion that strategic planning is a precondition for successful LED. Frequently, the effort in compiling a strategic plan seems to have been bigger than the effort in actually implementing it. The evidence that strategic plans have led to LED activities with a visible impact is thin.

Social policy instead of promoting competitiveness

In developing countries, there is more policy confusion around LED, often reinforced by donors who are under pressure to make their interventions more 'pro-poor'. This sometimes leads to LED being approached according to a social policy logic, not a business development logic. The main objective of this type of LED is to address low-income groups and to promote 'income-generating activities', often through temporary projects that depend on external support, funding and facilitation and never become sustainable; this has been amply documented for countries such as South Africa (Tomlinson, 2003). It is not rare to find that the prospect of sustainability is further undermined by secondary objectives, such as gender promotion, a focus at marginal groups, or affirmative action. This leads to overload and exaggerated expectations.

This problem of confusion between social and economic policy objectives has also been observed in industrialized countries, especially in the context of efforts to address long-term unemployment and social marginalization. In his critique of mainstream approaches to urban poverty in the US, Porter (1995: 66) observed that 'many programs train people for nonexistent jobs in industries with no projected growth'. Assessments of skills development schemes in West Germany in 2000/1 found that less than 50 per cent of participants were employed half a year later, and employment promotion schemes for long-term unemployed (which are typically organized at the local level) only managed to launch less than 30 per cent of participants back into the formal labour market (Hirschenauer, 2003). At the same time, the practical part of skills development and employment promotion schemes, for instance via work in public parks or as part of brownfield conversion schemes, created unfair competition for private SMEs in sectors like gardening and landscaping.

Confusing social and economic policy objectives under the umbrella of LED tends to lead to a situation where neither social nor economic objectives are achieved, and where actually the private sector in the local economy may be damaged.

Focus on an enabling environment

The focus on creating an enabling environment, which is currently the main thrust of the main donors' approach to private sector development in developing countries (cf. http://www.sedonors.org), encourages generic activities to the detriment of targeted interventions to create a competitive advantage in high potential sectors. There is nothing fundamentally wrong with addressing government failure and cutting red tape. But there is a good chance that this is an intervention that takes a lot of effort without rendering significant results because it does not address the main impediment for economic development; this kind of paradox, created by the application of standardized recipes, has recently been highlighted by Hausmann, Rodrik and Velasco (2006).

In poor locations, be it in peripheral regions or in declining industrial locations, private sector development tends to suffer more from market failure than from government failure. Perhaps the most important market failures are coordination externalities, which obstruct the emergence of those new economic activities that cannot be run by individual small businesses on their own. Typical examples would be tourism in poor regions, where a couple of small businesses need to complement each other to create an attractive package of activities – accommodation, catering, transport and supporting services – or new high-tech activities in declining regions. Developmental activities in poor locations and peripheral regions, as well as declining regions, need to address such coordination externalities. A focus on the enabling environment may make it easier to close down a business that is no longer viable in a declining region. But the developmental challenge is to sustain business retention and to promote the creation of new companies, not to facilitate the shut-down of established firms.

The locational policy paradox

LED tends to focus on small business since large companies, especially branches of large corporations, tend to be disinterested in LED initiatives that focus on creating a local competitive advantage (Meyer-Stamer, 2003). Companies of all sizes are interested in traditional, generic LED activities, such as development of real estate, infrastructure development and investment promotion. Yet when it comes to targeted activities to create a local competitive advantage, LED practitioners are battling to get large companies' participation, especially those that own hundreds if not thousands of facilities in almost as many locations across the globe. While companies may be strongly involved in local development activities at their home base, it is difficult to get them involved in genuine LED activities at branch level (as opposed to community involvement, sponsorship and similar activities).

Effective collective action at the local level is more than a rationally driven activity of maximizing utilization of economic actors. It is based on strong interpersonal networks. Creating them, and building the trust that is crucial for them to be effective, takes time. However, managing directors of local branches change frequently. Even if they have a mandate to engage in local relationships, they tend to find it hard to quickly build such relationships. Opting for sponsoring activities offers a much more attractive cost/benefit ratio.

Things are complicated even further by the habit of large corporations of acquiring, selling or spinning off business units. A local firm that plays an important role in LED may abruptly cease to do so because it has just been taken over by a multinational corporation, and the local founder-owner has been replaced by a foreign manager. A local branch plant that pursues an approach of actively engaging with the local community, thanks to the parent corporation's corporate citizenship principles, may abruptly cease to do so after it has been sold to another corporate. A local unit that is spun-off will usually start its life as a medium-sized or big company and will be busy positioning itself in the world market, rather than contributing to a local collective upgrading effort.

So is it good news for SMEs if they are the primary target of LED activities? The answer is both yes and no. SMEs benefit from generic interventions, be it infrastructure development or an effort to create a local enabling environment by cutting red tape. Large companies tend to be in a strong position vis-à-vis local government in both respects, especially when they can threaten with the downsizing or shut-down of local plants. SMEs need strong collective organizations to make their voice heard. A proactive effort by local government reduces the need for SMEs to get organized (and the transaction and opportunity costs involved in this). So with respect to generic LED activities, SMEs will usually enjoy benefits.

Things are more complicated with respect to targeted activities, and this is not only the result of the problems in involving local large firms. We have argued above that dynamic locations are the result of market forces, entrepreneurship and chance, and to some extent government intervention. This statement refers to the initial phase in the life cycle of a dynamic location. There is not really evidence that local government can play an active role at this stage, for instance, through 'local industrial policy', trying to target a specific emerging sector. Many local governments have tried this, and they have usually failed or created what Enright (2000) calls 'wishful thinking clusters'. Local industrial policy tends to be driven by fashions, not by competence and solid evidence. Following a widely acclaimed fashion ('nanotechnology is *the* future growth sector') makes it much easier for local policy-makers to justify their selective intervention, but it also minimizes the chance of success. A selective intervention that does not follow the fashion of the day, on the other hand, is difficult to justify and to sustain over a period of time.

In the growth phase it is common to observe the emergence of collective action within the local private sector, especially in areas with a strong propensity to market failure, such as skills development. In the maturity phase, the focus of collective action often expands to political articulation, trying to defend the achievements of the past. Local government sometimes plays a role in the growth phase, and it frequently plays a role in the maturity phase; and if the interventions at the maturity stage were not sufficiently effective, it will try to play a strong role in the decline phase. However, maturity and decline are typically phases of consolidation, that is, local SMEs merge into big companies or are acquired by large external companies, and this limits the latitude for local government action. In other words, there is only a limited time window for promising selective local government interventions during the growth phase of an emerging local cluster.

Interim conclusion: LED and SMEs

LED can make some difference. It can turn a given location into a place where it is easier to do business, for example, where the infrastructure is more efficient and transaction costs are lower than elsewhere. This is the result of generic LED. Efforts to pursue targeted LED are difficult, and there is little evidence that it has made a significant difference in the past.

LED can in particular make some difference to SMEs. Business owners often spend a disproportionate share of their time complying with government regulations so streamlining regulations and procedures generates an immediate benefit. One can make a strong argument that generic LED, which also includes infrastructure development, creating a more transparent real estate market, and other activities, benefits SMEs more than large companies.

At the same time, LED puts a burden on SMEs. A large business will typically send somebody from the corporate social responsibility department to LED strategy workshops, while an SME has to delegate somebody who otherwise would create direct value for the business; thus, the elaboration of an 'LED strategy' creates an opportunity cost for SMEs. SME projects that assist poor communities in generating some income sometimes create unfair competition for small local businesses.

More important, though, is the fact that LED rarely succeeds in launching catalytic interventions that open new growth opportunities for SMEs. Traditional national-level industrial policy focused mainly at large enterprises, but their growth created huge business opportunities for suppliers in the SME sector. Other national-level approaches, such as export promotion, were effective in some countries in opening new markets to SMEs. There is little evidence that the demise of these national-level, strategic interventions has been compensated for through LED. The experiences with value chain initiatives are instructive in this regard.

Value chains

Value chain promotion is emerging as an approach to link local producers to global markets. It is based on the observation that many markets are far from being the anonymous meeting places of numerous sellers and buyers, as assumed in simple microeconomic models. Instead, access to global markets nowadays often is controlled by a limited number of gatekeepers, namely global buyers that act as the spiders-in-the-web of global value chains. Supplying these global buyers has created new opportunities for exports from developing countries, leading to employment generation, foreign exchange earnings and fast-paced but selective upgrading of local producers. Before we discuss the downside of value chain promotion, this section deals with the important stimulus that value chain promotion can provide to more realistic demand-driven interventions.

The upside of value chain promotion

Traditional development approaches often upgraded local producers and then battled to find markets for their improved or new products. In contrast, value chain promotion is based on the insight that successful interventions start by looking at what the potential demand for the new or upgraded products is and how entry to final markets can be achieved through the gatekeepers. The value chain perspective draws attention to the sequence of activities from product conception to final consumers, stressing the importance and interrelatedness of activities within and beyond the actual production, notably design, logistics and marketing (Gereffi and Kaplinsky, 2001; Kaplinsky, Morris and Readman, 2002). Value chain maps visualize how different firms carry out the various main activities destined for particular market segments, and it shows the types of product, price, quantity, and numbers of buyers and sellers involved in specific chains. Such maps allow local producers, as well as policy-makers, to quickly improve their understanding of:

- who bargains with whom for what,
- where in the chain value added is concentrated,

- what are the opportunities and constraints for growth within existing chains,
- what are the chances and limitations for upgrading into higher value added chains and
- how to achieve most intervention leverage by addressing main bottlenecks in chains.

The value chain tool has proven a very useful analytical device to assist both producers and policy-makers in rationalizing their decision-making process about how and when to upgrade. An important upside of value chain promotion is that it brings the consumer and buyer perspective into the decision-making process around upgrading interventions. It makes producers more aware of their relative position within the bigger (value chain) picture. Therefore, it can help producers in better identifying their core competence or niche, and more sharply orienting themselves to strengthening this core competence and to developing strategic alliances with key stakeholders in relevant value chains, instead of 'workshopping' with everybody on everything. Moreover, the value chain tool can be used to collect views from global buyers on the relative competitiveness of producers in various locations (Schmitz and Knorringa, 2000). Such comparative assessments of competitiveness in the eyes of the buyers can act as a strong lever to 'shake up the entrepreneurs and make them hungry for outside assistance' (Schmitz, 2005: 19).

These comparative assessments can also be used by policy-makers to 'find a focus for their policies, programs or projects' (Schmitz, 2005: 19). More generally, the value chain perspective helps policy-makers and business support agencies to develop more targeted interventions, and achieve more leverage by addressing main bottlenecks that affect a multitude of producers (like providing a testing facility, which firms increasingly need as an entry requirement but cannot individually afford to set up). While traditional business support often drives producers deeper into overcrowded sectors by pushing them to do better what they do already, value chain promotion provides ammunition to investigate *how* overcrowded specific market segments might be, and whether opportunities exist to enter more attractive value chains (Schmitz, 2005: 21). As a rule, traders and buyers know more about distant markets and consumer behaviour than industrial policy-makers and publicly funded BDS providers (see, for example, UNDP *et al.*, 1988). Value chain analysis gives policy-makers and BDS providers a better understanding of how local producers are linked to global markets, and how they can be supported more effectively. In this way value chain promotion and demand-driven BDS can reinforce each other. Embedded BDS, that is, service delivery to producers through buyers, may be one extreme but promising example of this interaction (AFE, 2004; Anderson, 2000; Lauridsen, 2004). So far, embedded BDS delivery seems limited to smaller and traditional producers such as in handicrafts, where buyers are often domestic intermediaries. Global buyers in main consumer goods seem – understandably – hesitant to act as for a source of assistance, but more experiments are needed (Schmitz, 2005).

Among researchers and policy-makers often two different types of value chain promotion are distinguished: interventions to assist producers in achieving initial entry into global value chains, and interventions to stimulate further upgrading of producers that operate as suppliers in global value chains. These require different interventions. To achieve initial entry into global value chains, one needs to get (a group of) local producers on the 'radar screen' of one or more global buyers (usually through regional intermediaries and or scouts that are always on the look-out for new attractive production spaces). Next to upgrading local capabilities and standards to a 'threshold level', preparing the local ground, which includes infrastructure and other broader LED phenomena, selective networking is often crucial to secure some trial orders. Once initial entry has been achieved, the global buyers, and especially their regional intermediaries, usually start playing an important role in product and process upgrading.[1] It is especially in this initial phase where incipient suppliers go through a process of fast-paced process and product upgrading (Schmitz and Knorringa, 2000), also leading to increased employment and foreign exchange earnings. Obviously, achieving significant levels of local employment and foreign exchange earnings through such processing plants is not a mean feat. For example, from an LED perspective it might well be important in bolstering local effective demand. Nevertheless, an increasing number of authors in the value chain literature appear to be doubtful about the extent to which such processing plants are a likely first step in a more endogenous LED strategy.

The downside of value chain promotion

The barriers to entry for developing country producers to being integrated into global value chains are high, since most value chains are subject both to a variety of codified standards and to direct inspection by buyers. Getting on the 'radar screen' of the global buyers is a difficult and expensive process, and substantial investments are necessary to acquire product and process certification. Leaving aside the processing plants in 'export processing zones', usually only the already somewhat larger and more dynamic local producers in more diversified developing countries with a sizable domestic market, or located in the 'China-plusregion', are able to successfully enter global value chains. Therefore, it is an approach to further strengthen, streamline and bolster the achievements of 'local champion' companies, rather than an approach to develop new firms or achieve direct poverty alleviation in poorer regions.[2]

Producers in developing countries are usually integrated into quasi-hierarchical value chains, where the rules of the game are defined by buyers from industrialized countries. A key issue is the extent to which these asymmetrical relationships with buyers provide local producers with opportunities for learning and upgrading. Recent studies (among others, Gereffi, 1999; Schmitz and Knorringa, 2000) argue that global buyers often play a significant role in process and product upgrading, especially for their more favoured suppliers. The controversial issue is whether firms are also able to achieve functional upgrading, and to determine the role buyers play in furthering, neglecting or obstructing functional upgrading by their suppliers. While Gereffi´s study on garments recognizes that there are many obstacles to functional upgrading, he emphasizes the dynamic learning curves that producers in value chains are exposed to: moving from mere assembly to monitoring the entire production process, to design and sale of their own branded merchandise. In contrast, Schmitz and Knorringa (2000) found that in the footwear industry global buyers tended to see attempts at functional upgrading as encroaching on their core competencies and actively discouraged such attempts. One way around this problem is that especially somewhat larger producers in, for example, the Brazilian footwear and furniture industry actually participate in several value chains at the same time, and leverage the different capabilities acquired in the various value chains (Navas-Aleman, 2006). For example, in the domestic market they may operate in market-based relationships with wholesalers and retailers, selling their own designs, while using the process and product upgrading acquired in the quasi-hierarchical relationship with the global buyer. Another example that provides a nuance to the gloomy picture of captive world-class producers without a parallel development of design, branding and marketing capabilities, is the recent experience in the Vietnamese footwear industry. Here sub-national associations are carefully supporting producers to functionally upgrade in new production units without antagonizing the global buyers (Knorringa and van Staveren, 2006). More generally, Schmitz and Knorringa (2000) have argued that while participation in quasi-hierarchical chains leads to fast-paced process and product upgrading, market-based relationships with a variety of smaller buyers offer better opportunities for a slower but more balanced development of process, product *and* functional upgrading capabilities.

Nevertheless, by far most developing country producers in global value chains operate in quasi-hierarchical chains and are under constant pressure to improve quality and reduce prices, and they face substantial obstacles when it comes to functional upgrading, that is, moving into the higher value-added activities in the value chain. As local producers are constrained to processing activities under tight control by outside inspectors the local spin-offs are usually much more modest than initially anticipated. It turns out to be extremely difficult to forge a multitude of local horizontal, forward and backward linkages with such processing plants. Moreover, entrepreneurs and managers in such production plants often feel more 'attached' to their vertical value chain linkages, with outside actors, than to their horizontal local cluster linkages, which further limits the potential for local spin-offs. More generally, the conditions for locational upgrading efforts change profoundly once a local cluster has been spotted by global buyers. There is a strong incentive for local efforts before, while the focus of local producers shifts from local coordination to international interaction after. However, a crisis in the relationship with the global buyer may well lead to a new period in which local relationships become crucial again in achieving more broad-based functional upgrading at cluster level (Bazan and Schmitz, 1997).[3]

Notwithstanding the selective success stories of (clusters of) firms that have entered global value chains, and a widespread enthusiasm among industrial policy-makers, in recent years some analysts have become increasingly hesitant to advise policy-makers to try to follow this route (Kaplinsky, Morris and Readman, 2002; Knorringa, 2002). For example Kaplinsky, Morris and Readman (2002: 1175) wonder whether we are not guilty of a fallacy of composition in advising firms and regions to upgrade in order to enter global value chains as processors, as rents in processing are extremely low and too many new producers are fighting for the remaining crumbs in a market increasingly dominated by producers from the China-plus region.

In this context Kaplinsky has put forward the concept of immiserising growth,[4] where 'growing ... participation in industrial activities – reflected in the level of industrial activity, the growth in physical trade and the increase in industrial employment – may in fact become associated with declining overall standards of living' (Kaplinsky, 1998: 4). This negative macro effect is not because of an inefficient allocation of resources, but because of the pressures arising from economic globalization. Revenues from processing are very limited as compared to the revenues from, for example, designing and branding, and all competing potential suppliers are also busy upgrading, which leads to a situation of 'running to stand still'.

Especially in those labour-intensive sectors where developing countries have in recent decades become successful exporters, this trend is likely to lead to immiserising growth unless the firm or country in question can outpace competitors in process or product upgrading, or, even better but also more difficult, in functional upgrading. While individual firms or a specific country may use this as a successful development strategy, the tenet of the concept of immiserising growth is that this survival of the fittest can not constitute the basis for a broader and more inclusive development strategy that also benefits weaker economic actors and regions.

Kaplinsky concludes that: 'in previous eras, participation in industrial segments of the value chain provided the source for sustainable income growth. But, increasingly, in a globalising economy these industrial niches have become highly competitive, raising the spectre of immiserising growth' (Kaplinsky, 1998: 31). He argues that firms or countries need to identify and exploit specific rents from competitive advantages, but that the main lesson from recent history is that all rents are transitory and that new suppliers in GVCs basically carry out 'rent-poor' activities. Again, escaping from this immiserising-growth trap is something that might be achieved by some individual firms or countries, but the general trend is expected to be one of:

> declining real wages and declining real incomes in those countries specialising in rent-poor products.... The challenges thus confronting producers everywhere is to upgrade by appropriating whatever categories of rents are within their grasp, but to do so more rapidly than competitors in the knowledge that a rate of innovation lower than the average will result in immiserising growth. (Kaplinsky, 1998: 34)

This compelling and gloomy picture raises the question of how many niches in the global market can successfully be supplied by developing country suppliers to global value chains in a way that also provides a stimulus for local development. Even though global buyers will probably remain wary of becoming completely dependent on sourcing from the

China-plus region, producers from other regions will most likely also need to be able to target rather substantial and sophisticated market niches in their domestic (or regional) market to remain competitive. These domestic or regional market niches may well require producers to be well versed in design and branding activities, next to supplying to global buyers through quasi-hierarchical relationships. For more peripheral localities, with lots of low-potential SMEs but without some clear local champion firms with export potential, entry into (attractive) global value chains is likely to remain a remote option.

Conclusions

A country that addresses productive sector development, and in particular SME promotion, exclusively through LED and value chain promotion has effectively discarded the ambition to move upwards in the global economic hierarchy. The limits to the locally focused LED approach are not only related to the dependent integration of local producers into GVCs and the finding that the options for functional upgrading, that is, higher value added, are seriously limited once local producers have been integrated into a global value chain. The limits are also due to the intrinsic limitations of local approaches, which are the consequence of limited capabilities and resources of local policy-makers. LED and value chain promotion are incremental upgrading approaches. They are devoid of a vision for national development based on a consistent catch-up effort that involves not only upgrading within existing economic sub-sectors but also moving into new sub-sectors.

Latecomer countries need strategic interventions to build competitive sectors with a strong growth effect. This implies defining a new role for local government. It must not only create an enabling environment, but also pursue meso-level activities to shape a knowledge-based competitive advantage. This requires targeted support by higher levels of government, both in terms of funding and regarding conceptual guidance. The promotion of high-potential clusters would be one element of a strategic approach, which would be based on sectoral targeting. Recently, authors such as Dani Rodrik have pointed at issues such as persistent market failure, which stand in the way of purely market-driven development processes, and which condemn poor countries to remain stuck with a weak productive base (Rodrik, 2004; Rodrik and Hausmann, 2006). Esser et al. have argued since the early 1990s that 'systemic competitiveness' is the result of a collective effort of various societal actors (Esser *et al.*, 1996; Meyer-Stamer, 2005). This does not imply a call for traditional 'picking winners' policy but rather network-based governance patterns to shape economic upgrading efforts.

Strategic upgrading efforts are not an alternative to LED and to localized efforts to integrate producers into value chains. All these approaches have important roles to play, and ultimately they complement each other. The point is that all of them need to be in place. Relying on a partial approach only is unlikely to pull countries out of poverty.

Notes

1. Upgrading, in value chain literature, is usually broken down into: process upgrading (doing things better); product upgrading (producing better goods); and functional upgrading (engaging in additional and higher value-added activities) (Humphrey and Schmitz, 2000).
2. There also exists an increasingly rich literature on using the value chain tool in the context of poverty alleviation, by finding ways to strengthen the bargaining position of survival and micro businesses, and, for example, industrial home workers, in particular value chains and/ or to connecting to more attractive value chains (Dawson, 2003; McCormick and Schmitz, 2002). In this chapter we focus only on more formal small, medium and large firms that have a potential for international competitiveness.
3. In the case of the Sinos Valley, an American buyer that moved its sourcing to China (Bazan and Schmitz, 1997).
4. The phrase was initially coined by Bhagwati in 1958, and further developed in Bhagwati, 1987.

References

AFE (2004), *Promotion of Embedded Business Services in the Ghanaian Craft Export Sector. Summary Report*, Action for Enterprise, Arlington, VA. Full version of report on www.actionforenterprise.org

Anderson, G. (2000), 'The Hidden MSE Service Sector: Research into Commercial BDS Provision to Micro and Small Enterprises in Vietnam and Thailand', SEED Working Paper No. 5, International Labour Office, Geneva.

Andersson, Thomas, Serger, Sylvia Schwaag, Sörvik, Jens and Hansson, Emily Wise (2004), *The Cluster Policies Whitebook*, IKED, Malmö.

Bachtler, John and Wren, Colin (2006), 'Evaluation of European Union Cohesion Policy: Research Questions and Policy Challenges', *Regional Studies*, 40(2) pp. 143–53.

Bazan, L. and H. Schmitz (1997), 'Social Capital and Export Growth; An Industrial Community in Southern Brazil', Discussion Paper 361, IDS, Brighton.

Becattini, G. (1990), 'The Marshallian Industrial District as a Socio-economic Notion', in F. Pyke, G. Becattini and W. Sengenberger, *Industrial Districts and Inter-firm Co-operation in Italy*, International Institute for Labour Studies, Geneva, pp. 37–51.

Bhagwati, J.N. (1958), 'Immiserizing Growth. A Geometrical Note', *Review of Economic Studies*, 25, pp. 201–5.
Bhagwati, J.N. (1987), 'Immiserizing Growth', in J. Eatwell, M. Milgate and P. Newman (eds), *The New Palgrave: A Dictionary of Economics*, Macmillan, London.
Cunningham, Shawn and Meyer-Stamer, Jörg (2005), 'Planning or Doing Local Economic Development? Problems with the Orthodox Approach to LED', *African Insight*, 35(4), pp. 4–14.
Dawson, J. (2003), 'Facilitating Small Producers' Access to High-value Markets: Lessons from Four Development Projects', *Small Enterprise Development*, 14(2), pp. 13–25.
Enright, Michael J. (2000), *Survey of the Characterization of Regional Clusters: Initial Results*, University of Hong Kong, Hong Kong.
Esser, Klaus, Hillebrand, Wolfgang, Messner, Dirk and Meyer-Stamer, Jörg (1996), *Systemic Competitiveness. New Governance Patterns for Industrial Development*, GDI Book Series, No. 5, Frank Cass, London.
Gereffi, G. (1999), 'International Trade and Industrial Upgrading in the Apparel Commodity Chain', *Journal of International Economics,* 48(1), pp. 37–70.
Gereffi G. and Kaplinsky R. (eds) (2001), *IDS Bulletin – The Value of Value Chains: Spreading the Gains from Globalisation*, 32/3, July.
Gereffi, Gary, Humphrey, John and Sturgeon, Timothy (2005), 'The Governance of Global Value Chains', *Review of International Political Economy*, 12(1), pp. 78–104.
Hausmann, Ricardo, Rodrik, Dani and Velasco, Andrés (2006), 'Getting the Diagnosis Right', *Finance and Development*, 43(1), pp. 12–15.
Hirschenauer, Franziska (2003), Eingliederungsquoten sprechen eine deutliche Sprache. IAB (Kurzbericht Nr 17), Nüremberg.
Humphrey, John, and Schmitz, Hubert (2000), 'Governance and Upgrading: Linking Industrial Cluster and Global Value Chain Research', (Working Paper 120), IDS, Brighton.
Kaplinsky, R. (1998), 'Globalisation, Industrialisation and Sustainable Growth: The Pursuit of the Nth Rent', IDS Discussion Paper, 365, p. 43.
Kaplinsky, R., Morris, M. and Readman, J. (2002), 'The Globalization of Product Markets and Immiserizing Growth: Lessons from the South African Furniture Industry', *World Development*, 30(7), pp. 1159–72.
Knorringa, Peter (2002), 'Cluster Trajectories and the Likelihood of Endogenous Upgrading', in M.P. van Dijk and H. Sandee (eds), *Innovation and Small Enterprises in the Third World*, Edward Elgar, Cheltenham, pp. 48–65.
Knorringa, Peter and Staveren, Irene van (2006), *Social Capital for Industrial Development: Operationalizing the Concept*, UNIDO, Vienna.
Lauridsen, L. (2004), 'Foreign Direct Investment, Linkage Formation and Supplier Development in Thailand during the 1990s: The Role of State Governance', *European Journal of Development Research*, 6(3), pp. 561–86.
Linde, Claas van der (2002), *Findings from the Cluster Meta-Study*, Harvard Business School, Cambridge, MA.
McCormick, Dorothy and Hubert Schmitz (2002), *Manual for Value Chain Research on Homeworkers in the Garment Industry*, IDS, Brighton.

Meyer-Stamer, Jörg (2005), 'Systemic Competitiveness Revisited. Conclusions for Technical Assistance in Private Sector Development', mesopartner, Duisburg (Mimeo).

Meyer-Stamer, Jörg (2003), 'Why is Local Economic Development so Difficult?' mesopartner Working Paper No. 4, Duisburg.

Meyer-Stamer, Jörg, Maggi, Claudio and Seibel, Silene (2004), 'Upgrading in the Tile Industry of Italy, Spain and Brazil: Insights from Cluster and Value Chain Initiatives', in Hubert Schmitz, *Local Enterprises in the Global Economy. Issues of Governance and Upgrading*, Edward Elgar, Cheltenham, pp. 174–99.

Navas-Aleman, Lizbeth (2006), 'Opportunities and Obstacles for Industrial Upgrading of Brazilian Footwear and Furniture Firms: A Comparison of Global and National Value Chains', PhD thesis, IDS, Brighton.

Pack, Howard and Saggi, Kamal (2006), 'The Case for Industrial Policy: A Critical Survey. Policy Research Working Paper 3839, World Bank, Washington, DC.

Piore, Michael J. and Sabel, Charles F. (1984), *The Second Industrial Divide. Possibilities for Prosperity*, Basic Books, New York.

Porter, Michael (1995), 'The Competitive Advantage of the Inner City', *Harvard Business Review*, 73(3), pp. 55–71.

Porter, Michael E. (1990), *The Competitive Advantage of Nations*, Free Press, New York.

Rauch, James E. (1999), 'Networks Versus Markets in International Trade', *Journal of International Economics*, 48(1), pp. 7–35.

Rodrik, Dani (2004), 'Industrial Policy for the Twenty-First Century', Faculty Research Working Papers Series, John F. Kennedy School of Government, Cambridge, MA.

Rodrik, Dani and Hausmann, Ricardo (2006), *Doomed to Choose: Industrial Policy as Predicament*, Harvard University, Cambridge, MA (Mimeo).

Schmitz, Hubert (2005), *Value Chain Analysis for Policy-Makers and Practitioners*, ILO, Geneva, p. 81.

Schmitz, Hubert and Knorringa, Peter (2000), 'Learning from Global Buyers', *Journal of Development Studies* 37(2), pp. 177–205.

Sölvell, Örjan, Lindqvist, Göran and Ketels, Christian (2003), *The Cluster Initiative Greenbook*, Ivory Tower AB, www.cluster-research.org

Tomlinson, Richard (2003), 'The Local Economic Development Mirage in South Africa', *Geoforum*, 34, pp. 113–22.

UNDP, Government of the Netherlands, ILO and UNIDO (1988), *Development of Rural Small Industrial Enterprise: Lessons from Experience*, UNIDO, Vienna.

World Bank, (1993), *The East Asian Miracle. Economic Growth and Public Policy* Oxford University Press, Oxford.

World Bank, (2004), A Better Investment Climate for Everyone. World Development Report 2005, World Bank, Washington, DC.

2
Issues in Financing Small Enterprises

*Deborah L. Riner**

It is hardly surprising that small companies, no matter in what country they are located, share a common problem – access to financing. Preferably, policy prescriptions should be based on factual information and so it is to be expected that research on the reasons why small firms have more difficulty tapping financing began in the developed world, where data and the scholars to analyse it are more available.

The conclusions drawn from studies financing small and medium-sized enterprises (SMEs) in developed economies provides interesting conclusions and a good jumping-off point for studying the question of facilitating SME financing in other countries. More than anything, though, it underscores how critical institutional solidity is to the efficiency of the economy and the effectiveness of its financial intermediation system. By definition, institutions are more developed in the OECD (Organization of Economic Cooperation and Development) countries: that is an important part of the reason why they are called "'developed countries'. Also, by definition, in 'developing countries', the institutions of a market economy are not so well entrenched. While the lessons drawn from analyses of the constraints on SME financing in the OECD countries may well hold true, there are other, more fundamental factors constraining the availability of financing to SMEs in developing countries, ones that bear further analysis.

This chapter will summarize the major findings of the SME literature and, drawing on the experience of Mexico, discuss their relevance for developing countries as well as the institutional constraints on SME financing in developing countries.

---

* The author would especially like to thank Jon Hoy for his research of the SME literature.

Mexico was elected as the context in which to examine financing to SMEs for several reasons. First, it is not a typical developing country. Mexico is, depending on the year and exchange rate, the tenth or eleventh largest economy in the world. International organizations classify Mexico as a middle-income country. In the financial world, it is an 'emerging market'. Thus, Mexico is closer to the experiences on which the SME literature is based than many developing countries. Second, while the state has had an important presence in the economy, Mexico has a long experience with market-driven economics that the many formerly socialist countries in the developing world are just acquiring. Third, Mexico's capital markets are among the most developed and liquid in the world, outside of the 'developed economies'. Fourth, Mexico receives foreign investment, both direct and portfolio. The presence of multinational companies and portfolio investors in significant amounts is an indication of the relative sophistication of the Mexican financial system. Finally, the Fox Administration (2000–6) made improving the access of SMEs to financing one of its top priorities. If the findings from the literature on SME financing in the developed countries do not apply to Mexico, it is a strong argument for probing further into the hows and whys of SME financing.

Banks: the place to go?

Where should SMEs go for finance? A 2002 article[1] based on an empirical study of UK firms based on 1990–5 data argues that SMEs show a preference for certain types of financing over others, based on cost. At the top of the financing 'pecking order' are retained earnings.[2] If those don't suffice, SMEs chose debt, a more expensive option: SME owners have more information than lenders, who price the higher risk they face into the loan. The SMEs' third choice is issuing new shares, the most costly financing: when an SME's owners opt to issue equity instead of using retained earnings or debt, it signals a still higher level of risk – and cost – since the owners prefer risking other people's capital to their own. The more closely held a company (that is, the greater the extent to which the decision-maker is the primary financial stakeholder), the more pronounced the pecking order preferences.

Once, then, SMEs must go outside for financing, banks are the places they are most likely to look. At least, that is true in the developed countries. The pecking order of preferences in developing countries is not necessarily the same. Neither is it likely that the pecking order will be the same in all developing countries. Tax laws and accounting conventions will also influence the decision. Mexico provides a good example.

In 1995, the Mexican government had to intervene to stave off a collapse of the country's banking system. At the end of 2005, commercial bank lending to the private sector was only 45 per cent (in real terms) of its December 1994 level.[3] In 2002, credit to the private sector finally stopped contracting. It was not until 2004 that there was any noticeable increase in the balance of commercial bank loans to the private sector. Even then, credit to businesses and individuals with business activities continued to drop as a percentage of commercial banks' outstanding portfolios: in December 2000, loans to businesses constituted 71.3 per cent of commercial banks' outstanding loan portfolio to the private sector; in April 2006, it had dropped to 44.1 per cent – in spite of the 21.8 per cent real increase in the size of the outstanding portfolio.

Governments must answer several thorny policy questions about the design of the banking sector, whether or not banks are lending to SMEs. One is their position on concentration in the banking sector. If there are fewer banks in the market, do SMEs have less of a chance of receiving a bank loan? Another is about ownership. Should banks be publicly or privately owned? Should foreign banks be allowed into the market? If foreign-owned banks buy out or supplant nationally owned banks, will SMEs' access to bank financing be improved or diminished?

Bank concentration

Banking has been transformed in the last several decades. The development of capital markets, nationally and internationally, has given larger firms direct access to capital, bypassing banks. The information technology (IT) revolution forever altered banks' back-office operations, slashing employment and allowing banks to expand the geographical scope of their business. Mergers and acquisitions have changed the face of banking, creating mega-bank giants and eliminating many local institutions. Research on the relationship between bank size and financing to SMEs argues both that SMEs benefit from 'relationship lending'[4] and that higher concentration in the banking sector is not detrimental to small and medium-sized firms' access to financing.

One analysis indicates that SMEs' access to bank financing suffers disproportionately from banking concentration, although the effect is weaker in developed economies.[5] Small banks have advantages over larger institutions in obtaining and processing information from less transparent firms.[6] Bankers in small, local institutions know their customers and will use that knowledge to assess creditworthiness – relationship lending. In contrast, large institutions, which do not have such a close, personal relationship with the customer, base lending decisions on a numbers-driven financial analysis that does not necessarily capture the SME owner's vision, business acumen, or commitment to his firm – transactions-based lending.

On the whole, the literature argues that higher concentration does not decrease the loans available for small businesses. Post-merger developments can offset the decrease in 'relationship lending'. Bank structure is more important than the size of the individual bank: the probability that a business has a loan with a bank of a certain size is proportional to the concentration of that size bank in the market.[7] Very importantly, small businesses pay less for loans in markets dominated by large banks.[8] Other research argues that as the distance between small firms and their lenders increases, local market concentration may become less important.[9] Because monopoly power creates deadweight losses, increased concentration can decrease growth, but it also allocates more capital towards 'financially dependent' firms. Since these are more likely to be younger and more innovative firms, this can lead to technological increases that can offset the depressed growth.[10]

The literature also argues that mergers do not necessarily reduce the amount of small-business lending.[11] While the banks involved tend to cut back on SME lending following a merger, loans to SMEs rise following mergers. The explanation might be that other small banks pick up the SME clients discarded by the merging banks or that new, small banks enter the market.[12] Reconciling the apparent discrepancies between findings that greater concentration in the banking sector can hurt or facilitate SMEs' access to bank credit, Berger and Udell[13] argue that while larger banks are at a disadvantage at relationship lending, they have advantages in transactions-based lending, such as factoring and credit scoring, that are appropriate for loans to SMEs.

Greater concentration in the banking system does not necessarily restrict SME financing. However, it is important to examine the effects of concentration in particular institutional and legal contexts. For example, does concentration have the same effect in countries in which the banking system is competitive as in countries with an oligopolistic banking system? The prior question is the relationship between concentration and competition: does greater concentration impede competition?

Bank ownership

Does the ownership of banks affect lending to SMEs? Are SMEs more likely to receive financing if their capital is in national or foreign hands? Does it matter if banks are publicly or privately owned?

A survey of over 4,000 companies in 38 developing and 'transition' economies studied borrowers' perceptions of the relationship between the presence of foreign banks, interest rates and access to credit.[14] Most studies conclude that greater penetration by foreign banks in developing markets benefits firms of all sizes, bettering their access to long-term credit and reducing interest rates. Later work[15] supports the finding that a higher concentration of foreign banks leads to enhanced credit availability for firms, including small and medium-sized companies, even though foreign banks may prefer lending to large firms.[16]

There are various reasons why foreign banks are more successful in lending to SMEs in developing countries than nationally owned institutions. Foreign banks are likely to have better 'information technologies' for collecting and evaluating financial information, giving them a comparative advantage in transactions-based lending.[17] Foreign banks based in countries with well-developed capital markets and exigent regulators are also likely to have much more sophisticated risk-management systems and the financial instruments to hedge risks. Because they are expanding into new markets, foreign-owned banks are likely to have strong capital bases. If they are better capitalized than nationally owned banks, the foreign banks will have more lending power. And the entrance of foreign banks into a new market almost assuredly means more competition for nationally owned banks.

In Mexico, the entrance of foreign-owned banks has changed the face of banking. The foreign-owned banks brought capital and new financial instruments into the market. Banking hours are longer, customer service is better and credit has begun to flow to the private sector. Thanks to macroeconomic stability, foreign banks have been able to use their ability to hedge credit risk to make fixed-rate mortgage financing available – a fantasy ten years ago. Mexican-owned banks have not been left behind: when forced by competition to innovate, they have done so.

The evidence on public versus private ownership comes out clearly against public ownership: state-owned financial institutions are generally at a disadvantage compared to privately owned banks.[18] However, the arguments against public ownership rest on the inefficiency of publicly owned banks, the 'crowding out' effect of subsidized loans and the generally adverse macroeconomic consequences of a large state role in the economy. State-owned banks can be an effective vehicle for funnelling money to specified sectors, regions and activities, including SMEs. That does not mean that the SME beneficiary uses the subsidized funding efficiently or effectively, but it does get the SME-needed financing at a lower price. Whether the resources go to creditworthy projects or sound businesses depends on development banks' ability to assess credit and project risk. The quality of most development banks' loan portfolios raises doubts about that ability. In addition, lending decisions may well be politically motivated.

The very nature of the criteria on which management's success is evaluated often encourages shovelling money out of the door to the detriment of the longer-term objective of repayment. For example, as publicly owned entities, a development bank is a tool at the president's disposal in converting campaign promises into programmes. The amount of money the bank disburses is evidence that the president is delivering on his commitments. The repayment record is an issue for his successor. The temptation to confuse performance with inadequate indicators is enormous and appears in all sorts of ways in the private as well as the public sector. In education, for example, citing the number of free textbooks distributed does not say much about improvements in the quality of education.

Mexico's Ministry of Economy documents the success of its programmes to help *pymes* (small and medium-sized companies) by the number of financing entities created, the number and amount of loans made, and consultations and training programmes offered. That is important information. It does not, though, tell us how cost-efficient and useful the programmes are for the economy as a whole, whether the funds could have been used to greater effect elsewhere, or whether there are more effective ways to channel funding into *pymes*.

The poor quality of the loan portfolios of Mexico's development banks and state-owned banks in the past corroborates the findings that state-owned banks are inefficient. Certainly, banks like Nafin have been used at times to promote political objectives and to channel funds to favoured companies. During the Salinas administration, for example, Nafin (and other banks) financed, in part, the private sector buyers of some state-owned companies being privatized. So long as the acquired companies were worth the price paid and could service the debt used to finance the purchase, there was no problem. Unfortunately, that often wasn't the case .

Ironically, if the recommendations for creating an environment conducive to bank lending became reality, they would also spur economic growth and development and reduce financing costs in general.

Alternatives to bank financing

One of the fascinating questions raised by the Mexican experience is: how could the economy grow at an average annual rate of 3.7 per cent between 1996 and 2005 without bank financing for private companies in most of the period?[19] The answer is that other sources of financing appeared and that existing alternatives to bank financing acquired more importance. In Mexico, suppliers' credits became the principal source of financing for companies of all sizes; new financing mechanisms like *Sofoles* (*Sociedades Financieras de Objecto Limitado* or Limited Purpose Financial Societies) became a part of the financial landscape; and, it is likely, firm owners repatriated capital from abroad to keep their companies operating. The former two factors will be discussed in detail later in this chapter.

Retained earnings

Support for the thesis that owners used retained earnings to keep their companies in Mexico alive is found in the movements of assets held abroad in the capital account of the balance of payments. First, we assume that firm owners transfer some of the profits generated by their businesses to accounts held outside Mexico. It is a reasonable assumption, one justified theoretically and practically. The theoretical justification is diversification. Just as stock portfolios benefit from diversification, so do currency holdings, especially when the home country currency has experienced major devaluations. It makes perfect sense for Mexicans, in this case, to convert some percentage of their pesos into dollars as a hedge against an economic crisis. Although it may not be possible to trace a direct line from companies' profits to financial accounts outside of Mexico, the distinction between firm assets and family assets, especially in small, family-owned firms in developing countries, is often rather blurred. Anecdotal evidence abounds that many well-to-do Mexicans feel more comfortable with dollars than pesos.

Between 1990 and 1992, Mexicans drew down their assets held in foreign banks in small amounts (US$3.9 billion in three years). In 1993, the North American Free Trade Agreement (NAFTA) was signed, reinforcing the promise of a modern, rapidly growing economy that had made Mexico the 'flavour of the month' in international capital markets. Banks were lending to businesses; Mexicans built up their assets in foreign bank accounts in 1993 and 1994 (US$5 billion). The economic crisis unleashed on 20 December 1994 was reason for Mexicans to continue building up their assets in foreign bank accounts in 1995 and 1996 (US$9.2 billion). By 1997, however, there had not been any bank financing available for two years and Mexicans were becoming increasingly confident that the crisis was past. They drew down their assets

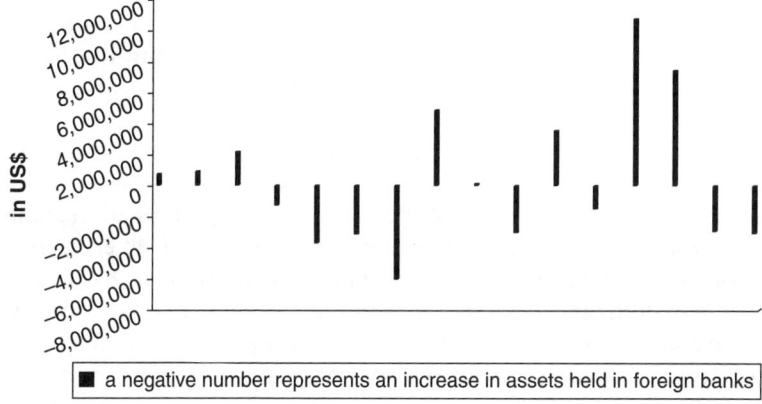

Figure 2.1 Assets held abroad by Mexicans in foreign bank accounts, 1990–2005

held in foreign banks in 1997 and 1998 (US$5 billion). In 1999, the year before the presidential election, when, traditionally, anything can happen, Mexicans opted to diversify, holding more dollars in foreign bank accounts (US$3.6 billion). Between 2000 and 2003, Mexicans reduced their assets held in foreign bank accounts significantly (US$20.3 billion).

Then the political situation began to deteriorate. Voters delivered a clear defeat to the President's party, the PAN, in the July 2003 mid-term elections. Since 2004, through the last half of the Fox *sexenio* (six-year presidential term), there was a widespread perception that the administration could not push through its legislative programme. At the same time, banks slowly began extending credit to the private sector and the development of Mexican capital markets offered very large firms new, cheaper sources of financing. Also, Mexicans have built up their assets held abroad (US$6 billion in 2004–2005),[20] a trend that picked up dramatically in the first quarter of 2006 (US$7.3 billion), a presidential election year.

Suppliers (trade credit)

An alternative to bank financing is credit extended by suppliers (trade credit). It has many advantages for SMEs in particular and, in Mexico, it is the method of financing to which firms of all sizes resort. First, we will outline the theoretical advantages of suppliers' credits. Then, we will discuss the Mexican experience.

Firms turn to suppliers for credit for several major reasons. One is that they are 'credit constrained'.[21] That may be because banks are not lending to companies in general (the case in Mexico for nearly a decade), because banks do not deem a particular firm creditworthy, or because of tight monetary policy. Another is cost: supplier credit is less expensive than bank credit.

Suppliers theoretically can finance their customers at a lower cost than banks for two major reasons.[22] First, the supplier has a natural advantage over financial institutions in gathering information about the firm receiving credit. The supplier acquires valuable, current information about its customers' financial condition in the normal course of doing business, selling its products and managing accounts receivables. For example, suppliers monitor their customers' payment patterns, data that serves as an early warning system of financial distress. Banks can also acquire that information, but it costs them more to do so.

Another tool that suppliers use in the normal course of business, discounts, also provides a wealth of information about customers' financial positions and strategies.[23] When suppliers offer homogeneous financing terms, they offer companies that are credit risks financing at a lower price than borrowing from banks.[24] Because of their in-depth knowledge of their customers' financial situations, suppliers can also use the credit they extend to price discriminate effectively:[25] the discount offered can be used to signal the buyer's financial condition.

Second, suppliers have tools to encourage customers to pay that can be quickly employed and have more immediate repercussions than banks'. Suppliers can threaten to cut off future product flow. In contrast, banks can only threaten to withhold future credit, the consequences of which are not so immediate for the borrowing firm. In the event of default, suppliers have an important cost advantage over banks in that they are often liquidating their own goods. Suppliers can more easily seize, repossess and re-sell their product than a bank: suppliers already have a network in place for selling seized goods in the case of a default by the customer.[26]

Even when it is difficult to seize assets, suppliers' credit may still be commonly used. In France, for instance, trade credit is heavily used even though suppliers rarely are able to seize any assets in bankruptcy proceedings.[27] In Mexico, it is also the case, suggesting that the information asymmetry considerations better explain the choice of trade credit than the ability to seize and liquidate assets.

The Mexican experience suggests that supplier credit (or trade credit), along with factoring, appear to be the most feasible financing options for SMEs in developing economies. Suppliers are generally able to offer less expensive credit than banks, especially to small businesses that keep their financial information close to their chests (it is not unusual for the financial assets of companies and their owners to be commingled) or in idiosyncratic forms (financial statements might be audited or they might be kept on the back of an envelope). In the absence of reliable, cost-effective legal channels, suppliers have a definite advantage over banks in the case of payment problems. First, because suppliers routinely track their customers' ordering, payment and inventory patterns, they are likely to pick up on financial problems sooner. They also can use the carrot of prompt payment discounts or the threat of shutting off future supply to persuade customers to pay.

In 1998, Mexico's central bank began surveying companies to ascertain their principal source of financing and reasons for using or not using bank credit.[28] Since the survey started, small, medium and large companies have routinely cited suppliers as their principal source of financing (Figure 2.2). The only companies that ever cited commercial banks as their principal source of financing were the AAA companies, and even they did not do so consistently. Frequently, AAA firms have also said that suppliers are their principal source of financing. Each year between 1998 and 2005, the smaller the firm, the higher the percentage of respondents that said suppliers were their most important source of financing.

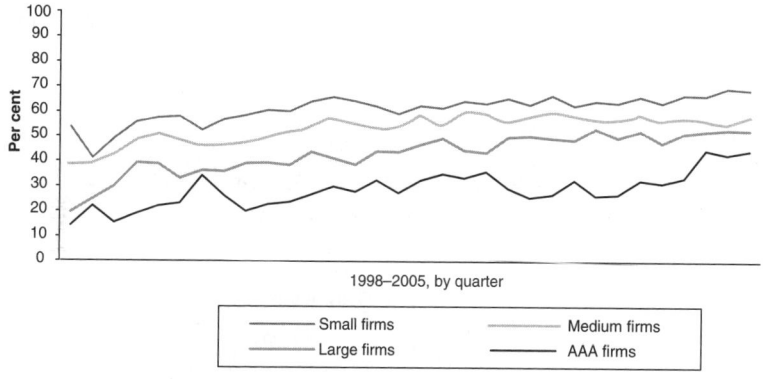

Figure 2.2 Companies citing suppliers as their principal financing source, by size of firm

In all cases, though, suppliers became a more important financing source as the years passed and this was in spite of the fact that commercial bank lending to private sector companies finally began to grow in real terms in 2002. In the fourth quarter of 1998, 55.7 per cent of small firms used suppliers as their principal source of financing; in the fourth quarter of 2005, 69.0 per cent did. The percentage of medium-sized companies using suppliers as their main financing source climbed from 48.1 per cent in the fourth quarter of 1998 to 58.0 per cent in the fourth quarter of 2005. For large companies, the percentages were 39.3 per cent and 52.8 per cent and for AAA firms, 19.2 per cent in the fourth quarter of 1998 and 44.4 per cent seven years later.

Of those companies in Mexico that used bank credit, the majority used it to finance working capital needs (Figure 2.3). Three-fifths to four-fifths of the small and medium-sized companies that used bank credit between 1998 and 2005 used it for working capital. The same was true for half to three-fifths of large companies. About half the AAA firms used bank credit for working capital financing. It was not until 2004 that AAA companies began to use bank credit to finance investment in any noticeable percentage (14 per cent to 30 per cent).

The most frequent reason that companies in Mexico cite for not using bank financing is cost (Figure 2.4). Between 1998 and 2005, one-fifth to one-third of small companies consistently said they did not use bank financing because it cost too much. A slightly lower percentage, but still typically one-fifth to one-third, of medium-sized companies said the same. Starting in 2003, about one-fifth to a quarter of large companies cited cost as the primary reason they did not use bank financing; between 1998 and 2002, however, frequently two-fifths of large

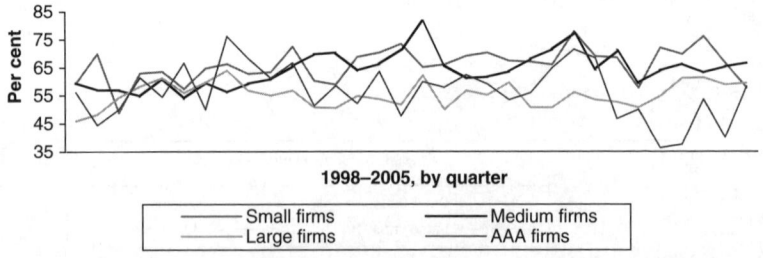

Figure 2.3 Companies using bank credit: percentage borrowing for working capital

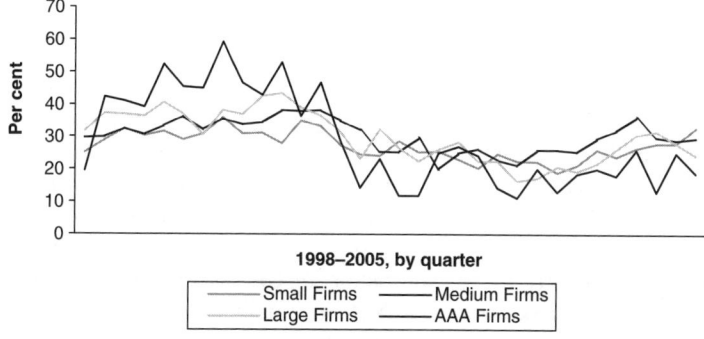

Figure 2.4 Reasons for not using bank credit: percentage citing high interest rates

companies said they didn't use bank credit because of its cost. Between 1998 and 2000, half of the AAA companies that answered the Mexican central bank's quarterly survey typically said they didn't turn to banks because of the cost. Beginning in 2001, the percentage of AAA companies citing cost fell dramatically, typically running at around a quarter of responses.

It is hardly surprising that when privately owned commercial banks began lending again, the first firms to benefit from the access to credit were the AAA companies, followed by large companies. Neither is it surprising that when foreign-owned banks acquired Mexican banks and recapitalized them, the increase in competition reduced costs for prime borrowers.

The reliance on supplier financing can create major collection headaches for companies. The size of those headaches can be measured by the number of days outstanding (DSO) of a firm's accounts receivables (A/Rs), a financial indicator on which the Finance people in multinationals' head offices often like to focus. In Mexico, where DSO typically runs at 60 to 90 days, controlling the DSO on A/Rs has an important impact on profitability. However, managing A/R exposure does not have the same importance in all developing countries. In Brazil, for example, the DSO on A/Rs is very low: customers generally pay their suppliers on time. Both Mexico and Brazil have suffered through long periods of high inflation (including triple-digit inflation); both are now enjoying low inflation. Executives of multinational companies say that prompt payment in Brazil and painfully slow payment in Mexico are cultural phenomena – 'the way the system works' – and, in this respect, companies adapt to the business practices of the environment in which they are operating.

Factoring

Factoring can be seen as a variant of supplier financing in that a company sells (actually, discounts) its A/Rs to a third party. The seller benefits from the transaction because he obtains his money quickly; in a high-inflation economy, which, until recently, most emerging economies suffered, that was a very important consideration. Because the buyer has working capital, he can buy more. The factor, of course, makes money by his ability to assess risk accurately. Not only does factoring provide firms short-term financing at a lower cost, it also bundles services by outsourcing at least part of firms' credit and collections function.[29]

Factoring can be particularly beneficial for smaller companies without access to bank credit that sell to large, creditworthy firms – a form of factoring know as 'reverse factoring'. The factor buys from firms without access to credit or with poor credit ratings the A/Rs owed it holds from high-quality suppliers (single or, sometimes, multiple suppliers) who are transparent and have good credit records.[30] The large firm's credit rating determines the discount the factor applies to the A/Rs, putting cash in the hands of the credit-constrained firm at a rate it could not otherwise obtain. For example, Wal-Mart arranged for its Mexican suppliers automatically to factor their Wal-Mart A/Rs through Heller Financial. The small Wal-Mart supplier obtains short-term working capital from Heller, who in turn is paid by Wal-Mart on its normal payment cycle. The small firm receives working capital up-front and reduces collection costs. Wal-Mart saves on billing costs by consolidating payments to one firm and, more importantly, alleviates its small suppliers' working capital constraints. The rate at which Heller Financial discounts the A/Rs covers the cost of operating the programme and produces its profits.

In this arrangement, the payment risk is that the high-quality debtor(s), not the more risky SME supplier, will default. Reverse factoring permits creditors to finance high-risk borrowers at the price the high-quality, low-risk debtor would pay. This process is especially efficient in emerging markets, where larger multinational buyer firms with more readily available and accurate financial information are often more creditworthy than their domestic suppliers.

Factoring has the potential to be especially useful for small businesses in those developing economies in which inadequate commercial codes, dubious contract enforcement and dysfunctional bankruptcy laws discourage bank lending. However, if factoring is to be an important financing tool for companies, the country must have a strong credit information system. Thus, factoring is a financing mechanism that requires a more sophisticated institutional infrastructure than supplier financing.

Although factoring has long existed in Mexico, it only recently acquired any importance with the establishment of the Mexican government-owned development bank, *Nacional Financiera*'s (Nafin) 'Productive Links' (*Cadenas Productivas*) programme. The programme offers online factoring services[31] to small and medium-sized companies (SMEs; *pymes* in Spanish). Large firms and government institutions initiate the chain in which their suppliers and distributors are invited to participate. The programme finances smaller, riskier companies that supply large firms: Nafin buys the accounts receivable of larger, creditworthy firms held by the *pymes*. In Mexico, where delaying payment is the norm, the ability to discount (factor) A/Rs is a boon.

The Nafin programme is mounted on an electronic platform, which reduces the cost of operating it and makes it more efficient.[32] If a *pyme*'s customer is listed as a qualifying participant in the 'productive chain', then the *pyme* is eligible to use the financing programme. Companies are delighted with the ease and rapidity of *Cadenas Productivas*. In a country in which companies constantly complain of the cumbersome and excruciatingly slow pace at which banks and the government process paperwork, *Cadenas Productivas* has won kudos for the agility with which it is administered.

The *Cadenas Productivas* programme has proven an effective channel for funnelling financing to *pymes*. The real test of the effectiveness of the programme, though, will come when the programme has a longer track record. Its success will depend on Nafin's ability to assess risk and immunize from political criteria its decisions on which firms' receivables to buy. The development bank has a poor track record so far as direct lending goes. Will it prove a better judge of A/Rs than it did of balance sheets?

Policy recommendations

In the business world, the most appropriate source of financing for an SME depends on what sources of financing are available to it. That depends, in large part, on the institutional and business context in which the firm operates. The realities of that context are very different in developed and developing and 'transition' economies and there are frequently significant differences among countries in each category.

Policy recommendations must take into account the context in which they are being implemented. Retained earnings may not be at the top of the financing 'pecking order' for SMEs in developing economies. Any SME owner who has lived through devaluation, followed by high inflation and negative real interest rates, fully appreciates the value of leverage. In countries in which bank credit is a small percentage of gross domestic product, policy recommendations might more profitably focus on facilitating access to other forms of financing in addition to stimulating bank lending. For example, in countries with inadequate legal and institutional frameworks to protect lenders' rights, bank credit is likely to be scarce, especially for SMEs. The impact of policies that strengthen the legal framework is more long term. Meanwhile, policies that facilitate factoring, for example, could potentially provide SMEs more immediate relief from their financing constraint.

Regulation and the 'rule of law'

To improve SME access to finance, governments should support the creation of an environment in which bank financing will be more likely to exist in the future.[33] That means supporting the development of countries' banking systems and strengthening their legal frameworks.

Banks must be adequately capitalized and supervised. Banks must develop risk assessment and management systems appropriate for their portfolios. Banking supervision must be more efficient and effective. The 1995 'tequila crisis' revealed the profound problems of the Mexican banking system. To prevent the collapse of the banking system, the government began to buy portfolios from troubled banks,[34] take over the banks that still could not survive, and permitted foreigners to invest in Mexico's three largest banks. (As part of NAFTA, foreigners were allowed to own shares in all but the three largest banks. With the crisis, that provision was waived.) Subsequently, the banks have been recapitalized: Mexico's three largest banks are now owned by foreign financial institutions, two Spanish and one American, and all but one of the other major banks are in foreign hands. Along with capital, foreigners have brought risk assessment and management systems. The CNBV (National Banking and Securities Commission) has dramatically improved banking regulation. And, banks began to lend again, first to consumers, then for mortgages and to businesses.

A country's legal framework can encourage or discourage bank lending. Not only must the laws on the books offer creditors protection in the case of a default by the borrower, the laws must be enforced. When banks weigh a lending decision, the clarity, consistency, cost and convenience of collecting loans all affect the price and availability of financing. The laws and procedures governing bankruptcies, the securing of collateral, the accuracy and availability of property registries, and the relative sanctity of property rights are all critical. In Mexico, until Congress passed a new collateral law in the late 1990s, the mechanics of collateralizing a loan effectively ruled out secured lending. For example, if a creditor lent to a shoe manufacturer and wanted to collateralize the loan with inventory, the creditor had to perfect a collateral interest in specified pairs of shoes. When those particular shoes were sold, the collateral was gone. Although the creditor could perfect a collateral interest in another pair of shoes, the cost and operational difficulties of identifying and tracking inventory turnover ruled out secured lending.

In Mexico, new laws governing bankruptcy proceedings, for securing collateral, protecting minority shareholders' rights and improving corporate governance have created a legal framework more conducive to lending.[35] However, the emphasis business organizations put on the 'rule of law' in their lobbying campaigns suggests how much remains to be done. A single example suffices to make the point. The client of a foreign insurance company operating in Mexico disputed the insurer's decision on a particular claim. An arbitrator upheld the insurance company. The client took the case to court, then to another court and to another court, shopping the case around until it found a congenial judge. The civil case was converted into a criminal case and the insurance company's top management had to run the business from outside of Mexico for several years or go to jail. Other insurers say that the foreign firm was in the right but wasn't sensitive to how things are done in Mexico.

Information: credit bureaus

It would be ideal if governments were to pass and enforce laws that better safeguard creditors' rights, facilitate the perfecting of collateral and limit what owners can do once a company is in bankruptcy proceedings[36] – actions that foster lending by banks. Is there anything else governments can do to help get credit to SMEs through market mechanisms? Yes. Government policy can actively support financing in the form of supplier credit and factoring without getting into the business itself by promoting the development of a credit information infrastructure. A credit bureau reduces the cost of gathering information. More complete information on companies' credit histories reduces payment risk.

Better assessment of risk, over time, reduces the rates at which A/Rs are discounted, benefiting companies.

In Mexico, several privately owned credit bureaus were established in 1995. Of those, only the Credit Bureau belonging to commercial banks has prospered.[37] Interestingly, factoring still has not taken off as a business in the private sector. The Credit Bureau has proven its worth, though. In 2001, banks began to grow their consumer lending business. The commercial banking system's outstanding consumer loan portfolio expanded over 30 per cent (discounting inflation) that year and in 2002. Since 2003, consumer lending has grown at 40 per cent-plus rates,[38] virtually tripling its share of commercial banks' outstanding portfolio to the private sector (from 10.3 per cent in December 2000 to 29.8 per cent in April 2006). Mortgage lending surged in 2005; at the end of 2005 and in the first four months of 2006, mortgage lending exploded, growing at 80 per cent-plus year over year rates. The Mexican commercial banks' mortgage lending business climbed from 12.9 per cent of their outstanding private sector credit portfolio in December 2000 to 20.1 per cent in April 2006. Perhaps factoring's turn will come.

There are several key issues that must be addressed when credit bureaus are established. One is: who supplies the information and what do they get in return? Another is: who has access to the information and at what price? In Mexico, access to and the sharing of information were thorny issues, ones that delayed the opening of the Credit Bureau. Not surprisingly, the banks with the largest customer bases wanted to condition access to the information in the Bureau on the amount of information supplied. While limiting access to information protected the banks that had acquired it, it was not the best way to advance the broader goal of making credit information available to all potential lenders.

Other issues for policy-makers to consider are whether credit bureaus should have a monopoly and whether they should be publicly or privately owned. In Mexico, the bank-owned Credit Bureau enjoys a monopoly. Market size may justify the lack of competition:[39] the market may be too small to support more than one credit bureau. It may also be that banks' refusal to share credit information doomed competitors to failure. The relationship between market size and competition in the credit bureau market is one that deserves study. Is there a conclusive argument to be made for public or private ownership of credit bureaus? In Mexico, a government-owned credit bureau preceded the privately owned bureaus started in 1995. It was not effective. However, the government also owned the commercial banks for about a decade, starting in 1982. The

Mexican experience clearly shows that when the commercial banks' lending decisions are politically motivated, portfolio quality can quickly decline. In such a context, that the credit bureau was ineffective does not necessarily lead to any conclusions about whether ownership should be private or public.

The informal economy

An area that deserves investigation is the relationship between the informal economy and financing sources. As the informal economy becomes more significant and vibrant, do banks become less important as providers of finance to companies? Might not suppliers become more important? It is a particularly relevant question for SMEs, which are more likely to operate in the informal economy than large companies.

There are *a priori* reasons to suppose that the more important and vibrant the informal economy, the less likely it is that banks will be the major sources of financing for businesses, especially SMEs. That has certainly been the case in Mexico. First, companies in the informal economy do not have the documentation banks required for processing a loan application. Second, audited financial statements are not characteristic of firms operating in the informal economy. Third, if companies operating in the informal economy opt to borrow from banks, they might expose themselves to the tax authorities. In the case of Mexico, taxes typically produce only about 11 per cent of the government's revenues and voters have clearly manifested their distaste for levying value-added tax on foods and medicines. In such an environment, adding companies operating in the informal economy to the tax rolls would help generate much-needed revenues as well as pay political dividends.[40] Suppliers, on the other hand, finance customers in both the informal and the formal economies.

Non-bank financing entities

An inspiring characteristic of the financial system in Mexico is its resilience. After the then-president of Mexico, Jose Lopez Portillo, nationalized[41] the banks in 1982, a flourishing private sector credit market developed. Through *casas de bolsa* (stock brokerage houses) or foreign banks' representation offices, companies with excess cash lent overnight to cash-short companies who could provide a guarantee or standby letter of credit. When the publicly owned banks were lending to the government or at the government's instruction (government-dictated portfolio distribution), a 'non-bank bank' market appeared to fill in the missing link and perform financial intermediation for the private sector.

Following the 1995 crisis, when the owners and management of Mexican banks were sorting through the remains of the near collapse of the banking system, digesting acquisitions, developing and imposing modern systems of credit analysis, risk allocation and control, and restructuring loans to salvage what they could of their portfolios, banks basically stopped lending. Of course, the need for credit did not evaporate. Into the vacuum created by the withdrawal of the banks stepped new financing vehicles and existing ones became more active. For example, automotive companies' financing arms financed the sales of vehicles; retailers financed the sale of their merchandise. Legislation created a new legal form in Mexico in the 1990s, the *Sofoles* (*Sociedades Financieras de Objecto Limitado* or Limited Purpose Financial Societies), which blossomed following the crisis.

Sofoles have helped satisfy the unstated thirst for financing and opened new market segments in the process. *Sofoles* moved into mortgage lending, for example. Subsequently, successful *Sofoles* became acquisition targets for commercial banks anxious to grow their mortgage lending business and acquire expertise quickly. A commercial bank interested in tapping into new market segments has even acquired a *micro-financiera*, a 'non-bank bank' that lends to low-income clients who have been ignored by the commercial banks.

There is a common moral to be drawn from the very different Mexican experiences in the 1980s – the nationalization of the banks – and in the 1990s – the near collapse of the banking system. If, for some reason, banks are not serving the function of financial intermediation, other entities will develop to move funds from savers to investors. The forms they take will depend on a country's legal framework and economic realities.

Conclusion

Which sources of financing are most appropriate for SMEs depends on the institutional and economic context in which the firms do business. That context is different in developed countries and developing countries and between the developing countries themselves. The particular economic, business, political and legal realities of each country will determine the 'best practices' for SME financing. What works well in the US or Canada probably won't be as efficient, effective, or, perhaps, even possible in Mexico. And what works well in Mexico may be as ineffective in Vietnam or Zimbabwe as what works well in the US is to Mexico.

Researchers and policy-makers interested in designing and implementing effective programmes to increase financing to SMEs must understand the institutional and business environment in which the SMEs operate and respond accordingly. If, for example, banks are not lending to the private sector, they will certainly not lend to SMEs. If the laws for securing collateral are unworkable, then inventory financing can hardly be an option. If taxes are levied on the sale of accounts receivable operations, then factoring is probably not viable.

In economies with well-developed, smoothly functioning legal systems and a financial infrastructure, banks are a logical choice for SMEs, since SMEs do not have the size to access capital markets directly. In countries with certain characteristics in which SMEs can borrow from banks, relationship lending can be more appropriate than transactional lending. If the quality and quantity of financial information available is limited or problematic, relationship lending has much to recommend it, from the lender's perspective. Relationships – a mechanism for creating and assessing trust – acquire extra importance in countries in which the legal system offers lenders little protection.

In countries in which a large share of economic activity takes place outside the formal economy, banks are not a likely financing source for companies operating informally.[42] Suppliers might be a more feasible source of financing.

Neither are banks the place to which SMEs should turn if the banking system makes its money by financing the government. That can take several forms. One is that the government imposes requirements on sectors to which banks must lend. In the past in Mexico, governments used the *encaje legal* to channel savings into financing the government deficit. In the last half of the 1990s and into the beginning of this century, when interest rates were high, Mexican banks made their money by paying depositors a low single-digit rate and investing in government debt instruments that paid several times more. The *Fobaproa* debt obligations issued by the federal government as it staved off the collapse of the banking system have also been a source of attractive risk-free profits for banks. So long as banks had a risk-free, no-brainer way to make good money, why wouldn't their managements opt to hold government debt and use their limited institutional resources to sort out portfolio problems, digest an acquisition, engineer new systems and create a new corporate culture?

The economic, business, legal and political realities of the context within which SMEs operate will determine their optimal sources of financing. Policy recommendations should be based on analyses of the most efficient and effective financing sources for SMEs, given the very different national realities within which they operate. Certainly, the Mexican experience has demonstrated that there is an impressive capacity for creating financing channels when the standard ones aren't active. Mexico is not unique in that respect. While it would be desirable if governments could create the institutional and legal conditions that would permit bank financing to SMEs to flourish, that is a long-term solution. In the short term, there is much to be learned from studying how SMEs currently obtain financing in developing countries and devising ways to facilitate those credit flows.

Notes

1. Watson and Wilson, 2002.
2. While retained earnings are the best way for SMEs to fund their growth, according to an article by Beck, Demirgüç and Maksimovic (2005) smaller firms report higher levels of financial and legal obstacles to earnings growth. Beck, Demirgüç and Maksimovic cite higher collateral requirements, corruption in banks, bureaucracy, high interest rates and lack of credit as significant financing obstacles. On the legal front, the speed with which courts rule, enforcement of court decisions, and the amount of revenue paid in bribes hurt growth. The study surveyed firms worldwide. Firms were asked to rate how different aspects of society impacted their ability to grow. Respondents' answers were compared to their firms' actual growth. The authors controlled for several factors, including country of operations, firm size, age and industry. Even controlling for these factors, there was a stronger correlation between reported impediments and actual lack of growth in small firms.
3. The balance of commercial bank credit extended to the private sector (excluding restructured loans and loans rediscounted through government banks or agencies), adjusted for inflation, plummeted 55.5 per cent in real terms between December 1994 and December 2005. These figures are derived from data contained in the monthly *Agregados Monetarios y Actividad Financiera* reports published by the *Banco de Mexico*, Mexico's central bank (www.banxico.org.mx).
4. Berger and Udell, 2002.
5. Beck, Demirgüç and Maksimovic. The article surveys firms and compares responses with concentration in the country, controlling for firm size, inflation, overall growth of the economy and other factors. The results suggest that firms face higher financing obstacles in more concentrated banking systems. The authors control for GDP per capita, finding that this relationship only holds for low-income countries, with the relationship being insignificant for middle- to high-income countries.
6. Berger and Udell, 2002. Also see Williamson, 1967, and Stein 2002.
7. Berger, Rosen and Udell, 2001.
8. Berger, Rosen and Udell, 2001.
9. Peterson and Raghuram, 2002.

10. Cetorelli and Gambera, 2001.
11. Peek and Rosengren, 1998.
12. Berger, Rosen and Udell, 2001.
13. Berger and Udell, 2002.
14. Clarke, Cull and Peria, 2001.
15. See Berger and Udell (2004) for those studies.
16. Berger and Udell, 2004. This is especially the case when foreign banks are going into formerly socialist countries.
17. Berger and Udell, 2004.
18. Berger and Udell (2004) cite the research findings on the question of public ownership of banks and SME lending.
19. Of course, another question is: how quickly could the economy have grown if banks had been acting as financial intermediaries?
20. Movements in assets held abroad are in the balance of payments data (*La Balanza de Pagos*) published quarterly by the *Banco de Mexico* (www.banxico.org.mx).
21. Biais and Gollier (1997) construct a model to explain the extension of trade credit.
22. Petersen and Rajan, 1997.
23. In a 1987 article , Janet K. Smith constructs a model that shows buyers are ultimately faced with the choice between a cash-discounted payment and a net payment. The supplier firm monitoring this choice naturally and quickly obtains valuable information about the buyer default risk. In a 1993 article, Y.W. Lee and J.D. Stowe examine the other side of the information exchange. They analyse how the terms of cash discount offer insight into the quality of the product and explain why the same company offers different credit terms for different products, as well as why credit terms vary across firms and industries. Since the product can be returned for a refund at any time prior to payment, the authors construct a model in which higher amounts of cash discounts signal lower-quality products. Higher discounts are intended to encourage cash purchasing, which shares the risk between the customer and the supplier.
24. Since poor-quality borrowers are typically credit rationed, suppliers' credits allow these 'non-bankable' firms to acquire goods at a lower price than they would pay if they borrowed from a bank to pay in cash.
25. Smith (1987) and Brennan, Maksimovic and Zechner. The latter article also demonstrates that vendor financing is optimal when demand is less elastic in the credit markets than in the cash market.
26. This point is also made by Mian and Smith, 1992.
27. Biais and Gollier, 1997. In another article in the *Review of Financial Studies*, Petersen and Rajan (1997) also discuss this advantage, noting that the amount of trade credit offered is inversely proportional to the ratio of finished goods to inventory.
28. Banco de Mexico, *Resultados de las encuestas de evaluacion coyuntural del mercado crediticio*, Dirección General de Investigación Económica, Banco de México, www.banxico.org.mx
29. Bakker, Klapper and Udell, 2004.
30. Klapper, 2005.

31. As well as a source of finance, *Cadenas Productivas* is also designed to serve as an electronic marketplace, linking up participating companies with large firms and government institutions to inform *pymes* of the products and services Nafin offers them (See Nafin's web page: www.nafin.com/portalnf/ ?action=content&sectionID=6&catID=153&subcatID=178).
32. The Philippines has a similar programme.
33. Beck, Demirgüç and Maksimovic, 2004. Also see Beck, Demirgüç and Maksimovic, 2005. For a discussion of accounting standards and information sharing, see Berger and Udell, 2004 and Board of Governors of the Federal Reserve System, 9 May 2006, at http://www.worldbank.org/research/ projects/sme/Financing_Framework_berger_udell.pdf>
34. The final cost of the banking sector rescue programme, *Fobaproa*, is about 18 per cent of GDP. It has been a political albatross for any politician identified as promoting it. The PRD's candidate in the 2006 presidential election, Andres Manuel Lopez Obrador, used *Fobaproa* against his PRI and PAN opponents.
35. In less than a decade, Mexico passed new collateral and bankruptcy laws, which, while not perfect, are a vast improvement in the legal environment to facilitate lending. The rights of minority shareholders have been granted more protection and laws to strengthen corporate governance have been part of the fallout from the corporate scandals in the US that produced the Sarbanes-Oxley Act (SOX).
36. Bakker, Klapper and Udell, 2004, and Klapper, 2005.
37. A paper by Jose Luis Negrin (2001) analyses the development and impact of credit bureaus on financing in Mexico. Negrin labels the bank-owned Credit Bureau a monopoly. He argues that the credit bureau owned by the Mexican government in earlier decades did not work.
38. In 2000, the Banco de Mexico began reporting the 'outstanding credit to the private sector' extended by commercial banks as well as the balance of credit to the private sector. In 2000 and 2001, the latter figure was 30–40 per cent larger than the former. Since 2002, the balance has been 1–2 per cent smaller than the outstanding credit figure. In 2002, both the commercial banks' outstanding portfolio to the private sector and their historical balances began to rise in real terms.
39. Negrin, 2001.
40. Tax income represented about 10 per cent of GDP in 2005. IVA (value-added tax) collections, 17.0 per cent of the government's income, grew at a 17.1 per cent real rate in the first four months of this year compared to the first four months of 2005. Several factors contributed to the improvement in IVA collections. One is the transformation of the commercial sector: as more people shop in large stores like Wal-Mart instead of *changarros* (small, locally run neighbourhood stores), more IVA gets collected. Another is a programme to put point of sale terminals in many more locations. Improvements in the SAT, the Mexican equivalent of the IRS, have also helped.
41. Technically, he 'statized' them since the banks were owned by Mexicans.
42. INEGI, the Mexican government organization (soon to be an autonomous entity) responsible for compiling information on the economy and country generally, now distinguishes between the 'informal' and the 'illegal' economies. That INEGI differentiates the two activities is testimony to the size

and growth of the informal economy's share of GDP and the extent of drug trafficking and contraband.

References

Bakker, Marie H.R., Klapper, Leora F. and Udell, Gregory F. (2004), 'Financing Small and Medium-Size Enterprises with Factoring: Global Growth and Its Potential in Eastern Europe', World Bank Policy Research Working Paper No. 3342 (May).

Banco de Mexico, *Agregados Monetarios y Actividad Financiera*, http://www.banxico.org.mx/fBoletines/Boletines/FSBoletines.html

Banco de Mexico, *Resultados de las encuestas de evaluacion coyuntural del mercado crediticio*, Dirección General de Investigación Económica, Banco de México, http://www.banxico.org.mx/fBoletines/Boletines/FSBoletines.html

Beck, Thorsten, Demirgüç, Asli and Maksimovic, Vojislav (2005), 'Financial and Legal Constraints to Growth: Does Firm Size Matter?', *Journal of Finance*, 60(1), pp. 137–77.

Beck, Thorsten, Demirgüç, Asli and Maksimovic, Vojislav (2004), 'Bank Competition and Access to Finance: International Evidence', *Journal of Money, Credit and Banking*, 36(3), pp. 627–48.

Berger, Allen N. and Udell, Gregory F. (2004), 'A More Complete Conceptual Framework for SME Finance', *World Bank*, 15 October, at <http://www.worldbank.org/research/projects/sme/Financing_Framework_berger_udell.pdf>

Berger, Allen N. and Udell, Gregory F. (2002), 'Small Business Credit Availability and Relationship Lending: the Importance of Bank Organizational Structure', *Economic Journal*, 112(477), pp. 32–53.

Berger, Allen M., Rosen, Richard J. and Udell, Gregory F. (2001), 'The Effect of Market Size Structure on Competition: the Case of Small Business Lending', *Federal Reserve*, Federal Reserve Board, October, at http://www.federalreserve.gov/pubs/feds/2001/200163/200163pap.pdf> (accessed 27 April 2006).

Biais, Bruno and Gollier, Christian (1997), 'Trade Credit and Credit Rationing', *Review of Financial Studies*, Oxford University Press for Society for Financial Studies, 10(4), pp. 903–37.

Brennan, M.J., Maksimovic, V. and Zechner, J. (1998), 'Vendor Financing', *Journal of Finance*, pp. 1127–41.

Cetorelli, Nicola and Gambera, Michele (2001), 'Banking Market Structure, Financial Dependence and Growth: International Evidence From Industry Data', *Journal of Finance*, 56(2), pp. 617–48.

Clarke, George R.G., Cull, Robert and Peria, Maria Soledad Martinez (2001), 'Does Foreign Bank Penetration Reduce Access to Credit in Developing Countries? Evidence from Asking Borrowers', *The World Bank*, November, at http://www-wds.worldbank.org/servlet/WDSContentServer/WDSP/IB/2001/12/17/000094946_01113004020846/Rendered/PDF/multi0page.pdf> (accessed 8 May 2006).

Frank, Murray Z. and Maksimovic, Vojislav (2005), 'Trade Credit, Collateral, and Adverse Selection' (26 October), at SSRN:_http://ssrn.com/abstract=87868 or DOI: 10.2139/ssrn.87868

Klapper, Leora F. (2005), 'The Role of Factoring for Financing Small and Medium Enterprises', World Bank Policy Research Working Paper No. 3593 (May).

Lee, Y.W. and Stowe, J.D. (1993), 'Product Risk, Asymmetric Information, and Trade Credit', *Journal of Finance and Quantitative Analysis*, 28(2), pp. 285–300.

Mian, S. and Smith, C.W. (1992), 'Accounts Receivable Management Policy: Theory and Evidence', *Journal of Finance*, 47, pp. 169–200.

Nafinsa, *Cadenas Productivas*, www.nafin.com/portalnf/?action=content&sectionID=6&catID=153&subcatID=178)

Negrin, Jose Luis (2001), 'Credit Information Sharing Mechanisms in Mexico: Evaluation, Perspectives and Effects on Small Firm Credit', paper prepared for the 5–6 October, Conference on Financial Markets in Mexico, organized by the Stanford University Center for Research on Economic Development and Policy Reform.

Peek, Joe and Rosengren, Eric S. (1998), 'Bank Consolidation and Small Business Lending: It's Not Just Bank Size That Matters', *Journal of Banking and Finance*, 22(6—8), pp. 799–819.

Peterson, Mitchell A. and Raghuram, Rajan G. (2002), 'Does Distance Still Matter? The Information Revolution in Small Business Lending', *Journal of Finance*, 57(6), pp. 2533–70.

Petersen, Mitchell A. and Raghuram, Rajan G. (1997), 'Trade Credit: Theories and Evidence', *Review of Financial Studies* (3rd series), 10, pp. 661–91.

Smith, Janet K. (1987), 'Trade Credit and Information Asymmetry', *Journal of Finance*, 42, pp. 863–72.

Stein, Jeremy C. (2002), 'Information Production and Capital Allocation: Decentralized Versus Hierarchical Firms', *Journal of Finance*, 57(5), pp. 1891–921.

Watson, Robert and Wilson, Nick (2002), 'Small and Medium Size Enterprise Financing: A Note on Some of the Empirical Implications of a Pecking Order', *Journal of Business Finance and Accounting*, 29, pp. 557–78.

Williamson, Oliver E. (1967), 'Hierarchical Control and Optimum Firm Size', *Journal of Political Economy*, 75(2), pp. 123–38.

3
The Unsuspected Player: Small Firms in Business with Low-income Sectors

Patricia Márquez and Ezequiel Reficco

In the late 1980s, Jorge and Javier Añaños watched how guerillas threatened the supply of soft drinks in their region of Peru and looked into the business. They mortgaged their family home for US$20,000 and began producing 'Kola Real', a cola beverage offered at a lower price than leading brands, targeted to low-income areas, and distributed through the informal economy truckers. Concerned that its low price might be viewed by consumers as cheap, they employed the slogan *'la bebida de los precios justos'* (the fair-price beverage). Operations soon expanded and by 2006 Kola Real and other beverages were being produced and marketed in Mexico, Central America and Venezuela (Lozano, 2005). How did a company with such small beginnings – known today as the Aje Group – take over a significant share of the soft drink market from giants such as Coca-Cola and Pepsi? Do SMEs hold a competitive edge when doing business with low-income sectors (LIS)? What managerial practices were critical for the company to succeed with LIS consumers?[1]

Peru's Aje Group became a prospering multinational in little more than a decade. It competed with large soft drink companies by means of a creative marketing, built on a keen understanding of the needs, buying habits and expectations of poor consumers. As a small player outside Lima, it exploited a market niche of poor consumers long ignored by large corporations, and gained competitive advantage. By working with informal economy trucks on commission, the family company avoided the high cost of operating warehouses and a fleet of vehicles, let alone attending to a large payroll. Although some may question the benefits of marketing sweetened soft drinks to the poor, the success of Aje Group invites thinking about how the lives of the poor can be changed by means of market-based initiatives.

Of the world's 6.2 billion people, two-thirds live in poverty. There is growing evidence that profitable market opportunities may be tapped by engaging LIS as consumers, suppliers, or business partners, which in turn hold the promise of improved well-being for the poor. The pioneering work of Prahalad, Hart and Hammond on 'serving the poor profitably', coupled with the widely shared view that development organizations failed to mobilize major social transformation, have uncovered a world of possibilities. Current debate centring on this premise has triggered links between issues that heretofore were perceived to lack any real connection: the fight against poverty, business performance and social development.

To be sure, LIS have long participated in trade, but for the most part in a technological and organizational context of limited opportunity and multiple hurdles – sometimes even exploitation. The possibility of inserting the poor in the global economy – 'democratizing the economy', as Prahalad puts it – may provide a passkey to social transformation. A follow-up book, *The Fortune at the Bottom of the Pyramid* (Prahalad, 2005), led both the academic and business communities to reflect on market initiatives as a basis for social change. Prahalad's work focused on LIS as potential consumers; he correctly noted these currently underserved by large companies, and pointed to the revolutionary impact on the poor that broadening consumer choice could bring about in terms of economic growth and individual self-esteem. According to Prahalad, multinational corporations (MNCs) are best positioned to tackle the daunting task of truly impacting global poverty; in his view, only this type of organization features the financial clout, global distribution channels and brainpower needed to address the challenge. Nonetheless, that view has come to be questioned. A growing BOP literature suggests that MNC performance in dealing with LIS has been mixed; more interestingly, small and medium-size enterprises have achieved previously unsuspected successes.

A second shortcoming often noted in the literature on BOP is undue emphasis on viewing the poor as an untapped consumer market.[2] Clearly, successful integration of LIS in the global economy will broaden consumer choice and raise their disposable income by way of the price reductions that enhanced competition will bring. Nonetheless, significant progress in poverty reduction will not likely be achieved without increasing LIS real income, that is, improving their 'balance of payments' vis-à-vis the rest of society, with more money flowing in and less coming out.[3] To achieve this, the next step is to 'turn LIS into partners' (Marwaha et al., 2005).

This chapter builds on growing interest in LIS as consumers, and explores the largely untapped benefits of LIS as business partners and suppliers. In keeping with the current LIS focus, a series of case studies are reviewed to show how market initiatives with LIS can change the lives of the poor and contribute to social and economic development.

SMEs in business with LIS: what they do well

In practical terms, a number of first-generation LIS strategies led by MNCs failed to fulfil expectations. For the globally extended, multilayered and generally slow-moving MNC a shift in mind-frame from the top to the base of the pyramid is riddled with challenges. Companies often expand on their corporate model by making small adjustments in a) lowering unit cost by repackaging existing products with smaller content; b) reducing overall costs by outsourcing production to low-wage developing countries; or c) expanding distribution to urban shantytowns and rural areas by using the 'Avon saleslady' model (Hart, 2006). There is little doubt that MNCs stand to play a leading role in serving LIS markets; but whether they feature the most appropriate organizational skills and capabilities for doing so is open to question. The field of the micro-credit industry is a case in point. Micro-finance institutions were working with LIS long before the 'bottom of the pyramid' phrase was coined.[4] After some hesitation, certain multinational banks entered the micro-credit market once it proved to be economically attractive. However, they do not appear to have displaced other organizational forms, such as cooperatives or NGOs, with which they compete in serving the financial needs of the poor.[5]

The relative strengths of SMEs vis-à-vis larger companies in responding to market change has been a subject of academic debate,[6] and whether SMEs hold special advantage when it comes to engaging in business with LIS is as yet unknown. As it happens, this aspect is currently being explored as part of a wider research project in which the authors are involved.[7] The three studies reviewed below were uncovered by this research, and each illustrates the relative strengths of SMEs when it comes to engaging in business with the poor.

Mission centrality

It stands to reason that building a business from scratch by targeting a particular market holds advantages over adapting ongoing operations to serve other markets, particularly when these represent a challenge. Some SMEs were created with the explicit purpose of circumventing barriers that prevented the poor from participating in mutually enriching market exchanges. Not surprisingly, they tend to be good at it. To many of these SMEs, the poor are their main market and *raison d' être*, for which they developed an original, customized value-proposition. Alternatively, large corporations tend to approach LIS as an incremental gain, for example, 'reaching the next 20 per cent'. Transposing to LIS markets a value-proposition that has worked well with a middle-income market may not meet with success. For the global firm that centres its mission on products or services geared to the needs and wants of better-healed consumers, adapting to the LIS markets represents a strong departure from past business practices.

Small-scale retailing illustrates the influence of mission centrality. D'Andrea and Herrero found that the 'preferred format' of LIS consumers in metropolitan areas is the small shop, which caters to their specific needs, as against large retail establishments with expanded sales space that target broader consumer segments. The authors hold that the flexibility of small shops enables them to tailor operations to the needs of LIS consumers, among others, in terms of location, cost of purchase and service. Despite the lower prices offered by large-space retailers, LIS customers often view price as being less important than the 'total purchase cost', which takes into account both displacement and opportunity costs for time invested in making the purchase. Because few among the poor have access to a vehicle, ample storage space and ready cash, they tend to purchase small amounts frequently, indeed often daily. The proximity of the small shop to LIS dwellings responds to LIS needs. Moreover, the small shop, which is generally run by its owner, offers personalized service, generates customer loyalty, allows for product recommendations and fosters the exchange of relevant community information. Then too informal credit (purchase on trust), enables the customer to pay 'next time', thus suiting LIS needs and promoting loyalty (D'Andrea and Herrero, 2006).

Proximity

SMEs tend to be closer to the poor, and thus to better understand their needs. For small firms with LIS at the core of their mission and business model, the extent to which they truly understand the poor and are able to relate to them probably determines their success or failure. Developing 'local' solutions can be more important than having 'global' reach,[8] as the aforementioned experience of Peru's Aje Group shows.

The idea of 'proximity' is not merely spatial: opening a small branch office in a poor neighbourhood is easy enough to do. Proximity entails long-time presence on the ground – being 'part of the landscape' – as well as affinity in various dimensions: social, cultural and even ethnic. This affinity, which has been termed 'social embeddedness' (London and Hart, 2004), can become in fact a competitive advantage for firms that work with LIS. Entrepreneurs that launch SMEs are more likely to fulfil such criteria in engaging in business with LIS than *expat* managers of global corporations. This proximity helps develop empathy, and provides an overall perspective that is more consistent with those LIS customers' needs. This is no small feature; overcoming cultural barriers represents a key step towards successful integration of LIS in productive value chains (Austin *et al.*, 2006). Cultural proximity can facilitate learning from 'native capability': from the large community of livelihood activities of the poor (Hart and London, 2005).

In emerging markets, proximity can also mean ease for operating concurrently in both the formal and informal economy, which in some countries can harbour as much as 50 or 60 per cent of the labour force. Noted earlier for the Aje Group, start-out SMEs are not generally on the radar screen of large corporations and, we might add, governments or tax agencies. Small firms are small fish in the pond. For a number of reasons, developing business relations with the informal economy is more difficult for MNCs than SMEs.

LIS markets are noted for *variability*. Income levels can vary greatly from shack to shack, as well as its flow, which can be daily, weekly or monthly; changes in climate can push distribution times from hours to days. Proximity allows for 'specificity', that is, the ability to react and to adjust to those variations. Large companies generally focus on economies of scale, and technology-intensive business models built on top of the pyramid consumer markets, which can be a hindrance when it comes to serving LIS (Dawar and Chattopadhyay, 2002).

Flexibility and innovation

SMEs targeting LIS generally employ processes that are simpler, with lower fixed costs, and conceived to deliver goods and services to consumers with little purchasing power. By starting with a clean slate, there is no need to alter the 'company way of doing things'. Corporations that have long served more affluent markets and seek to adapt operations for the LIS context must overcome a strong inertia that tends to suppress departures from established practices. As Hammel (1999) notes, it is no secret that large bureaucracies tend to stifle innovation.[9]

Micro-finance shows how SMEs focused on LIS (*mission centrality*) can deliver groundbreaking change (*flexibility* and *innovation*) through the applications of lessons derived from field experience (*proximity*). As *The Economist* recently recognized, 'What is now generating so much hope and excitement [in micro-lending] is... the effect of the rapid innovation that has taken place in the past three decades' (Easton, 2005a). Long discarded by traditional banking as a non-viable business proposition, until the mid-1970s funding the poor was assumed to be the domain of subsidies. That changed when a small group of entrepreneurs correctly surmised that there would not be enough resources to mitigate poverty, unless it was done profitably. Although non-profit organizations are still important in that field, and a few large banking corporations are now entering the fray, the micro-lending industry came to be dominated by SMEs: regulated micro-finance institutions (MFIs) that target LIS as their main line of business.

The organizational innovation that unleashed this process was rather low-tech: the leverage of social capital as a substitute for the lack of collateral, through group-lending. But what made this innovation possible was a keen understanding of both the needs and behaviour patterns of the poor by means of ongoing engagement on the ground.[10] Lending to the poor is contact-intensive – requiring high levels of close interaction with each customer – and entails a high credit risk over a limited asset pool (Chu, 2005). Traditional banking applied to the LIS market the same logic employed for higher income groups, and concluded that the poor could not be served profitably.

However, the interest rate paid by the middle classes was not a relevant reference point for the poor. Medium-sized MFIs discovered that LIS were ready to pay interest rates much higher than those charged to higher-income consumers, which could be the basis of an entirely different business model. First, the length of loans targeted at LIS is shorter, which limits the impact of high interest rates. Second, where capital is so acutely scarce, its marginal productivity tends to be quite high, which allows LIS to absorb high interest rates. Finally, for LIS *direct financial costs* are only one component of total costs, together with *transaction costs* (those imposed by the lender as a result of their delivery systems) and *accessibility costs* (opportunities lost because of transaction costs imposed by lender), which are taken for granted in mass banking. If those additional costs are factored in, the net result can be surprising. A loan provided to the poor by a credit union, with a 2 per cent monthly interest rate, could cost twice as much as another loan provided by a street lender at 10 per cent interest (Chu, 2005).

The track record of SMEs operating as regulated banking institutions – with average ROE rates for 2002–4 that range from 25–50 per-cent (Figure 3.1) – gained them some respectability. Some, such as Bolivia's BancoSol, were top profit-makers in the national financial markets where they operated.

This fact defies the conventional view that SMEs are doomed to operating in substandard conditions, which prevent them from 'graduating' to more affluent markets. Given such ROEs, and repayment rates of around 97 per cent (Figure 3.2), one may ask why anyone might want to ever leave these markets. Rather, the reverse is actually happening: established banking corporations have followed this lead, and are timidly entering the LIS micro-lending market – a very welcome development for the poor.

There is no reason why multinational corporations could not replicate the innovations originally developed by SMEs. However, these niche

BancoSol (Bolivia)	26.30%
Compartamos (Mexico)	52.20%
Confía Banco Procredit (Nicaragua)	39.30%
Findesa (Nicaragua)	32.00%
Edpyme Crear Arequipa (Peru)	29.70%
FIE (Bolivia)	25.20%

Figure 3.1 Average ROE of leading micro-lending SMEs in Latin America (2002–4)
Source: Adapted from Marulanda & Otero

1–30 days	2.9%
31–60 days	0.5%
61–90 days	0.3%
91–180 days	1.0%
More than 180 days	2.2%
Total	3.4%

Figure 3.2 Delinquency among the most representative MFIs in 2004 (% overdue of loans)
Source: Adapted from Marulanda & Otero

players appear to have something valuable to contribute, as most large banking corporations are entering LIS markets in partnerships with MFIs. For example, ABN Amro has established in Brazil 'Real Microcrédito', a joint venture with ACCION International. ACCION is a network formed largely (although not exclusively) by SMEs that have upgraded from the third sector into fully regulated private banking institutions. The world's largest financial corporation, Citigroup, does not deal with individual micro-finance customers, and has established relationships with micro-finance institutions in 20 countries. Most large banks are reluctant to bring micro-lending to the core of their business, and are still treating it as a part of their CSR programmes (Easton, 2005b).

Lower opportunity costs

Entrepreneurs that create SMEs generally operate within a limited market: their chessboard is substantially smaller than that of, say, Procter & Gamble's. For SME entrepreneurs, their country (or region, or town) is not an option among many, but rather their whole frame of reference. For global players the opportunity cost of capital and – most importantly – management time, is quite high, which makes for an intense internal competition among alternative projects. Those ideas that cannot aspire to make a dent on MNCs' quarterly earnings reports have little chances of seeing the light, as no manager will invest the energy required to mobilize the internal bureaucracy towards change if the potential pay-off does not justify it. Thus, prospective lines of business that may be insignificant for a company with 12-digit revenues may be interesting for an SME that may not have access to juicier alternatives. SMEs, in short, tend to spot and exploit LIS market niches that would not show on the radar screen of large companies.

We now review three experiences where SMEs do business with LIS in different capacities. The first aims for LIS as its sole customer target for providing quality healthcare services; the second sources from reliable, high-quality LIS suppliers in an export-oriented industry; and the third is an SME partnered with LIS in developing a profitable jointly run eco-lodge with significant economic, social and environmental pay-offs. For each experience, we describe the business, and review the barriers that had prevented LIS from becoming part of the broader formal economy, and identify innovations implemented, and results achieved. We then offer tentative lessons that may be drawn from these experiences.

LIS as customers: bringing health to the barrios

Cruzsalud is an SME offering prepaid healthcare for low-income groups in Caracas, Venezuela, known as *barrios* (poor neighbourhoods).[11] From the start in 2004, the company targeted to the LIS market, using a high-volume/low-margin model. Two years later the firm employed 60 staff members including physicians, paramedics and sales force. Cruzsalud works with 70 affiliated external physicians, drawn from several medical specialities, and 25 independent salespeople.

According to standard market research, 80 per cent of Caracas's population, roughly 4.6 million, is classed in the two lowest income groups, D and E. Household income is estimated to range from US$150 to US$320 per month. A survey commissioned by Cruzsalud found that 95 per cent of the low-income groups interviewed were willing to pay up to US$8.4 per month for basic healthcare protection. As many as 97 per cent of respondents expressed no knowledge of a private service that catered to their market, and reported channelling 6.9 per cent of their income to health services.[12]

Cruzsalud is the only private company that offers comprehensive health coverage[13] to Caracas LIS at a price consumers can afford. The cost of their prepaid plans offered range from US$4.2, per month to US$32.6, the latter plan applying to full services for people 64 or older. Most urban poor make a living in the informal economy, with no access to employee health plans. Given their low income, private healthcare is often beyond their reach; only 15 per cent of the city's population is estimated to belong to a health plan.

Overcoming barriers that hindered market access and social inclusion

Despite its size, the LIS market in Caracas has not attracted health insurance companies, not only because of its low-margin slow-profit outlook. Delivering prepaid healthcare to the poor represents a daunting challenge. Selling an intangible (coverage of the risk of illness) to a population where spending decisions are subject to high opportunity costs (with too many alternative uses) is no easy task. Moreover, physical remoteness and limited infrastructure require the developing ad hoc distribution channels with minimal fixed costs in order to render the operation economically viable. At first glance, Caracas shantytowns might appear to be located close enough to downtown health services; yet for all practical purposes, they are a world away. The steep hills, coupled with poor transport and everyday violence, make access to public hospitals in downtown Caracas impractical, and limit available health facilities to primary care.

Although purportedly cost-free, public health facilities can be costly for the LIS patient. Those requiring surgery must buy their own hospital kit, including all materials such as cotton gauze, povidine, etc. and to mend fractures, rails and screws used in the procedure. Throughout time governments have installed some small medical units (*ambulatorios*), where doctors-in-training provide primary care, but they tend to be located in the lower parts of the Caracas hills where older – and often more well-off – shantytowns are located. Physical access remains a challenge. The Chávez administration has set up a system of primary healthcare units in LIS areas called *Barrio Adentro*, staffed by some 30,000 Cuban physicians and paramedical personnel. According to most estimates, the system has worked reasonably well – despite some shortcomings.[14]

Cruzsalud sought to construct a business that incorporates the best of both public healthcare worlds: the traditional model (where patients visit a downtown hospital) and the new model (where house calls are made, or out-patients attend a nearby facility). For the latter service, the company opened a clinic in a downtown area, close to a very large LIS slum community. Prepaid healthcare is a contingent service; featuring such facilities helps consumers feel they pay for a tangible good. Cruzsalud also sought to build trust by strengthening its presence in LIS areas served. Teams of physicians and nurses routinely patrolled slum communities to bring their services to the target market, generate customer trust, and deepen knowledge of consumer needs.

Servicing LIS lies at the heart of Cruzsalud's mission; operational practices had to be adapted to the everyday dynamics of urban poverty. As noted earlier, medical training in Venezuela is capped by an internship that must take place in a poor community. Physicians affiliated with Cruzsalud's were all familiar with at least one such community, and had experience in developing local bonds to reduce threats to security. The problem was that prior to *Barrio Adentro* there was no institutional platform for round-the-clock presence of medical care in those areas.[15] The government-sponsored programme signalled that perhaps a similar model could be developed profitably. Cruzsalud examined the experience and created a model where socially committed physicians and nurses were hired at market rates to serve LIS under a prepaid medicine scheme.

By operating in LIS communities, on an everyday basis, Cruzsalud has found ways to innovate in service delivery. To attract new customers, Cruzsalud relies on word-of-mouth promotion. The teams of physicians and nurses that visit the urban slums help build goodwill and shield company staff from security risks. Cruzsalud's fleet of small-sized fully equipped 'ambulettes' is able to attract potential customers as they manoeuvre in the narrow alleyways of Caracas's *barrios*. Start-up sales did not come easily. Cruzsalud first tried out an 'Avon-lady'-type sales force, with mixed results, recruiting 200 affiliates in two months. Subsequently, a mixed model was developed adding an independent sales force of 25 people paid entirely on commission. This alternative has fared better, quickly bringing in 1,600 new affiliates.

To render Cruzsalud economically viable, managers became obsessed with cost-control. SAP, a fairly developed IT system for small Venezuelan companies, was selected to centralize process management. They also kept costs under control by working on prevention, following patients through their life cycles. The creation of patients' complete histories also speeded diagnosis and led to better treatment. Other cost-related measures included replacing checklists of medical exams that tend to generate additional tests, insisting that attending doctors write down the required exams – the logic being that, if the doctor has to write by hand, she will think carefully about what the patient really needs.

Assessing social and economic value

For Cruzsalud, building a critical customer base to pay for fixed costs was crucial. In two years, the company reached the break-even point, with a net income in 2006 just under US$100,000. With a customer base of 5,000 affiliates, the company's long-term goal of becoming a going concern offering prepaid healthcare for the poor is now in sight. Cruzsalud managers are increasingly confident that growth of affiliations will continue, thus hastening profitability.

Yet daunting challenges remain. A main issue is how to persuade poor consumers to keep up payments to cover a contingent need. Those who do not need health services tend to discontinue payments, which threatens Cruzsalud's financial viability.[16] To address this issue Cruzsalud is mounting an educational campaign to promote customer awareness of their growing need for healthcare and the benefits of keeping up payments.

LIS as suppliers: linking the global economy to poor farmers

Costa Rica Entomological Supplies (CRES) is a small company founded in 1984 by Joris Brinckerhoff, aimed at exporting Costa Rican butterflies.[17]

This SME was conceived as a sustainable venture offering an entrepreneurial opportunity for low-income farmers. CRES buys butterfly cocoons from a network of as many as 100 independent suppliers across a wide region, for each butterfly species requires a different microclimate. The company's competitive strength rests on its capacity to offer customers a portfolio of widely different species, with emphasis on high quality, quick delivery and customer service.

Overcoming barriers faced by Lis suppliers

The economy of rural Central America is based on agriculture. Those who are not engaged in subsistence farming, work as low-skilled employees in large corporations. Few opportunities are available for small entrepreneurial farmers to bypass traditional middlemen – who often exploit them – in order to improve their livelihoods. A key barrier is poor education: these farmers lack access to information on world markets for crops they produce. Without CRES, these 100 suppliers on the way to becoming micro-entrepreneurs might still be working as *jornaleros* (day-workers) for large companies.

CRES has worked extensively with its suppliers, training them for harvesting quality butterflies at competitive costs. CRES has teamed up with the non-profit *Instituto Nacional de Biodiversidad* (INBIO) to produce pedagogic materials that would promote biodiversity micro-entrepreneurship. In working with LIS suppliers, the company stressed the importance of reliable supply, product quality and building customer loyalty. Although not always well attended, CRES organized quarterly meetings to review results and address forthcoming challenges. The company also organized an annual meeting of foreign buyers to which suppliers were invited with the purpose of exchanging information.

To design appropriate incentives, CRES ranks suppliers in different categories based on the quality of their caterpillars. Suppliers who failed to meet the company's minimum standards were dropped. The supply ranking also enables customers to acquire knowledge of the origin of the butterflies, and provides a guarantee of quality.

Assessing economic and social value

CRES's successful butterfly export business developed over a span of 20 years. Benefits are split with suppliers on a 70/30 basis; in 2005, the average price of a single butterfly was US$2.12, for which the CRES supplier received US$1.40. In that year, CRES's return on net sales was 2.67 per cent; for suppliers, their average income averaged some US$800, which, reportedly, is three times their previous earnings.

CRES has also worked closely with several communities where the farmers are based, promoting the butterfly as a valuable means for sustainable development.

LIS as partners: collaborating to promote ecotourism

Posada Amazonas is a joint venture between a small Peruvian company – Rainforest Expeditions (RFE) – and an organized indigenous community, *Ese'eja de Infierno*. In 1997, both parties teamed up to create an eco-lodge located in the heart of the Peruvian Amazon region (Pérez, 2003). Years earlier, the state had granted the *Ese'eja* community property rights over some 24,700 acres, the Tambopata-Candamo Reservation, much of which was known for its environmental richness. The *Ese'eja*s partnered exclusively with RFE to carry out tourism-related activities in an eco-lodge to be built in that area. In return, RFE agreed to get the necessary funding to construct the lodge, to manage it and to hire all community members in need of work, on a rotating basis – contracts were awarded for two years. The agreement was signed for a period of 20 years; after that, the community would have the choice of continuing their engagement with RFE or terminating the partnership.

Insofar as the *Ese'eja*s lacked any sort of business experience, the initiative required enormous training and knowledge-transfer efforts. Successive community members were taught operational skills as guides, cooks, housekeepers, as well as maintenance and management functions. Jobs were awarded on merit-based selection, following a period of mandatory training.

Overcoming barriers that hindered market access and social inclusion

Few business ventures are as geographically remote and isolated as *Posada Amazonas*. To reach the lodge, visitors must travel on a canoe-type boat for several hours. Accordingly, the operation was well beyond the flow of ordinary trade and investment. Access to credit became a serious hurdle: most investors and traditional banking turned their backs on the idea, which appeared too risky. After nine months of negotiations, RFE was at long last able to obtain a soft loan from an international development agency, the Peru-Canada Fund (FPC).[18]

The financing agency conditioned its loan on partnering with the community. By doing this, it created a complex problem for the company: How do you 'partner' with an indigenous community with no experience in business relationships? Not only did they lack any formal training or experience in running a business. They had been brought up in an environment where one works only a few hours a day, a few times per week, on a need basis.[19] By all accounts, community members lacked not only technical knowledge, but the discipline and work ethos required to succeed in a competitive market.

The company eventually embraced the idea of co-ownership with the community. By giving the *Ese'eja*s a stake in the success of the venture, they created the incentives for them to educate themselves and rise up to the challenge. Instead of establishing a vertical relationship, in which the company maintained full control, spurred by FPC's imposition, RFE built a horizontal arrangement in which they ensured community buy-in and widespread commitment. Moreover, it did so balancing opposing imperatives: on the one hand, the need for fairness and social inclusiveness; on the other, the need for expediency and pragmatism in decision-making.

The *Ese'eja* community and RFE run the joint venture on an equal footing: each party has 50 per cent of voting shares. The former participates in decision-making through the Management Committee (MC), which despite its name does not have any managerial functions. Rather, its attributes are closer to a traditional governance role, such as monitoring and evaluating the performance of the business, so as to safeguard the interests of the *Ese'eja*s. Through this committee, commoners have unfettered access to information pertaining to all operational aspects of the business, and define strategies jointly with RFE. Thus, the MC functions as an effective representation and decision-making body.

In turn, MC members are accountable to the community's Executive Board, made up of a chairman, a vice chairman, a member and a treasurer, all serving for a term of two years. The community plenary organ, where decisions are made, is the Commoners' Assembly, composed by all those family heads who owned their own farm. An absolute majority makes most decisions (51 per cent of all votes), while crucial decisions – such as the decision to partner with RFE – require a qualified majority of two-thirds of the votes.

Assessing economic and social value

This rather unique joint venture generated social and economic value for all concerned: the company, the community and society at large. For RFE, key competitive assets were client access to an outstandingly rich ecosystem, led by trained guides in their own habitats. By partnering exclusively with the community, the company erected an entry barrier to potential competitors, which sustained good profit margins. Despite slight variations, *Posada Amazona*'s competitors[20] offer a comparable product. However, the originality of the latter's value proposition, which combined an economic, an environmental and a social component, allows it to charge a price premium ranging from 10–40 per cent over its competitors. Moreover, its unique relationship with the indigenous community provided RFE an additional competitive advantage in free publicity.[21] In 2002, *Posada Amazonas* made a net profit US$111,000, a healthy return on investment considering the initial investment of US$250,000.

The *Ese'eja* community also benefited. In 2000, 1,225 tourists visited the lodge, for a total of 3,239 nights.[22] Given that the lodge charges a daily rate of US$90, during that year the venture injected around US$300,000 – assuming no additional expenses – in an economically depressed region. As co-owner of the joint venture, the *Ese'eja* community received half the profits produced by it. A good share was invested in social infrastructure, as decided by the community's Executive Board; included were a childcare centre, a radio antenna, a lightning conductor and a secondary school.

Besides earning dividends, those employed at the *Posada* earned wages, and those who did not – jobs rotated among community members every two years – still benefited from the venture through the sale of timber, bamboo, crop and crafts to the lodge. Additionally, the typical *Ese'eja* family continued to practise traditional customs in agriculture, hunting, collecting Brazil nuts and raising livestock. A community that in the past faced cyclical fluctuations in the price of farm goods now enjoyed a stable income.[23] Overall, the *Ese'eja*'s involvement in tourism related activities roughly doubled their disposable incomes.

Remarkable progress was also made in developing local skills, and attitudes readily transferable to other activities, leading to economic value creation. Some community members launched micro-enterprises that sell goods and provide services to the visitors. For example, the *Centro Ñape* offering ethno-botanic tours, which focus on the medicinal properties of the local flora, in 2002, generated US$10,000 in revenue. Another micro-enterprise, the *Comité de artesanías* (Crafts Committee) trained 17 families to create craftwork with seeds, fabrics and pottery, generating, in 2002, US$6,000 in revenue.[24] Moreover, the *Ese'eja* community as a whole has become more entrepreneurial. Spurred by the success of their agreement with RFE, *Ese'eja* leaders recently concluded agreements with three other Peruvian tourism companies to run lodges along the Tambopata river. Each of the three companies agreed to pay a toll for entering community territory by road from Puerto Maldonado, connecting to boats that will await them in the community's river port.

Finally, *society and the environment* also gained. The *Ese'eja* community had long been plagued by a lack of employment opportunities that threatened their ethnic identity, as the young tended to emigrate to nearby Puerto Maldonado in search of new horizons. According to local observers and community leaders, the process of social disintegration has been reversed.[25] Nowadays, community leaders talk about 'cultural rescue' and the need to return to tradition and authenticity; they are working on relearning their native *Ese'eja* language, eclipsed by Spanish, and teaching it consciously to their children (Stronza, 2000).

For society, *Posada Amazonas* generated environmental gains, creating powerful incentives to protect the regions flora and fauna. The community now recognizes that birdwatching has become their mainstay. Tourism and conservation are positively linked; as more individuals become employed in tourism-related ventures, fewer engage in activities that may harm the environment – such as unregulated hunting or fishing.

Lessons from SMEs

Cruzsalud, CRES and *Posada Amazonas* illustrate how SMEs targeting LIS generate social and economic value. The mission centrality of LIS markets for SMEs such as those described, their flexibility, capacity to innovate and their proximity to LIS enabled them to become 'socially embedded'. These features made possible effective integration of LIS into economically vibrant value chains.

Cruzsalud reaffirms Prahalad's underlying insight: bringing the market to the slums is likely to generate dignity and choice, together with an improvement in the living standards of the poor. At the same time, Cruzsalud defies predominant logic regarding public health and low-income groups. All too often, the health services delivered by public agencies to the poor are not only inadequate, but also inefficient. As the experience shows, the poor are used to paying for health services even when delivered by a public agency, and will reward private health service providers that tailor service delivery modes and charges to their needs; the poor – like everyone else – seek good health services and are willing to pay if given the opportunity.

The remaining experiences – CRES and *Posada Amazonas* – depict fairly successful and creative market-driven experiments in which LIS became engines of economic value creation. What makes them particularly interesting is the salutary effect that the experiences have had on individuals who had previously lacked access to the global economy.

CRES has ably contributed to developing Costa Rica's market for butterflies. Key to its success was the centrality of LIS to its strategy. This was not a side project to help out the poor; developing a network of reliable suppliers among LIS butterfly producers was crucial for company survival. In exchange, CRES's network of loyal suppliers have learned that selling indiscriminately to one or other buyer, either to take advantage of the opportunity or fearing a price drop, renders their future vulnerable. Bringing LIS into a SME-led value chain is not new per se. What is innovative in the CRES experience is that these value chains are turning geographically isolated low-income producers into efficient, quality-driven entrepreneurs. This process entails not only improvement in productivity, but also empowerment by means of a deeper understanding of the promise and intricacies of supply and demand forces in the broader economic setting.

In the *Posada Amazona* experience, RFE made vital inputs to render the venture viable – management expertise, financing and access to travel networks that linked world demand for ecotourism with local supply. Yet it can be affirmed that an even more valuable contribution may have been the *critical thinking* that went into this innovative experience. After all, the ability to develop a vision and to carry it out is the spark that ignited the process of change; all other inputs can be tapped in the open market and were simply means to facilitate success.

The involvement of community representatives as decision-makers on an equal footing in the partnership fostered the transfer of skills that would have been extremely difficult to acquire in any other way. This interaction triggered a process of learning, compelling community members,

> to ask questions about themselves and their own futures; to discuss how best to represent themselves and their community to the world... to notice with new eyes their own resources, talents, and skills, and then to think critically about how they might be used... to [reach] variously defined local goals. (Stronza, 2000)

At the end of the 20-year period, the community is to decide autonomously whether to renew their partnership with RFE, choose another partner, or manage their own operation. Compare this with the traditional scenario of a MNC landing on a remote location and hiring a local workforce; the community would remain a passive player, learning little about business operations beyond acquiring basic skills. 'When local residents are *not* participating actively and something goes wrong, outsiders who are directing the project can pull out, leaving locals with little of benefit and a greater dependency on others for help in the future' (Stronza, 2000).

Lessons from these three experiences mirror in some sense the debates that took place in the 1950s, when strategies for economic development were being shaped. Poverty was then understood as deprivation of critical needs – essentially health and education – that infringed on basic human rights and impaired economic growth. Development was seen as providing the means for addressing those needs. Some argued that skills and capabilities had to be developed from the ground up: 'Teach a man to fish; and you have fed him for a lifetime.' Recently, some came to see that technical knowledge is not enough. What is really crucial to overcome poverty is the critical thinking of *deciding what to* fish, and the *ability to organize* human and physical resources to make it happen. SMEs hold the potential to become instrumental in fostering that process among LIS, in effect empowering them.

Yet the integration of LIS in SMEs value chains is no easy matter. As experiences show, the process is fraught with challenges. Besides, SMEs also have their own built-in weaknesses. They usually endure diseconomies of scale, which result in higher costs and loss of competitiveness. Their limited geographic reach usually implies depending on more intermediaries to attain global markets, which chips away their profit margins. They tend to endure diseconomies of scope, with a limited product portfolio, which block the creation of synergies between market segments – that is, top of the pyramid and base of the pyramid – and limits choice for consumers. They sometimes use below-par technology, and tend to be constrained in the development of proprietary new technologies, due to the substantial fixed costs of mounting an R&D effort, which they cannot spread over a sizable output. Finally, they are usually constrained in access to external sources of financing, particularly in the developing world. This usually creates financial bottlenecks that condition growth and scalability.

Here, too, the field of micro-finance showcases clearly the weaknesses of SMEs, much as it exemplified their strengths. The connection between supply and demand of capital is eased by the work of rating agencies, which provide consistent credit benchmarks to investors. Asked about what would most encourage their institutions to become more involved with micro-finance, three of the world's largest banks' reply was: 'The presence of credit-rating agencies.' However, the small size of most MFIs makes it expensive to pay for rating (Easton, 2005c). According to some observers, the next big leap in productivity in this sector will come through the widespread application of information technology. However, the small size of most MFI makes it very difficult for them to underwrite this type of investment (Marulanda and Otero, 2005). A possible way around these bottlenecks could be for some SMEs operating with similar business models in different markets to form networks, which allow them to capture economies of scale through the pooling of their resources in investments that may deliver solutions to shared problems.

Returning to the three experiences spotlighted earlier, many a hurdle may yet emerge before any of them can be deemed an unqualified success. It remains to be seen if Cruzsalud can generate and sustain affiliations among LIS consumers. Convincing LIS to pay for an intangible they do not actually *need* 'right here, right now', will entail a sustained educational effort. Given the public nature of this cause, some of the costs associated with it could be externalized, through a partnership with NGOs or government agencies, which might prove more effective at it. CRES must craft a strategy that offsets the low entry barriers of its business, for suppliers with less concern for quality may erode the company's market. *Posada Amazonas* will need to prove that superimposing a social organization (the *Ese'eja* community) onto an economic organization (RFE as a company) is sustainable. This characteristic is not without its critics; some find the concept behind this joint venture obtuse. Their critique is that the business of business is to make a profit, and that whoever wants to enmesh a social dimension in an eco-lodge will have both mediocre economic and social results.[26]

In sum, the successful integration of LIS into a wider economy is too difficult a task to be accomplished by any one type of organization. Overcoming the barriers that hitherto have limited LIS involvement as consumers, suppliers and partners of mainstream businesses will require bold thinking and innovative solutions. Despite their shortcomings and challenges, the experiences examined above suggest that SMEs can provide some of that.

Notes

1. In this chapter the term 'low-income sectors' (LIS) will be used synonymously with the widely used 'base-of-the-pyramid' (BOP). The term BOP lends itself to the reification of the poor, and suggests a kind of homogeneity that can be misleading.

2. C.K. Prahalad (2005) indeed considers the 'social transformation' that will emerge by drawing the poor into the global economy. However, emphasis is solely placed on LIS as consumers of different goods and services: 'As BOP consumers get an opportunity to participate in and benefit from the choices of goods and services made available through market mechanisms, the accompanying social and economic transformation can be very rapid.'
3. 'Increasing income generated in the low-income community requires interventions or changes that alter one or more of these balances – that increase consumption that is locally-produced, that increase investment activities using local materials, that provide government services using inputs from the local community, or that expand exports.' See Leonard, 2005.
4. 'Micro-finance has been used as a tool for alleviating global poverty for about 40 years.' Epsteinand Crane, 2005. *Micro-finance*
5. In Africa, for example, both NGOs and cooperatives seem to have the upper hand in that market. 'While unregulated MFIs [NGOs] are reaching poorer clients, they have higher costs and smaller operations volume; these institutions will need to scale up, transform, or merge with other institutions to achieve levels of efficiency that can guarantee their continued operation. Cooperatives compare favorably for savings mobilization, even though, on average, they do not lend as much as other MFI types. Given their lower operating costs, cooperatives are well poised to improve financial performance and remain competitive.' Lafourcade *et al.* (2005). Micro-financeMicro-finance
6. For a summary of the arguments of both camps, see Beck, Thorsten, Asli Demirgüç-Kunt, and Ross Levine, 2003.
7. The Social Enterprise Knowledge Network (SEKN) is a research partnership encompassing ten leading management schools, eight in Latin America (EGADE, INCAE, IESA, Pontificia Universidad Católica de Chile, Universidad del Pacífico, Universidad de los Andes, Universidad de San Andrés, Universidad de Sao Paolo), one in Spain (ESADE) and the Harvard Business School. SEKN's mission is to advance the frontiers of knowledge and practice in social enterprise through collaborative research. The network has embarked on a three-year research project on market initiatives with LIS. The cases discussed in this paper are part of our collective research output. For more information: www.sekn.org
8. Some are advocating 'a shift in emphasis from the "global" to the "local" consumer, and from globally standardized to locally adapted marketing programs'. Dawar and Chattopadhyay, 2002.
9. 'Big companies are not markets, they're hierarchies. The guys at the top decide where the money goes. Unconventional ideas are forced to make a tortuous climb up the corporate pyramid. If an idea manages to survive the gauntlet of skeptical vice presidents, senior vice presidents, and executive vice presidents, some distant CEO or chairman finally decides whether or not to invest. You wanna try something new, something out of bounds, something that challenges the status quo? Good luck.' Hamel, G., 1999.
10. 'A lesson...is that commercial success in serving the poor must start with a fundamental understanding of the day-to-day realities of low-income lives....Accordingly, theory-down approaches have a dismal record in the history of micro-finance; successes have always flowed street-up" (Chu, 2005). The above analysis of micro-finance relies to a large extent on Chu's paper.

11. This experience is based on a case prepared by IESA professors Rosa Amelia Gonzalez and Horacio Viana, under the SEKN project.
12. For segment E, monthly expenditures in health averaged US$10.35 and US$22.1 for segment D.
13. The Cruzsalud portfolio of services includes medical attention offered at its *Centro de Atención Integral*, together with home visits by physicians and nurses, medical consultations and tests in several specialties, dental care and ambulance services for emergencies.
14. There is concern about the long-term sustainability of the programme given its dependence on oil subsidies made available to Cuba, and how long Cuban staff will remain willing to live in similar conditions to the LIS they are serving.
15. The service module programme started in Venezuela in the 1990s offered a wide range of public services in poor communities, including primary healthcare. Unlike Barrio Adentro, however, doctors did not reside in the facility and were not on call 24 hours.
16. Only 23 per cent of affiliates have kept up with payments, while 29 per cent of affiliates have actually needed Cruzsalud medical services. The similarity among both rates suggests that only those in real need of medical services feel compelled to pay.
17. This experience is based on a case prepared by INCAE Business School professor John Ickis, with researchers Juliano Flores and Catalina Ickis, under the SEKN project.
18. The FPC funded 100 per cent of the initial investment of US$250,000, of which 40 per cent was a donation to the community, and the remaining 60 per cent was to be repaid in three years, at 9.5 per cent interest rate.
19. In the words of Juan Pesha, native community member, 'we haven't yet gotten used to certain things, like having a permanent job, Monday through Friday, or all month long. Things are different here. A regular native's job implies working two or three times a week, and not eight hours. It mainly means hunting animals, collecting nuts, etc., but it isn't a full-time job. Also it is not uncommon for someone to be drunk for two or three days in a row.' Pérez, 2003: 9.
20. Locally, Posada Amazonas competed with at least six lodges (Cusco Amazónico, Sandoval Lake Lodge, Tambopata Jungle Lodge, Explorers Inn, Corto Maltés and Ecoamazonía), and internationally, with various eco-lodges in Ecuador and Bolivia.
21. For example, the tourist guide of choice in this industry, *Lonely Planet*, featured a ten-sentence description of Posada Amazonas, while other lodges were given a sentence or two. According to Kurt Holle, marketing director and founding partner of RFE, 'They are not saying we are better, but we get more press; they talk more about us. So, we become more interesting for the same price. Why? Because they talk about our relationship with the community, about the community owning the place, and so on. The same happens with travel agencies. Many agencies mention that the lodge belongs to the community, and tourists view the fact that part of their money goes to community development as an additional benefit.' Austin *et al*. (2004). *labour*
22. Company documents.
23. In the words of Hernán Arrospides, a community member: 'Here you have some security; if you work so many days, you get so much money. To the

contrary, in agriculture, there is no security...you take your products and prices are too low...Then, it means you worked very hard for almost nothing., Austin et al., 2004. *labour*
24. Company documents.
25. According to Patricia Herrera, manager of the Posada Amazonas, 'The most beneficial aspect of this relationship for the community is the fact that they don't need to leave....I came to the community before the Posada Amazonas was built, and, at that time, many of them were leaving for Puerto Maldonado to work at any odd job...The community was running out of youngsters. Now, with the Posada, it's like young people, kids at school, know they have a job opportunity so they can stay here...They love it here, in their homeland.' Pérez, 2003: 10.
26. Barry Roberts has coined the term "ecotourism", and has wide experience running eco-lodges. He is currently in charge of Costa Rica's country-branding campaign. According to Roberts, "it is clear that Rainforest Expeditions (RFE) has been seriously mistaken from the beginning of the Posada Amazonas project, in sharing lodge management, decision-making and service quality control with Ese'ejas and settlers, on an equal basis. There is only one captain on a ship, and nobody should expect an inexperienced person to have the knowledge and the capability to produce the kind of service required in this kind of operation. If they continue to have a 50 percent share in management, they are bound to fail in the short run...RFE executives should be aware of the fact that company management should focus solely on running a company to make it successful." Roberts, B. (March 2003). "The Ese'eja Can Change." *INCAE Magazine* XIII(1): 76.

References

Austin, J.P. et al. (2006), 'Building New Business Value Chains with Low Income Sectors in Latin America', in K. Rangan, J. Quelch, G. Herrero and B. Barton, *Business Solutions for the Global Poor: Creating Social and Economic Value*,. Jossey-Bass, San Francisco, CA.
Austin, J., et al. (2004), *Social Partnering in Latin America: Lessons Drawn from Collaborations of Businesses and Civil Society Organizations*, Harvard University Press, Cambridge, MA.
Beck, Thorsten, Asli Demirgüç-Kunt, and Ross Levine (2003), 'Small and Medium Enterprises, Growth, and Poverty: Cross-Country Evidence', World Bank Policy Research Working Paper (3178) (December).
Chu, M. (2005), 'Commercial Returns and Social Value: The Case Of Microfinance', paper presented at the Business of Reaching the Global Poor symposium at Harvard Business School, Boston, MA.
D'Andrea, G. and Herrero, G. (2006), 'Understanding Consumers and Retailers at the Base of the Pyramid in Latin America', in K. Rangan, J. Quelch, G. Herrero and B. Barton, *Business Solutions for the Global Poor: Creating Social and Economic Value*,. Jossey-Bass, San Francisco, CA.
Dawar, N. and Chattopadhyay, A. (2002), 'Rethinking Marketing Programs for Emerging Markets', *Long Range Planning*, 35(5), pp. 457–74.
Easton, T. (2005a), The Hidden Wealth of the Poor, *The Economist*.

Easton, T. (2005b), Giants and Minnows, *The Economist*.
Easton, T. (2005c), Critical Acceptance, *The Economist*.
Epstein, M.J. and Crane, C.A. (2005), 'Alleviating Global Poverty through Microfinance: Factors and Measures of Financial, Economic, and Social Performance', paper presented at the Harvard Business School Conference on Global Poverty, Boston, MA.
Hamel, G. (1999), 'Bringing Silicon Valley Inside', *Harvard Business Review* (September–October), pp. 70–84.
Hardin, G. (1968), 'The Tragedy of the Commons', *Science*, 162, pp. 1243–8.
Hart, S. (2006), 'What Have We Learned?', paper presented at Research at the Base of the Pyramid: 'Developing a New Perspective', The William Davidson Institute, University of Michigan, Ann Arbor.
Hart, S. and London, T. (2005), 'Developing Native Capability: What Multinational Corporations Can Learn from the Base of the Pyramid', *Stanford Social Innovation Review*, pp. 28–33.
Lafourcade, A.-L., et al. (2005), Overview of the Outreach and Financial Performance of Micro-finance Institutions in Africa, Micro-finance Information exchange (MIX).
Leonard, H.B. (2005), 'When is Doing Business with the Poor Good – for the Poor? A Household and National Income Accounting Approach', paper presented at the Harvard Business School Conference on Global Poverty, Boston, MA.
London, T. and Hart, S.L. (2004), 'Reinventing Strategies for Emerging Markets: Beyond the Transnational Model', *Journal of International Business Studies*, 35, pp. 350–70.
Lozano, G. (2005), 'Aje Group en México: no hay enemigo pequeño', EGADE Teaching Case, Instituto Tecnológico de Monterrey, Monterrey.
Marulanda, B. and Otero, M. (2005), *The Profile of Micro-finance in Latin America in 10 Years: Vision & Characteristics*, ACCION International, Boston.
Marwaha, K., et al. (2005). *IBENEX: Business Effectiveness – the Next Level: Being Served by the Poor, as Partners*. Paper presented at the Harvard Business School Conference on Global Poverty, Boston, MA.
Pérez, F. (2003), 'Posada Amazonas', SEKN Teaching case no. SKE002, Harvard Business School Publishing, Boston, MA.
Prahalad, C.K. (2005), *The Fortune at the Bottom of the Pyramid: Eradicating Poverty through Profits*, Wharton School Publishing, Upper Saddle River, NJ.
Roberts, B. (2003), 'The Ese'eja Can Change', *INCAE Magazine*, XIII(1) (March), p. 76.
Stronza, A. (2000), *Because It Is Ours: Community-Based Ecotourism in the Peruvian Amazon*, Department of Anthropology, University of Florida, Gainesville, FL, p. 201.

4
Innovation and Entrepreneurship among Born Global Enterprises

Maija Renko and Jerry Haar

The globe keeps on getting smaller. It is not a surprise that at the same time, small businesses are increasingly global. The phenomenon of global start-ups, 'born globals', international new ventures and global high-tech start-ups has been documented in business literature as well as academic research since the 1980s (Rennie, 1993; Doz, Santos and Williamson, 2001; Harveston, Kedia and Davis, 2000; Rasmussen, Madsen and Evangelista, 2001; Rialp-Criado, Rialp-Criado and Knight, 2002; Zahra, Ireland and Hitt, 2000).

Oviatt and McDougall (1994) provide a comprehensive definition for an international new venture, which has since 1994 been adapted in a large number of empirical investigations of the phenomenon. According to Oviatt and McDougall (1994: 46), international new venture is 'a business organization that, from inception, seeks to derive significant competitive advantage from the use of resources and the sale of outputs in multiple countries'. In this chapter, we look at innovativeness and entrepreneurial orientation of these international ventures. We use the terms international new ventures and born globals interchangeably to refer to young, small firms that internationalize at an early age. Furthermore, we make a claim that both innovativeness and entrepreneurial orientation are necessary characteristics for small firms to succeed in global competition.

There are few small firms in today's world that are not affected by the globalization of competition; even those small businesses that choose to stay local face this global competition in the form of foreign firms entering their domestic markets. A small coffee shop practically anywhere in the world has to be aware that its home market may be the next step in the global expansion of Starbucks. The same holds true for a myriad of foreign franchises, such as Wendy's, Minuteman Press and Dryclean USA, that challenge local businesses. It has been also documented that despite the larger public's tendency to believe that small ventures are growth-oriented, actually only a small proportion of new firms aim at high growth in foreign markets (see, for example, Autio, 2005). Personality traits, organizational factors and environmental factors have been studied by entrepreneurship researchers as causes of new venture success and growth (Baum and Locke, 2004). For example, entrepreneurial climate in a society as well as role models have been linked to firm growth (Davidsson and Henrekson, 2002). However, early firm growth has been predominantly explained by the individual characteristics of the founder or founders of the business; age, sex and experience (Stuart and Abetti, 1990), cognitive constructs such as perceived competence (Chandler and Jansen, 1992) and personal goals (Birley and Westhead, 1994). In the current chapter, we suggest that there are four key characteristics that are typical for growing innovative, entrepreneurial, global firms. These firms, again, are the engine of the growth of economies and expansion of technologies into new frontiers.

Innovativeness and entrepreneurial orientation as engines of a firm's international growth

Innovation is a process that defines problems and develops new knowledge to solve them (Nonaka, 1994). When defined this way, it is clear that innovation is not an exclusive territory of high-tech firms. Innovation is becoming increasingly important as a means of survival, not just growth, in the face of intensifying global competition and environmental uncertainty in practically every industry. Not only firms in industrial nations but those in developing countries, as well, embrace innovation to enhance their competitiveness. Companies such as Taiwan's Acer, which started up and then grew into a major corporation, along with high-tech clusters of small firms in countries like Brazil are excellent examples.

In fact a number of born-again global companies in countries like Taiwan, Korea and India, considered as 'born global', were founded by professionals who had migrated back from the US and brought their US network of business partners and technical contacts with them, so that they could tap into networks in two countries from the outset.

Conceptually, innovation has been closely connected to knowledge management, organizational learning and networks (Swan *et al.*, 1999; Hislop *et al.*, 1997; de la Mothe and Foray, 2003; McElroy, 2002).

Innovative activities are seen as complex search, learning and problem-solving processes, which are as much based on existing knowledge as on creating new. Innovation – the process of defining problems and developing new knowledge to solve them – is essential for small firms that aim at growth in today's global markets. In rapidly changing international business environments factors such as technological and regulatory uncertainties, ambiguous markets and high development costs are challenges that require innovativeness from the firm.

Innovativeness is also a key component in what has been called entrepreneurial orientation of a firm. Miller (1983) describes entrepreneurial orientation as one that emphasizes aggressive innovation, risky projects and proclivity to pioneer innovations that preempt competition. Covin and Slevin (1989) have developed a scale for the measurement of the three components of entrepreneurial orientation, namely innovativeness, proactiveness and risk taking. For Covin and Slevin (1989), innovativeness reflects a tendency to support new ideas, novelty and creative processes, thereby departing from established practices and technologies. Proactiveness refers to a posture of anticipating and acting on future wants and needs in the marketplace, and risk-taking is associated with a willingness to commit large amounts of resources to projects where the likelihood and cost of failure may be high (Lumpkin and Dess, 1996; Wiklund and Shepherd, 2003). Knight and Cavusgil (2004) talk about an 'international entrepreneurial orientation', that is, a characteristic of born global firms that enables them to see and exploit entrepreneurial opportunities in international markets. International entrepreneurial orientation reflects the firm's overall innovativeness and proactiveness in the pursuit of international markets, and it is associated with a global managerial vision and a proactive competitive posture.

By definition, exploring international markets by a small firm typically requires a great deal of innovative and proactive attitude as well as risk-taking in the form of economic commitments. Knight and Cavusgil (2004) conjecture that young firms with a strong innovation culture and a proclivity to pursue growth in international markets tend to internationalize earlier than internationally oriented young firms that lack an innovative culture. Furthermore, Knight and Cavusgil suggest that born global firms are inherently entrepreneurial and innovative firms that possess the characteristic of excellence in knowledge acquisition and learning. Whereas larger, long-established firms usually experience substantial bureaucratization that hinders their innovative activities, smaller and younger firms are more flexible, less bureaucratic and more innovative.

Below, we introduce four characteristics that are typical for innovative, entrepreneurially oriented small firms that aim at international growth: people, markets, technology and networks. In a way, these four characteristics can also be read as manifestations of an innovative and entrepreneurial company culture. Even though our perspective is mostly that of a firm and its management, it is important to note that the development of born global firms is affected both by the characteristic of the environment and those of the founder/entrepreneur simultaneously (Madsen and Servais, 1997).

Four characteristics of growing innovative, entrepreneurial, global firms

People

Successful start-up firms are composed of entrepreneurs and employees that form a 'winning team'. Research has tried to identify the characteristics of successful entrepreneurs in many respects, but the results have often been inconclusive and even contradictory. For example, empirical research has demonstrated a range of results regarding the relationship between education, entrepreneurship and success, with education frequently producing non-linear effects on the probability of becoming an entrepreneur, or in achieving success (Reynolds, 1997; Davidsson and Honig, 2003; Arenius and Minniti, 2005).

Even though the kinds of human skills and knowledge needed for successful growth of a firm cannot be specified in terms of education, we can still be certain that small-firm success stems from the contributions of people involved. Human capital of a new venture is mainly available from individuals in the start-up team. The larger this start-up team, the more human capital there is. The important role of the management team for the success of a start-up firm has been confirmed in several studies (Delmar and Davidsson, 1999). Bollinger, Hope and Utterback (1983) reviewed the then-existing knowledge on factors contributing to the success of new technology-based firms. The only empirical finding that they could cite was that the faster-growing technology-based new firms were started by greater management teams, and that more technology had been transferred from the incubating organization to the more successful new firms.

Research suggests that internationally oriented managers have low psychic distance to foreign markets, master foreign languages and have experience of foreign countries. In addition, they are less risk-averse and less resistant to change than managers with a domestic orientation. (For a review, see Nummela, 2004.) For those firms that aim at expanding into global markets, a 'global mindset' of managers is needed. This mindset includes the willingness to seize international market opportunities, ability to handle cultural diversity, and the preparedness to take risks in building cross-border relationships (Fletcher, 2000).

This global mindset of leaders and managers can serve as a trigger for the international growth of a firm; but in order for a company to grow successfully, it needs to be able to incorporate all its employees to work for a common purpose. Even though Starbucks today is a large firm with presence on multiple continents, one need only go back some years in company history to investigate the personnel policies that have, for their part, made the phenomenal growth possible. In 1987 Starbucks had 17 stores, all in the Seattle area. Today, it has over 11,000 locations on three continents. This growth can be, to a large extent, attributed to the hiring and retaining of high-quality employees and managers. In 1988, Starbucks became one of the first companies to extend full health benefits to part-time employees, and in 1991 it became the first privately owned US firm to offer a stock option programme. These moves have been pivotal in increasing employees' commitment to the firm in an industry that typically suffers from high employee turnover (Barringer and Ireland, 2006:, 307–9).

Markets

Innovative and entrepreneurial small firms typically prosper in growth markets. However, this is not only a matter of picking the right growth markets. Through their proactive market approach, the companies themselves actually foster market growth for the whole industry. Customer orientation in innovative and entrepreneurial firms is about visioning and finding a mutual matching between a marketer's offering and a customer's demand (whether present or created). Often, new small firms offer products that are new to the market. This emphasizes the role of proactiveness in customer search and market communication; customers will not line up on the supplier's door if they cannot even relate their problems to solutions offered by the supplier. Proactiveness in visioning customers' needs can be achieved through listening to potential customers themselves but also by listening to the other players and stakeholders in the markets.

Understanding customers and competition in foreign markets is a prerequisite for successful internationalization of small firms. The more traditional 'internationalization process' theory emphasizes the accumulation of foreign organizing knowledge (Johanson and Vahlne, 1990), whereas the 'new venture internationalization' theory (McDougall, Shane and Oviatt, 1994; Oviatt and McDougall, 1997) views international market knowledge more as an enabling resource than as a regulator of resource commitments. In the literature on new venture internationalization, the inherent mobility of knowledge allows for an early and rapid internationalization of new ventures (Yli-Renko, Autio and Tontti, 2000).

Some small ventures are able to grow by adopting a business idea that has proven to be successful in one country to a new geographical market. A great example of such an approach, made possible through the proactive and global outlook of founding entrepreneurs, is the car-sharing service Zipcar. Antje Danielson, one of the founders of Zipcar in the US, was impressed by the car-sharing concept that was catching on across Europe in the end of 1990s. Together with the other co-founder of Zipcar, Robin Chase, Danielson introduced the car-sharing business model to the US markets. Chase and Danielson built the firm and its technology infrastructure in the US around the core ideas of convenience, affordability and environmental friendliness (Hart, Roberts and Stevens, 2005). In 2006, Zipcar had a customer base of 60,000 consumer and business drivers, making it North America's largest car-sharing service. The company currently operates over 1,600 vehicles in 12 states and provinces, including metropolitan New York, Boston, Chicago, San Francisco, Minneapolis, Toronto and Washington, DC (www.zipcar.com).

Whether a small firm adopts the Zipcar approach of market expansion or develops a totally 'new-to-the-world' kind of an innovation, a critical characteristic necessary for firm growth is a proactive attitude towards markets.

Today's fast-paced economies are characterized by growth markets, where potential for superior economic rents is competed away in the matter of months, weeks, days, or even minutes, as is the case in online auctions. Hence, starting up a firm in a growth market is, in itself, an insufficient guarantee for long-term success. However, when a firm combines its position in a growing market with a proactive approach of being one of the pioneers in that market, it increases the chances of survival and success.

Technology

Rapidly changing technology has been one of the key foundations of accelerated internationalization of young, small firms. Widespread diffusion of email, Internet and other technologies has made internationalization a more viable and cost-effective option for firms of all sizes. Markets for technology and technological products are seldom bound to a certain physical location. Codified knowledge is easily transferable via various means of communication available today. Patent rights travel across country borders without much extra cost, and scientific communities within various disciplines are increasingly international. International air travel has also become faster and cheaper over time. The containerization of freight has made the international logistics of goods less expensive than it used to be. Also, the constantly decreasing costs of digital technology and its constant miniaturization have made computers and other information technology devices available throughout the world (Yu, de Koning and Oviatt, 2005). These technology trends are affecting all businesses, large as well as small, in the global marketplace. However, for small, young firms that internationalize at an early age advanced technology is often not only a factor that makes communication, transactions and logistics easier; advanced technology also forms the backbone of the competitive advantage for many of these firms.

The main concern for technology-based firms of any size is the development and exploitation of their very technology. These firms tend to be well 'plugged –in' to the marketplace and to external sources of expertise and advice. Often technology markets are international niche markets, in which case it is likely that internationalization of small, young technology-based firms may take place rapidly. Jones (1999: 20) points out that resource needs of small firms as well as the multidisciplinary nature of many technology fields suggest that the internationalization process may have an inward as well as an outward dimension, and that these firms are likely to be instantly or rapidly international.

As an example of internationalization of a technology-based sector, let us consider the software industry in the small, open economy of Finland. Finland, with its population of 5 million people, is one of the world's most competitive economies and most technologically developed welfare and information societies. Solid technological infrastructure, open competition, government's active role in the development of an information society, technology-oriented citizens and knowledge-based metropolitan areas provide a basis for the development of high-tech industries, such as software. High-tech exports from Finland have tripled over the past five years and in industrial productivity Finland has caught up with the United States (National Technology Agency of Finland, 2004).

The size of the Finnish software market in 2001 was slightly less than €1.1 billion (European Information Technology Observatory, 2002). The value of the software product business of Finnish companies was €892 million for the same period, with the share of exports rising to more than €400 million (Hietala *et al.*, 2002). In 2004, there were about 1,100 companies in Finland operating in software or closely related fields (Finnish Software Business Cluster, 2004). Most of these firms are small; in industry data from 2001, the median sales turnover of the Finnish software firms was about €500,000 and 70 per cent of firms employed less than 20 people (National Technology Agency of Finland, 2003).

Finnish software companies are mainly owned by their founders and their family members, with only minor foreign and external ownership. European companies have lagged behind the US firms in the packaged software segment, due to small and diverse home markets, low degrees of standardization and internationalization, and weak links to universities (Torrisi and Malerba, 1996). Currently, however, at least, the Finnish software sector is witnessing development from custom software developed for local markets towards mass-market software intended for international distribution (Finnish Software Business Cluster, 2004). The growth of the Finnish software business sector has been extremely rapid. In 1998, the combined sales of Finnish firms in the sector totalled €252 million, out of which the share of exports was €104 million. By 2001, the industry turnover had grown into €892 million, and at the same time the exports had increased to a yearly figure of €408 million (National Technology Agency of Finland, 2003). Despite industry growth, small software firms are struggling with profitability problems. In 2001, most of the companies that participated in a survey on Finnish software businesses made no profit. According to the same survey, Finnish software companies usually start internationalization with direct sales to other countries. About 37 per cent of the companies that participated in the survey had international sales. Internationalization most often begins with the Swedish, American and Estonian markets and the most important export countries are Sweden, Germany, United States and Great Britain (National Technology Agency of Finland, 2002).

Because of their small domestic markets – less than 0.5 per cent of the global software market – growth-seeking firms from these nations have to be competitive in international settings and aim at international markets. Findings of Finnish, Irish and Norwegian software internationalization by Bell (1995) supported to some extent the concept of psychic distance as an important factor in the selection of export markets. In his sample, 50–70 per cent of firms entered 'close' markets in the initial stages of export development. Finnish firms targeted Sweden, Norway and the former USSR – countries that are geographically and culturally proximate. However, the data also revealed that some 30–50 per cent of firms had initiated exports with sales to countries that could not be considered as either psychologically or geographically proximate. In Bell's study (1995) factors that strongly influenced firms' initial and subsequent market selection decisions in addition to distance were client following, sectoral targeting and computer industry trends.

Networks

For anyone starting a new enterprise the benefits of knowing the 'right' people materialize early on in the start-up process. Several studies report on the contribution of the entrepreneur's network to resource acquisition of new ventures (Birley, 1985; Honig, 1998; Baron and Markman, 2002). Eisenhardt and Schoonhoven (1996) show that growing ventures exploit their managers' social contacts for alliance formation. McDougall, Shane and Oviatt (1994) suggest that foreign personal contacts of key individuals can be used to identify new opportunities, obtain business advice and assistance in negotiations, and open doors in markets where the internationalizing firm has no previous presence. Personal contacts also increase the alertness of the internationalizing firm as its attention expands from domestic to international markets (Oviatt and McDougall, 1997). The findings of Bell's (1995) study of export behaviour among entrepreneurial software firms suggest that the network approach offers a strong explanation in the internationalization process of these firms.

Fernhaber and McDougall (2005) study strategic adaptation and networking capabilities as drivers of new venture growth in international markets. According to them, networking can have positive effects on international growth through a number of mechanisms. First, networks can lead to increased levels of growth by providing entrepreneurs with informational benefits. For example, strong ties with major customers in international markets can provide invaluable feedback regarding necessary product changes. Second, networks can increase the legitimacy and credibility of an internationalizing new venture. To illustrate, a new venture that belongs to a local business group or is a member of an industry trade association can be viewed as more credible among international buyers than a firm without such network support. Third, concrete exchange relationships can develop as a result of networking. Often, a firm's first international sales are to customers that the firm has got to know through a third party, who can serve as a reference for both sides of the transaction (Coviello and Munro, 1997).

The importance of networks in the global economy, however, goes beyond the bootstrapping activities and customer finding. As reported in a *Business Week* cover story on 14 August 2006, there is a large number of new firms in the online marketplace that is attempting to follow the path laid out by Google Inc. – build a global user community and hope the advertising from retail sellers will follow. One of the recent successes in adopting this business model is Digg.com, a website that lets the user community 'dig up' the most interesting stories on the web and vote them onto the online 'front page' of Digg.com. Last year the site that first saw daylight in the autumn of 2004 was the 24th most popular website in the US, easily beating, for example, Fox News (no. 62), according to industry tracker Alexa.com. Digg-registered users have been doubling every three months. More than 1 million people flock to Digg daily, reading, submitting, or 'digging' some 4,000 stories. As on many similar sites, people register and create online profiles. Of these users, 94 per cent are male and more than half are IT types in their 20s and 30s making $75,000 or more. These demographics combined with the global scope of online business make the site highly attractive for advertisers. The company's business idea is completely based on co-creation of value within the user community. The attractiveness of the site for users (customers) as well as for advertisers depends on the size of the user network.

Innovative and entrepreneurial firms not only take advantage of the networks that they have established with their suppliers, employees and other stakeholders; they also scout the network opportunities present in the marketplace. Instead of value chains, today's markets are composed of value networks and value constellations in which customers and sellers are linked to each other, often through multiple simultaneous ties. In such a marketplace, competitive advantage can often be derived from establishing a valuable location in the network. In this process of finding a valuable network position, however, serendipity may often play a larger role than strategic network management.

There are few better examples of the synergistic relationship between people, markets and technology than German's Fraunhofer Society, an expansive collection of 56 scientific research institutes. This non-profit organization invented the MP3 standard for digital music; and MP3 patents generate tens of millions of dollars in licensing fees for the Fraunhofer Society (*Business Week*, 2007a).

Discussion and conclusions

We have now introduced four characteristics that describe innovative, entrepreneurially oriented firms that aim at global growth. These characteristics are summarized in Figure 4.1.

New market conditions in many sectors of economic activity have made it possible for firms to internationalize even at an early age. Liberalization of world trade, the increasing importance of niche markets and the lowering cultural barriers between various country markets have made it possible for even small firms to market their products internationally. We have suggested that the more successful international small ventures operate in growth markets, and – in line with entrepreneurial orientation of a firm – adopt a proactive approach to marketing and sales.

Technological developments in areas like communication, transportation and production also play an important role in the emergence of born global phenomenon. A key to the sustainability of a competitive advantage of a small firm in global markets is the possession of (or access to) unique, rare, inimitable resources. Indeed, a wealth of empirical investigations

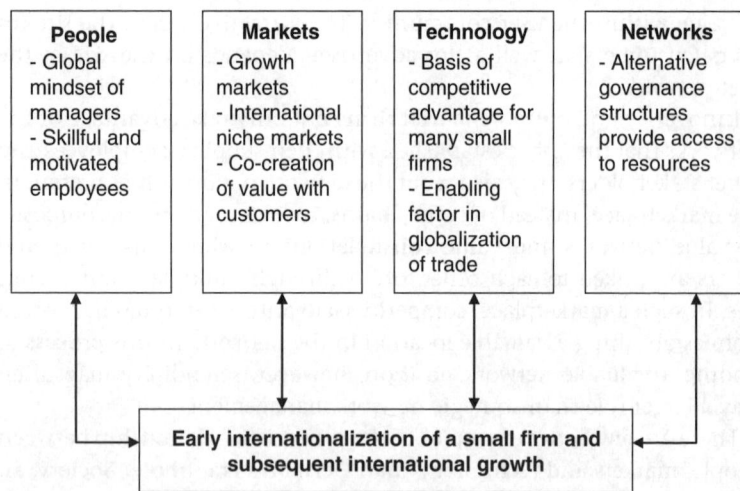

Figure 4.1 Innovative and entrepreneurial characteristics of born global firms

on international new ventures have applied the so-called 'resource-based view' of the firm and associated conceptual developments (dynamic capability perspective, knowledge-based view of the firm) as the core theoretical framework for explaining the emergence and growth of international new ventures (for a review, see Rialp *et al.*, 2005). Small firms seldom have the resources to build brands comparable to those of incumbents, nor does their size allow them to benefit from economies of scale or scope. It follows that the competitive advantage of a small, international firm is often based on technological capabilities and resources. In comparison to larger international firms, international new ventures are typically more niche-focused, usually applying cutting-edge technology to develop highly specialized products suitable for niche global markets (Rialp *et al.*, 2005).

Even if new, small ventures commonly lack sufficient financial resources to control many assets through ownership, hybrid structures such as licensing, franchising and strategic alliances are often useful alternatives to both internal control and market control of resources. Indeed, Oviatt and McDougall (1994: 35) find that a major feature that distinguishes new ventures from incumbents is the minimal use of internalization – resource ownership – and the greater use of alternative transaction governance structures, like networks. In addition to providing access to resources, innovative small firms can also benefit from network structures in their marketing. Instead of traditional value chains, where goods move stage by stage from producers to distributors and finally to end users, many of today's markets can be described as value constellations, where both customers and sellers participate simultaneously in value creation.

The more sophisticated entrepreneurial skills of people, including those of the founding entrepreneur who starts an internationalizing firm, have also contributed to the increasing number of born global firms worldwide. The managers of internationalizing new, small firms seem to perceive the entire world as a firm's marketplace from the outset. They neither confine themselves to a single country focus nor see foreign markets as purely complementary to the domestic one (Rialp *et al.*, 2005). They begin with a global vision, and devise a collection of capabilities at the strategy and organizational culture levels of the firm that give rise to early internationalization and possible success in a broad range of foreign markets. Early, small internationalizers quickly acquire a substantial base of international experience and knowledge that traditional multinational corporations typically have taken longer to acquire (Knight and Cavusgil, 2004).

This point is amply illustrated by developments in Europe's 'start-up culture'. US venture capital firms like Benchmark Capital and Accel Partners, as well as European ones like Luxembourg's Mangrove Capital partners, have been actively involved. Among the notable start-ups to emerge in Europe are: Skype, the Net phone company; Pageflakes; photo-sharing site Ofoto; MyQSL, open-source database software; Last. fm; and FON (*Business Week*, 2007b).

The characteristics presented here as typical for innovative and entrepreneurially oriented firms that internationalize at an early age are, in many respects, very similar to characteristics of companies that would succeed in domestic markets as well. The importance of people – the entrepreneur as well as employees – as well as unique (technological) resources as a basis for firm competitiveness do not only concern firms that operate in international markets. However, there are aspects in both the people dimension (global mindset of the entrepreneur) and in the technology dimension (unique technology that is aimed at a worldwide niche market) that relate to firm internationalization. Similarly, even though networking skills are important for all entrepreneurs, globally oriented entrepreneurs are likely to have access not only to domestic stakeholders but also foreign ones through their personal networks. And even though growth can be a characteristic of a domestic market of a small firm, it is the international growth markets that appeal to born global firms. However, given this ambiguity in distinguishing factors that are beneficial for firm success in general from those that trigger internationalization at an early age, future research in the area would benefit from investigation of the differences in drivers of domestic vs global growth, and to what extent the two really differ.

References

Arenius, P. and Minniti, M. (2005), 'Perceptual Variables and Nascent Entrepreneurship', *Small Business Economics*, 24, pp. 233–47.

Autio, E. (2005), *Global Entrepreneurship Monitor, 2005 Report on High-Expectation Entrepreneurship*, at http://www.gemconsortium.org (accessed 26 July 2006).

Baron, R.A. and Markman, G.D. (2002), 'Beyond Social Capital: The Role of Entrepreneurs' Social Competence in their Financial Success', *Journal of Business Venturing*, 18(1), pp. 41–60.

Barringer, B.R. and Ireland, R.D. (2006), *Entrepreneurship: Successfully Launching New Ventures*, Pearson Education, Upper Saddle River, NJ.

Baum, J.R. and Locke, E.A. (2004), 'The Relationship of Entrepreneurial Traits, Skill, and Motivation to Subsequent Venture Growth', *Journal of Applied Psychology*, 89(4), pp. 587–98.

Bell, J. (1995), 'The Internationalisation of Small Computer Software Firms – A Further Challenge to "Stage" Theories', *European Journal of Marketing*, 29(8), pp. 60–75.

Birley, S. (1985), 'The Role of Networks in the Entrepreneurial Process', *Journal of Business Venturing*, 1(1), pp. 107–17.

Birley, S. and Westhead, P. (1994), 'A Taxonomy of Business Start-Up Reasons and their Impact on Firm Growth and Size', *Journal of Business Venturing*, 9, pp. 7–31.

Bollinger, L., Hope, K. and Utterback, J.M. (1983), 'A Review of Literature and Hypotheses on New Technology-based Firms', *Research Policy*, 12, pp. 1–14.

Business Week (2007a), 'An Idea Incubator Tries to Grow Cash', 12 March.

Business Week (2007b), 'Techies Across the Pond', 12 March.

Chandler, G.N. and Jansen, E. (1992), 'The Founder's Self-assessed Competence and Venture Performance', *Journal of Business Venturing*, 7(3), pp. 223–36.

Coviello, N.E. and Munro, H.J. (1997), 'Network Relationships and the Internationalization Process of Small Software Firms', *International Business Review*, 6, pp. 361–86.

Covin, J.G. and Slevin, D.P. (1989), 'Strategic Management of Small Firms in Hostile and Benign Environments', *Strategic Management Journal*, 10, pp. 75–87.

Davidsson, P. and Henrekson, M. (2002), 'Determinants of the Prevalence of Start-ups and High-Grandowth Firms', *Small Business Economics*, 19(2), pp. 81–104.

Davidsson, P. Honig, B. (2003), 'The Role of Social and Human Capital Among Nascent Entrepreneurs', *Journal of Business Venturing*, 18, pp. 301–31.

de la Mothe, J. and Foray, D. (2003), *Knowledge Management in the Innovation Process*, Springer, New York:.

Delmar, F. and Davidsson, P. (1999), *Firm Size Expectations of Nascent Entrepreneurs*, Jönköping International Business School, at http://www.ihh.hj.se/eng/research/publications/wp/19997%20Delmar,%20Davidsson.pdf (accessed 23 August 2005).

Doz, Y., Santos J. and Williamson, P. (2001), *From Global to Metanational*. Harvard Business School Press, Boston.

Eisenhardt, K.M. and Schoonhoven, C.B. (1996), 'Resource-based View of Strategic Alliance Formation: Strategic and Social Effects in Entrepreneurial Firms', *Organization Science*, 7, pp. 136–50.

European Information Technology Observatory (2002), Annual Report. European Information Technology Observatory, Hamburg.

Fernhaber, S.A. and McDougall, P.P. (2005), 'New Venture Growth in International Markets: The Role of Strategic Adaptation and Networking Capabilities', *Advances in Entrepreneurship, Firm Emergence, and Growth*, 8, pp. 111–36.

Finnish Software Business Cluster (2004), 'Finnish Software Product Business in Brief', http://www.swbusiness.fi/portal/industry_information/what_is_software_business_/

Fletcher, D. (2000), 'Learning to Think Global and Act Local: Experiences from the Small Business Sector', *Education and Training*, 42(4/5), pp. 211–19.

Hart, M., Roberts, M.J. and Stevens, J.D. (2005), *Zipcar: Refining the Business Model*, Harvard Business School Cases, 9-803-096.

Harveston, P.D., Kedia, B.L. and Davis, P.S. (2000), 'Internationalization of Born Global and Gradual Globalizing Firms: The Impact of the Manager', *Advances in Competitive Research*, 8(1), pp. 92–9.

Hietala, J., Maula, M.V.J., Autere, J., Lassenius, C., Kari, N. and Autio, E. (2002), *Finnish Software Product Business: Results from the National Software Industry Survey 2002*, Centre of Expertise for Software Product Business and Helsinki University of Technology.

Hislop, D., Newell, S., Scarborough, H. and Swan, J. (1997), 'Innovation and Networks: Linking Diffusion and Innovation', *International Journal of Innovation Management*, 1(4), pp. 427–48.

Honig, B. (1998), 'What Determines Success? Examining the Human, Financial, and Social Capital of Jamaican Entrepreneurs', *Journal of Business Venturing*, 13(5), pp. 371–94.

Johanson, J. and Vahlne, J.-E. (1990), 'The Mechanism of Internationalization', *International Marketing Review*, 7(4), pp. 11–24.

Jones, M. (1999), 'The Internationalization of Small High Technology Firms', *Journal of International Marketing*, 7(4), pp. 15–41.

Knight, G.A. and Cavusgil, S.T. (2004), 'Innovation, Organizational Capabilities, and the Born-Global Firm', *Journal of International Business Studies*, 35, pp. 124–41.

Lumpkin, G.T. and Dess, G.G. (1996), 'Clarifying the Entrepreneurial Orientation Construct and Linking it to Performance', *Academy of Management Review*, 21, pp. 135–72.

Madsen, T.-K. and Servais, P. (1997), 'The Internationalization of Born Globals: An Evolutionary Process?', *International Business Review*, 6(6), pp. 561–83.

McDougall, P.P., Shane, S. and Oviatt, B.M. (1994), 'Explaining the Formation of International New Ventures: The Limits of Theories from International Business Research', *Journal of Business Venturing*, 9, pp. 469–87.

McElroy, M.W. (2002), *The New Knowledge Management-Complexity, Learning, and Sustainable Innovation*, Butterworth-Heineman, Oxford.

Miller, D. (1983), 'The Correlates of Entrepreneurship in Three Types of Firms', *Management Science*, 29, pp. 770–91.

National Technology Agency of Finland (2004), www.tekes.fi

National Technology Agency of Finland (2003), *Ohjelmistotuotteet SPIN 2000–2003-teknologiaohjelma*, Ohjelmistotuotteilla kansainväliseen menestykseen, Tekes Technology Reports 15/2003, Helsinki, Finland.

National Technology Agency of Finland (2002), 'Growth of Software Product Industry Continued Despite Slowdown in Market Growth', at http://akseli.tekes.fi/Resource.phx/tivi/spin/en/growth.htx. Original source: J. Hietala, M.V.J. Maula, J. Autere, C. Lassenius, N. Kari and E. Autio (2002), *Finnish Software Product Business: Results from the National Software Industry Survey 2002*, Centre of Expertise for Software Product Business and Helsinki University of Technology.

Nonaka, I. (1994) 'A Dynamic Theory of Organisational Knowledge Creation', *Organisation Science*, 5, pp. 14–37.

Nummela, N. (2004), 'Is the Globe Becoming Small or is the Small Becoming Global? Globalization and internationalizing SMEs', in M.V. Jones, and P. Dimitratos (eds), *Emerging Paradigms in International Entrepreneurship*, Edward Elgar, Cheltenham, pp. 128–51.

Oviatt, B.M. and McDougall, P.P. (1994), 'Toward a Theory of International New Ventures', *Journal of International Business Studies*, 25(1), pp. 45–64.

Oviatt, B.M. and McDougall, P.P. (1997), 'Challenges for Internationalization Process Theory: The Case of International New Ventures', *Management International Review*, 37 (Special Issue 2), pp. 85–99.

Rasmussen, E.S., Madsen, T.K. and Evangelista, F. (2001), 'The Founding of the Born Global Company in Denmark and Australia: Sensemaking and Networking', *Asia Pacific Journal of Marketing and Logistics*, 13, pp. 75–107.
Rennie, M. (1993), 'Global Competitiveness: Born Global', *McKinsey Quarterly*, 4, pp. 45–52.
Reynolds, P. (1997), 'Who Starts Firms? Preliminary Explorations of Firms in Gestation', *Small Business Economics*, 9, pp. 449–62.
Rialp-Criado, A., Rialp-Criado, J. and Knight, G.A. (2002), 'The Phenomenon of International New Ventures, Global Start-ups, and Born-globals: What do We Know After a Decade (1993–2002) of Exhaustive Scientific Inquiry?', Working Paper No. 2002/11. Dep. d'Economia de l'Empresa, Universitat Autònoma de Barcelona, Bellaterra (Barcelona), Spain.
Rialp, A., Rialp, J., Urbano, D. and Vaillant, Y. (2005), 'The Born-Global Phenomenon: A Comparative Case Study Research', *Journal of International Entrepreneurship*, 3, pp. 133–71.
Stuart, R. and Abetti, P. (1990), 'Impact of Entrepreneurial and Management Experience on Early Performance', *Journal of Business Venturing*, 5(3), pp. 151–62.
Swan, J., Newell, S., Scarborough, H. and Hislop, D. (1999), 'Knowledge Management and Innovation: Networks and Networking', *Journal of Knowledge Management*, 3(4), pp. 262–75.
Torrisi, S. and Malerba, F. (1996), 'The Dynamics of Market Structure and Innovation in the Western European Software Industry', in D. Mowery (ed.), *The International Computer Software Industry: A Comparative Study of Industry Evolution and Structure*, Oxford University Press, Oxford, pp. 165–96.
Wiklund, J. and Shepherd, D. (2003), 'Knowledge Based Resources, Entrepreneurial Orientation, and the Performance of Small and Medium-sized Businesses', *Strategic Management Journal*, 24, pp. 1307–14.
Yli-Renko, H., Autio, E. and Tontti, V. (2000), 'Social Capital, Knowledge, and the International Growth of Technology Based New Firms', Helsinki University of Technology, Institute of Strategy and International Business, Working Paper Series 2000, No. 4.
Yu J., de Koning, A. and Oviatt, B.M. (2005), 'Institutional and Economic Influences on Internet Adoption and Accelerated Firm Internationalization', *Advances in Entrepreneurship, Firm Emergence, and Growth*, 8, pp. 85–110.
Zahra, S.A., Ireland, R.D. and Hitt, M.A. (2000), 'International Expansion by New Venture Firms: International Diversity, Mode of Market Entry, Technological Learning, and Performance', *Academy of Management Journal*, 43(5), pp. 925–50.

Part II
Country Case Studies

5
Competitive Business Practices in Developing Economies: The Case of Small and Medium-size (SMEs) Companies in Mexico

Jaime Alonso Gómez

This chapter describes the current status and future prospects of Mexican small and medium-size companies. The first section presents a general view including the numbers, business sectors, size, geographic location, investment levels and composition of SMEs in Mexico. The second part describes the variety of needs and challenges that SMEs are facing in the presence of a business environment that is more global, demanding and competitive. Part three enumerates the efforts of the Mexican government at federal, state and municipal level to assist and support SMEs in their strategies to become more competitive. The fourth section shows that current efforts are not enough and that further reforms and policies need to be carried out. The fifth section introduces an emerging and innovative (at least in Mexico) set of trends developing in Mexican SMEs. Finally, section six integrates all the sections and presents a view ahead for SMEs in Mexico.

SMEs in Mexico: general overview

Mexico has an estimated population of 104 million people (2005). Its $752 billion gross domestic product in 2005 places Mexico as the 13th largest economy, the 11th and 12th largest importer and exporter in the world (2005).

Mexico's SMEs account for 99 per cent of the total number of businesses,[1] include 79 per cent of the labour force, represent approximately 60 per cent of the GDP, and generated 315,000 new jobs in 2004 (Secretaría de Economía).

English	Spanish
Number of companies by size	Número de empresas por tamaño
Micro, small, medium, large	Micro, pequeña, mediana, grande
Employment	Empleo
Contribution to GDP	Contribución al PIB

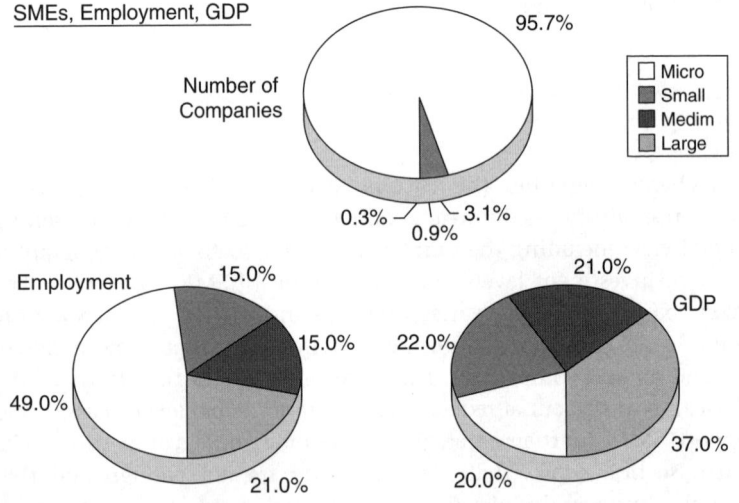

Figure 5.1 SMEs in Mexico
Source: SIEM, 2005.

In 2004, SMEs generated 62 per cent of the Gross National Product (GNP) (http:www.cipi.gob.mx/html/principal,html).

Classification of companies

Companies in Mexico are classified by the department of economic development as follows:

Figure 5.3 shows the composition of companies in terms of size and sector.

It can be seen that 99.6 per cent of industrial companies are SMEs, 99.8 per cent of commercial companies are SMEs and 99.6 of service

Classification	Industrial	Commerce	Services
Micro	Less than 10	Less than 10	Less than 10
Small	11–50	11–30	11–50
Medium	51–250	31–100	51–100
Large	More than 250	More than 100	More than 100

Figure 5.2 Companies by number of employees and sector
Source: Secretaría de Economía, 2005.

Size	Composition by size and sector (per cent)			Total
	Sector			
	Industrial	Commercial	Services*	2,844,308
Micro	94.4	94.9	97.4	95.7
Small	3.7	4.0	1.6	3.1
Medium	1.7	0.9	0.5	0.9
Large	0.4	0.2	0.4	0.3
Total	100	100	100	100

Figure 5.3 Composition of companies by size and sector (per cent)
Source: Censo Económico, 1999.
*Non-financial private services.

companies are SMEs. Total composition of SMEs in Mexico amounts to 99.7 per cent.

Commerce is Mexico's main economic activity and accounted for 52 per cent of the total number of SMEs in 2002. Most of the economic activity is concentrated in state capitals and other cities or urban areas. This is not different from other developing countries in which political and economic activity takes place in urban areas.

Close to 50 per cent of the SMEs in Mexico are located in the states of Guanajuato, Mexico, Veracruz, Jalisco, Puebla and Distrito Federal. The main drivers for this concentration are: high population density, large number of suppliers and distributors, availability of information,

Sector	Micro	Small	Medium	Large	Total
Industrial					
Agribusiness	997	355	91	10	1,453
Mining	155	36	40	37	268
Industrial manufacturing	28,149	8,338	4,444	2,240	43,171
Construction	10,637	3,406	582	86	14,711
Total industrial	**39,938**	**12,135**	**5,157**	**2,373**	**59,603**
Commercial					
Commercial	434,072	12,441	4,122	1,725	452,360
Total commercial	**434,072**	**12,441**	**4,122**	**1,725**	**452,360**
Services					
Communications	4,718	588	133	253	5,692
Services	127,478	12,001	1,723	1,531	142,733
Total services	**132,196**	**12,589**	**1,856**	**1,784**	**148,425**
TOTAL	**606,296**	**37,165**	**11,135**	**5,882**	**660,388**

Figure 5.4 Number of SMEs, by sector and size
Source: Sistema de Información Empresarial Mexicano (SIEM), 2005.

financial and commercial services, and access to technology, education and external markets (export-oriented business clusters) (SIEM, 2005).

SMEs in terms of business orientation

Independently from size, sector and geography, SMEs can be subdivided into pre-production, production and distribution, wherein marketing and sales are the main factors.

Pre-production implies research and development (R&D) and the design of products and services. Production considers the transformation activity by which products and services are created. Distribution means the commercialization of products and services. This last part – commercialization – is the weakest link for most SMEs in Mexico. This is why the Mexican government actively participates in implementing a set of policies to help small and medium-size companies get closer to

Employees	1989 UE*	1994 UE*	1999 UE*	Average annual growth of UE*		UE* as percentage of total		
				1989–94	1994–9	1989	1994	1999
TOTAL	1,313,944	2,184,558	2,726,366	10.7	4.5	100.0	100.0	100.0
Less than 2	963,514	1,646,133	2,066,581	11.3	4.7	73.3	75.4	75.8
2–5	224,195	356,892	432,586	9.7	3.9	17.1	16.3	15.9
5–10	57,271	91,646	115,694	9.9	4.8	4.4	4.2	4.2
11–15	21,244	29,460	36,788	6.8	4.5	1.6	1.3	1.3
16–20	11,387	14,751	18,318	5.3	4.4	0.9	0.7	0.7
21–50	21,236	26,702	33,181	4.7	4.4	1.6	1.2	1.2
51–100	7,564	9,505	11,012	4.7	3.0	0.6	0.4	0.4
101–250	4,810	6,206	7,620	5.2	4.2	0.4	0.3	0.3
251–500	1,675	2,059	2,709	4.2	5.6	0.1	0.1	0.1
501—1,000	764	881	1,251	2.9	7.3	0.1	0.04	0.05
> 1,000	284	323	609	2.6	13.5	0.02	0.01	0.02
TOTAL	1,313,944	2,184,558	2,726,366	10.7	4.5	100.0	100.0	100.0

Figure 5.5 Companies in Mexico
Source: Censos Económicos del INEGI 1989–1999.
* UE = Economic units or for profit organizations.

domestic and international markets. The purpose is to help companies with export-oriented logistics, financial support, training and development seminars (human capital), business management, market expertise and skills to become robust at exporting.

Economic growth may also imply an increase in the number of companies. In Mexico, the number of companies and business people has been increasing in recent years. Figure 5.5 presents the growing number of SMEs by sector.

The last figure shows that the number of SMEs has been growing but the rate of growth per number of employees (micro, small, medium and large companies) is different. It is observable that there was a decrease in the rate of growth (almost across all sizes) between 1994 and 1999 (correlated with economic crises of 1995). The lowest growth rate was for companies with between 51 and 100 employees. The largest annual average growth was for companies with more than 1,000 employees.

In the early 2000s, due to new and more demanding market and competition conditions, SMEs tend to be integrated or interrelated with other companies in terms of clusters, vertically integrated value chains (for exports), research and development collaboration. These new relationships with domestic and international firms have brought a higher level of competitiveness but also imply being exposed to the presence and/or influence of large corporations that have acquired, merged or made disappear many SMEs in Mexico (Kauffman, 2001).

An interesting factor in SMEs in the early 2000s is that they are increasingly buying more software and IT tools for business process consolidation and modernization. This is presenting provocative challenges for software companies which have to design and implement more company(SME)-specific business solutions (as opposed to generally implemented software such as SAP, ERP, CRM, etc.). This software purchasing grew close to 150 per cent in 2004. Due to an increase in availability of IT solutions for small and mid size companies and their importance as an element of the whole business model, the relative size of SME's as a percentage of the whole IT industry in Mexico changed from 19.2% in 2001 to 46.6% at the end of 2006.

In the first decade of the 2000s in Latin America, Mexico will be the country wherein SMEs acquire most IT software and information technology generally; even more than in Brazil (the other large economy in Latin America).

According to Edgar Fierro, IDC de Mexico analyst, 80 per cent of SMEs are in Mexico's north, centre and west. The southern area presents growth potential despite its not so robust level of business and social development. However, there is indeed a large development divide between the southern region in Mexico and the rest of the country.

Fierro mentions that SMEs invest 51 per cent of their resources in hardware, 33 per cent in software and services when these are related to increasing quality, productivity and competitiveness. A more generic distribution of SMEs' investment portfolios is presented in Figure 5.6.

This figure shows that manufacturing SMEs in Mexico have been investing mostly in a) production capacity and new product development, when it implies the pre-production and production phases, and b) in the modernization of their business process and in ways to understand and/or influence domestic markets (in the presence of a more open, de-regulated Mexican economy). This is as a result of more and more SMEs working in import substitution products and services.

Investment destiny for all SMEs and percentage of companies			
Manufacturing sector (machinery and equipment)			
Production capacity	New product development	Cost reduction	Production process automation
(37.9)	(29.8)	(29.0)	(21.4)
Commercial sector (equipment and facilities)			
Increase in sales	New technologies	Change in sales strategy	Cost reduction
(39.5)	(34.1)	(21.2)	(15.3)
Manufacturing sector (commercial area)			
Domestic market modernization of business processes	Strategic changes in domestic market	Domestic market research	Advertisement
(46.9)	(43.9)	(16.1)	(7.1)
Service sector (commercial area)			
Domestic market modernization of business processes	Strategic changes in domestic market	Business process efficiency	Domestic market research
(56.0)	(14.1)	(14.1)	(5.3)

Figure 5.6 SMEs: type of investment (percentage of companies that invested resources by concept)

Source: Encuesta del Observatorio PyME, 2002.

SMEs in the service sector are investing also in the modernization of their business process to increase sales, as well as in research to understand and influence domestic markets.

SME current status and challenges

Companies across all countries experience a highly complex, interdependent, competitive and global business environment. Palomo[2] mentions in his article how SMEs in Mexico are facing a set of problems as they enter the new millennium. At the micro-economic level, Mexican small and medium-size companies in general lack:

- Management know-how (effective and efficient planning, organization, execution and control systems)
- Technology for production and distribution
- Financial support to grow and become competitive
- Human capital
- Customer service and orientation
- Innovation orientation to differentiate products and services (South Korea companies invest 40 times more in innovation than Mexican companies).

Only 10 per cent of SMEs in Mexico export. This is a contrasting figure when compared with SMEs' exports in other countries: 84 per cent in the US, 79 per cent in Taiwan and 73 per cent in Japan. Only 10 per cent of Mexican SMEs have certifications. This complicates competing in international markets and integration to export-oriented clusters or business chains, and, finally but no less importantly, 86 per cent of Mexican SMEs say that they do not know about government support incentives or support (Observatorio PyMes in Mexico, 2003).

At macro-economic level, Kauffman (2001) report the following:

---

a. Lack of a clear industrial policy
b. Fiscal policy does not foster industrial development
c. Financial support and interest rates are not competitive
d. Depressed domestic market does not allow for scale economies
e. Lack of government support and incentives for SMEs
f. Public services are not competitive in quality, price and infrastructure
g. Big competitiveness asymmetric differences among the NAFTA companies (technology, financial, IT, human capital, etc.)
h. Environmental practices and regulations in Mexico are more costly than those enjoyed by commercial partners
i. Reforms in labour and energy policy are needed
j. Lack of innovation and technology development business culture
k. Lack of robust human capital training and development systems

---

Figure 5.7 Problems in Mexican SMEs
Sources: Kauffman, 2001, and Ramos, 2004.

> a. Limited participation in export-oriented commerce
> b. Limited access to sources of funding
> c. Out of touch with most dynamic and growing sectors
> d. Insufficient training and development of human resources
> e. Lack of contact with universities and technical schools
> f. Lack of innovation and technological development culture
> g. Idle production capacity across all sectors in manufacturing SMEs

Figure 5.8 Mexican SMEs' main challenges
Source: CIPI, 2001.

Similar problems were described by CIPI (2001):

Without doubt, SMEs in Mexico are challenged by a multiplicity of problems related to the lack or insufficiency of:

- Managerial strategic vision and know-how
- Export orientation
- Technical and logistics infrastructure
- Relationships with universities and/or research centres
- Financial support
- Capacity to respond to new environmental and social demands
- Understanding domestic markets due to deregulation of the economy
- Human capital
- Total factor productivity

Many of these have been present for at least 10-15 years. Even though Mexico's industrial policy to support and assist SMEs has become more and more robust, it is still insufficient. This will be observed in the next section.

Government policy for SMEs in Mexico

The scenarios described in the previous sections have propelled special responses of the Mexican government at federal, state and municipal levels to foster and develop SMEs. In particular, the design and implementation of industrial policy to fortify small and medium-size companies.

Due to the fact that 64 per cent of all Mexican SMEs are also family business (lacking management know-how and expertise on global competitiveness), the Mexican government has emphasized a wide variety of training and development seminars on these topics to help family business owners understand the dynamics of global competition, technological innovation and human capital.

An additional element that has been found is that 86 per cent of these family firm and SME owners have mentioned that they do not know of any government-based (federal, state or municipal) support or incentive dedicated to foster SMEs' competitiveness. Of these business owners, 12.65 per cent know about the incentives but do not use them, and only 1.8 per cent know and utilize these incentives and support.

Government support and incentives include the fortification of productive clusters and vertically integrated (for exports) groups of companies, technological modernization, basic and advanced technical training, supplier development, support to achieve international certifications (ISO 9000 like), programmes helping to export, acquisition of machinery and equipment, and managerial strategy.

In 2001, 2002 and 2003 the Mexican government created the following programmes to help and support SMEs:

FAMPYME: *Fondo de Apoyo a la Micro, Pequeña y Mediana Empresa* (Fund to support micro, small and medium-size companies)
FIDECAP: *Fondo de Fomento a la Integración de Cadenas Productivas* (Fund to foment SMEs' integration in productive chains)
FOAFI: *Fondo de Apoyo para el Acceso al Financiamiento de las Micro, Pequeñas y Medianas Empresas* (Fund to SMEs' financial access)
FACOE: *Programa de Centros de Distribución en Estados Unidos* (Fund to develop distribution centres in the US to facilitate SMEs' export activities)

All of these programmes had the objective of creating, developing and consolidating SMEs. Each *fondo* or fund was specific to a particular purpose. In 2004 all of these funds were integrated into a single one, *Fondo PYME*. The rationale for doing this was to:

- Integrate government policy and public image (for communication purposes) to help SMEs
- Unify efforts and integrally attend projects and initiatives asking for support
- Categorize specific incentives and needs
- Facilitate support and assistance by type of need
- Multiply impact of policies, plans and projects to strengthen SMEs' competitiveness
- Improve accountability, transparency and measurement of impacts.

This unified fund was directly derived from the *Plan Nacional de Desarrollo Empresarial* (Business Development National Plan) 2001–6 and the Law for the development of SME competitiveness.

In 2004, the *Secretaría de Economía* presented the following results (2000–4):

The unification of all funds into one strategic and system fund produced good numeric results as it can be derived from the figure. But, perhaps the most beneficial result was that SMEs registered in the fund became more formal and professional, and were able to train and de-

Concept	Annual data					January		
	Observed				Goal	2003	2004	Variation (annual percentage)
	2000	2001	2002	2003	2004			
Companies which were registered and assisted	6,312	8,404	10,266	10,780	7,729	5,207	4,178	−19.8
Successful cases*	5,047	6,813	8,468	9,086	6,956	4,567	3,941	−13.7
Referrals to external consultants (with economic support from the fund)	929	1,318	1,667	2,326	1,782	862	489	−43.3
Referrals to financial institutions	914	1,252	1,627	1,823	1,918	1,274	790	−38.0
Training and development (persons)	33,425	25,834	33,425	35,130	30,000	16,406	14,747	−10.1
Training and development (companies)	–	–	3,862	6,806	3,370	3,673	2,317	−36.9

Figure 5.9 SME fund: main results, 2000–4

Source: Secretaría de Economía, Censo Económico, 1999.

*El indicador mide los casos exitosos terminados

Institution	No. of programmes
Secretaría de Comercio y Fomento Industrial	31
Secretaría de Hacienda y Crédito Público	18
Secretaría de Contraloría y Desarrollo Administrativo	3
Secretaría del Trabajo y Previsión Social	5
Secretaría de Educación Pública	4
Banco Nacional de Comercio Exterior, S.N.C.	22
Nacional Financiera, S.N.C.	18
Consejo Nacional de Ciencia y Tecnología	7
Secretaría de Desarrollo Social	4
Secretaría de Agricultura, Ganadería y Desarrollo Rural	6
Secretaría de Medio Ambiente, Recursos Naturales y Pesca	13
TOTAL	**131**

Figure 5.10 Programme inventory (by government institution)
Source: CIPI, 2001.

velop many of their executives and employees with the new tools and methods to accomplish higher levels of competitiveness.

CIPI also conducted a study to identify the number and kind of programmes existing to help SMEs in Mexico.

Figures 5.10 and 5.11 show that the government institutions more proactive to help and assist SMEs were *Secretaría de Comercio y Fomento Industrial* (Economic Development), with 31 programmes, *Banco Nacional de Comercio Exterior* (Foreign Trade Bank) with 22 programmes, *Hacienda* (Treasury and Fiscal) with 18 programmes, and *Nacional Financiera* (National Development Bank) with 18 programmes too. Most of these efforts provided training, technical assistance and business consulting (27 out of 131), credit and financial services (25 out of 131), fiscal support an incentives (24 out of 131) and purpose-specific projects (22 out of 131).

Mexico's economic performance improved over the 1990s. GDP growth was strong, inflation was controlled, and the current account deficit was of only moderate size. When the US economy slow-down

Type of programme	No. of programmes
Fiscal support and incentives	24
Support to activities provided by states and specific agencies	22
Information systems*	1*
Orientation and inter-institutional services	13
Training, technical assistance and business consulting	27
Credit, risk capital and subsidies from CONACYT, SEDESOL and SEMARNAP	13
Credit and financial services from Mexican development banks and institutions	25
Regional development and business productive chains	6
TOTAL	**131**

Figure 5.11 Support programme inventory
Source: CIPI, 2001.
* Information system programmes were clustered by SIEM to facilitate access.

took place in 2001, the impact on Mexico was moderate by traditional Mexican standards (Mexico's exports to and imports from the US are more than 80 per cent). Additionally, the financial system and economic stability have been in good shape due to sound macroeconomic policies. Yet, the large number of reforms and the entry to NAFTA in the mid-1990s have not produced a substantial and sustained productivity increase for SMEs.

More macroeconomic and regulatory reforms are needed. All the programmes and institutions described in the last two figures have been positive and produced results. However, Mexico's SMEs are not yet competitive enough as different OECD and IMD competitiveness studies and surveys show.

Growth in Mexico, it has been said, is limited by:

(a) Low levels of human capital. This is particularly detrimental in a new global and knowledge-based economy;
(b) Lack of technical and physical infrastructure such as communications, roads, Internet highways, etc.;
(c) Large segments of population in poverty and informal economy;

(d) Wide segments of population in informal work and business activity;
(e) Lack of enforcement of the state of law that helps in providing certainty for foreign direct investment and business activity.

The business enterprise and SMEs in general are facing challenges and new expectations from customers, employers, investors and society as a whole. The stability and the well-preserved tradition of the business enterprise have been challenged. Business issues concerning innovation, business design, knowledge-based competencies, customer's changing lifestyles, capital efficiency, active pricing and marketing, acquisitions and alliances and new organization forms are, at the beginning of the new millennium the drivers of new rules of competition and sustainable development.[3]

There is thus a need for further and more robust reforms in Mexico that will raise the rate of growth of labour and total factor productivity. According to Mexican officers, growth needs to be increased from 4 per cent a year approximately to a minimum of 6 per cent. According to Mexico's OECD Survey in 2003 and Gabriela Ramos, director of OECD in Mexico, several challenges have to be addressed:

- Mexico needs to remain committed to macroeconomic stability
- Public revenue and expenditure need to be more solid and predictable
- Resources for education and training ought to be used more effectively
- Emphasis on strategic thinking and new business vision
- Raise and improve the stock of infrastructure capital
- Pursue labour-market reforms
- Pursue reforms in the electricity and telecommunications sector
- Eliminate corruption
- Alleviate extreme poverty and ensure that benefits of stronger growth are shared more broadly across population groups
- Assure the strengthening of legal system and financial/banking institutions.

Emerging/innovative business practices in SMEs in Mexico

Mexico's development in the second half of the 1900s was basically driven by becoming cost-attractive to companies and investors. The strategy was to substitute imports and develop local–national industrial infrastructure. Major efforts went instigated to bring investment to the region. The most important achievement was the *maquiladora* industry (which started in the 1960s and was related to low-cost and labour-intensive assembly of imported raw materials, which were then shipped back to the country of origin).

Many multinational enterprises installed *maquiladora* operations along the Mexican border with the US. This created, generally speaking, a good level of development, manifested in an industrial (low-skill manufacturing) culture, new jobs and better per capita income. But as we now see in a global economy, new players are taking Mexico's place regarding this strategy. China is the number one example that has changed the rules of the game, not only for Mexico but for many other countries too. The strategy to bring investment based on low cost of labour to countries with middle gross domestic per capita income (that is, US$4,000–10,000), such as Mexico, Brazil, Chile, Poland and the Czech Republic, is no longer sustainable. Countries like El Salvador, Honduras, Eastern European countries, and China and India in particular, are taking Mexico's place. The emergence of China, especially (which received almost $70 billion in investment in 2005 versus $17 billion each for Mexico and Brazil), has changed dramatically the flows of foreign direct investment.

To compete in a global economy, SMEs need to change from competition based on cost to positioning and differentiation based on value creation. Value added business strategy has been shown to be more sustainable and profitable than cost (Hamel, 2002), in particular, when the valued added (in products and services) implies the use of knowledge-intensive workers or more sophisticated technology.

A second element is the realization that investment in production capacity, process optimization and productivity increase is good. Yet investment to create or develop innovation capabilities is better. A number of studies by Hamel (2002) and Prahalad (2005) show the impact of this emphasis on innovation.

In this context in which cost-based competition is no longer sustainable for middle-income economies, there are four emerging trends in Mexican SMEs that are worth mentioning:

(a) Innovation-driven positioning and differentiation;
(b) Technology-based new venture creation;
(c) SMEs from Mexico and other countries that also have (or soon will have) free trade agreements with the US;
(d) Use of remittances (money sent back to Mexico by people who migrated to the US and work there) to start new companies.

SME innovation-driven positioning and differentiation

The region of León in the state of Guanajuato in central Mexico is well known for its shoe and leather-clothing industries. However, despite heavy competition from other regions of the world, these industries are still operating (but having a hard time). The future of the Mexican shoe industry in particular has been under severe threat by the arrival of both legal imports and illegal contraband from China and Brazil in recent years. Lower cost and higher/equal-quality shoes from these two countries are now available all over the distribution markets where León-made shoes are sold. To respond to this threat, leather and shoe manufacturers in León are implementing all sorts of modernization, efficiency and quality-oriented techniques such as total quality management, lean manufacturing, six sigma, 5-S, statistical process control and capital investment in equipment and machinery. These efforts have produced the expected results, such as lower cost, higher manufacturing efficiency and product quality. But as it has been know in the manufacturing industry in general, cost- and quality-based competitive advantage is harder to sustain, and in particular, against the gigantic and powerful China.

In an initiative that includes business and industry consultants, regional universities and their research centres, management training and private/public funds, several leather and shoe manufacturers have become not only able to sell their products to US and Europe, but also to China and other Asian markets. Exports to China and Asia include leather pieces, which are used for the car seats of luxury cars and shoes for the high-income, more sophisticated Chinese consumer. The key to accomplish this: innovation on process technologies to accentuate the quality specifications and the appearance characteristics of leather pieces used for the luxury cars; and shoe designs that emphasize elegance and style, plus comfort (qualities that the new professional Chinese are increasingly demanding). The group of León-based companies that are doing this has not only seen an increase in their revenues from exports but, most importantly, a new way of doing business based on innovation and design.

Technology-based new venture creation

This has been clearly understood by three entities in the Mexican business domain: CONACYT (Mexican Council for Science and Technology), *Secretaría de Economía* and several leading business schools (private and public) in the Mexican business realm.

By taking into consideration the notions of innovation, speed from concept to market, valued-added business activity, knowledge-based products and services and design (instead of manufacturing only), CONACYT and *Secretaría de Economía* (with their monetary resources) have allied with business schools (with management know-how and human capital resources) to support several initiatives:

(a) Training and educating groups of SME executives and company owners with the new rules of competition and a special emphasis on innovation and design;
(b) Technology/innovation-based new venture creation (generation of new economy wealth vs enhancing actual operation of current SMEs);
(c) Development of new generation incubators and accelerators to foster and/or create as many new companies as possible with new university graduates;
(d) Funds that provide up to 80 per cent of the total capital for the technology/innovation-based new venture. In case the new venture does not prosper, the entrepreneur does not need to pay more than 20 per cent of the total amount of money;
(e) New business models to support the management of the new business ventures.

This new alliance between CONACYT , *Secretaría de Economía* and leading business schools had, at the end of the first semester of 2006, more than 150 new companies in incubation or acceleration process and is creating a more rapid, more education-based, and more systematic process to generate new wealth in terms of the competition drivers inherent to the new global, knowledge economy. Very promising results, but not yet conclusive, are starting to appear. In particular in the areas of information technology for business processes, bio- and nano-technology (functional food), healthcare, mechatronics (inter-phase between mechanical and electronics) and environmental. This alliance is expected to continue.

Examples of these efforts include the leather and shoe industries in León and the information technology sector. A very good case to illustrate the information technology sector is Creswin, a Mexican SME that has won several international competitions and contracts due to its innovation capabilities. This organization produces Windows-compatible software for managerial process, which manages orders from mobile sales personal and/or electronic trade on real time by using PDAs or cellular phone technology on wide band communication technology. Estimates on productivity improvement on sales and delivery due to this business process technology amount to up to 800 per cent. This company and its founder and CEO have won international prizes such as the World Young Business Achiever (WYBA), the World Confederation of Business (Worldcob) and the Bizz Award in 2006, as the best business for software innovation. Currently, this company has implemented more than 16,000 applications in more than 20 countries and has grown 245 per cent with respect to its 2005 business operations. A key to this success is positioning and differentiation based on value added, innovation and speed in anticipating business needs.

A second example involving universities and young entrepreneurs is a design-oriented company that started when its founders were studying engineering and design at a state university in Mexico City. With the initial help of some professors, who provided business contacts and methodological guidance, this company started to sell advertising and publicity designs for small companies in Mexico. After that, they also obtained contracts for stands and sales displays for major multinationals in Mexico. Recently, this company has been able to win contracts with major multinationals that are interested in more technical designs for a variety of parts for their electro-domestic products. Currently this company has more than 180 customers of which 50 per cent are Mexican SMEs. According to its founders, the key for this success is skilled workers, innovation and design-based portfolio of products and services and a clear vision that competition is based on value added, not just in terms of cost.

The most interesting example involves the use of biotechnology and new lifestyles. The seed of the avocado, a Mexican fruit which is very popular in Mexican cuisine and whose consumption is growing around the world, has very interesting properties. In very simple terms, the seed produces pesticides and insecticides that impede the bugs and other plagues that eat the pulp of the avocado while it is growing in the avocado tree. Furthermore, the very same seed also fabricates natural-based antioxidants, which prevent the dishes that use avocado as part of their preparation (such as guacamole and chips, a very common snack in Mexico and the US in sportbars or fast-food restaurants) from becoming dark in colour and crispy in consistency; in more technical terms, they oxidize. A central Mexico SME, in conjunction with a biotechnology centre and a private business school (which is helping with the business plan and model), is already taking advantage of the avocado seed properties and is working in three directions. One is related to the food industry, in which the SME with the help of the biology research centre is, producing natural-based preservatives (versus more synthetic chemicals) to keep foods fresh for extended periods. This is particularly attractive for the health-conscious consumer; this is a growing worldwide trend. The second direction implies the use of the same antioxidant properties but in the cosmetics industry. By using special cosmetic technology, they are producing pastes and mascara creams for both men and women to use on the face, arms and other body parts to avoid wrinkling, darkening or dark specs on the skin. This aesthetics market niche is also growing exponentially around the world. The business school is working with the SME to prepare the business plans and business models on the two business opportunities: food and the cosmetics industry. The third area of joint work among research centres, business schools and entrepreneurs is on the development of a new pesticide that does not harm humans. This is still work in progress. Key elements in this project are venture capital from *Secretaría de Economía,* biotechnology from research centrers, business schools and market needs.

The following example emphasizes the alliances between companies and universities. Microsoft invites students from universities from all over the world to help the company invent the future through new technology projects. A group of students from a private school in Mexico's Pacific area won the contest at national level and then participated in a worldwide tournament with students from 40 countries, who presented 180 projects. The Mexican students developed software that diminishes wrong or erratic medical decisions. Students detected that some major sources of errors are: variance in the identification of symptoms and the medications from doctor to doctor and the lack of communication between general doctors and specialized doctors regarding patient information. Hospitals sometimes do not have the clinical history or file of the patients and doctors may ignore the fact that a particular prescription may be harmful to the patient because of some hereditary situation or particular allergy. Medical errors or prescriptions given by doctors who do not have enough patient information account for one of the ten most common causes of death worldwide.

Mexican students developed software that is capable of retrieving information about the patient and making it accessible from any PDA, laptop or similar electronic device. Some additional software features include history of similar cases, intelligent diagnostics, the possibility to publish cases and total security and privacy of information.

Key success points to this project were: the identification of a market need in the health industry; the entrepreneurial spirit of the students;

the business incubator at the private university; the support from Microsoft; and the office of patents at the regional level in Mexico.

SMEs from Mexico[4] and other countries that also have (or soon will have) Free Trade Agreement with the US

The G3 group (Mexico, Colombia and Venezuela) has a Free Trade Agreement (FTA) that has produced in general, a good increase in the amount of trade exchanged by the three countries. Recently, there have been negotiations regarding including Panama in this group. The opportunity here is related to the country of origin rule, for content of products that includes a country or a region within the FTA area. Mexican SMEs, and those from other Latin American countries such as Colombia and Panama (in process of an FTA with the US) or Chile (already with an FTA with the US), can have complementarity when exporting to the US. For instance, a product could have 45 per cent Mexican content and 30 per cent Colombian or Chilean. By doing this, the country/region rule of origin and content is accomplished (say, more than 55 per cent), and geographically integrated chains/clusters of SMEs can increase possibilities to enter the world's largest market; the US. Given the nature of business activities and development in the Latin American region, opportunities emerge in the mid- to high value added, manufacturing parts for some or all of the following industrial sectors: automobile, electronics, home appliances and metal-mechanic. Additional opportunities are emerging for Colombian and Mexican SMEs in the apparel and editorial industries; the Colombian fashion industry has been developing robustly in the last decade. For example, a joint venture (JV) between a Colombian SME that provides the fashion design and a Mexican SME that contributes with marketing, distribution and sales in the US is a natural one. Something similar can be developed for Colombian editorial companies, which are strong in the South American area and are exploring entering the US (Hispanic) market. JVs of this nature are already taking place, even before the signing of a FTA between Colombia and the US.

The use of remittances (money sent back to Mexico by people who have migrated to the US and work there) to start new companies

The tremendous economic asymmetries between the US (GDP/capita of roughly US$40,000) and Mexico (GDP/capita of roughly US$8,000), without mentioning the large divide between the 'haves' and the 'have nots' in Mexico, have historically caused a lot of migration from poor and rural areas from Mexico into the US.[5] First-generation male Mexican immigrants earn only half as much as Anglo men. But the second generation has overtaken black men and earned three-quarters as much as Anglos. Second-generation children enjoy more benefits than the first generation, too: they are twice as likely to have employer-provided pensions and one-and-a-half times more likely to have health insurance. And the adult daughters of Mexican immigrants, having learned English, are much more likely to have jobs than their mothers were.

Mexicans have grown much richer by going to the United States. And their children are doing even better. Whereas only 40 per cent of first-generation Mexican immigrants between the ages of 16 and 20 are in school or college, nearly two-thirds of the second generation are. Between the ages of 21 and 25 the leap is even more striking, from 7.3 per cent to 24.4 per cent.

Immigrants' children are typically American citizens, having been born on American soil. More than 90 per cent speak English fluently and Latinos seem to be very entrepreneurial; they open new firms at a rate three times the national norm.

Children of immigrants (legal or not) will have a double advantage over their parents. Not only are they native-born Americans, but they are 'native-born' to the information age. A prestigious Mexican national advisory board on the census, the *Consejo Nacional de Población*, has just released a study that says that 17 million Mexicans have emigrated out of Mexico in 40 years. The study says that the majority of those emigrating did so to the US, where 9.5 million of them now reside. The study says that if it were not for those emigrating, the total population of Mexico would be 120 million. The study says that there are now 8.2 million Mexicans who are sons and daughters of these emigrated Mexicans in the US and that 7.8 million are second-generation descendents.

In addition, the study states that the percentage of Mexican families that have relatives in the US or receive monies from Mexican workers in the US now exceeds 18 per cent of all Mexican households, representing 3.8 million in total. Mexico is divided into 2,350 municipalities or 'townships' and the study says that 96 per cent of these have some sort of connection with the US or receive monies from Mexican immigrants in the US. The study provided the following breakdown concerning this connection: 492 townships have a 'high' connection, 392 townships have a 'medium' connection, 466 townships have a 'low' connection and 93 townships have no connection.

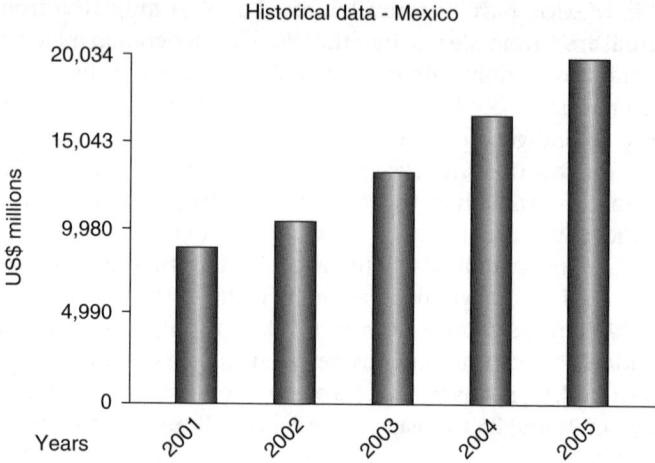

Figure 5.12 Remittances: historical data, Mexico
Source: Interamerican Development Bank, 2006.

These statistics are particularly relevant given the fact that more than $50 billion in remittances were sent from the US to Latin America in 2005. In 2003, Mexico captured more than $13,000 million and, at the end of 2006, Mexico is expected to receive $24,000 million in total remittances (the majority from the US). The following figure shows these statistics.

A small, but increasing, percentage of people who migrated to work and live in the US have started an SME by sending money to their friends and relatives in Mexico. The Mexican recipients of this money, who previously used it for immediate consumption, have now changed their approach. They now use it, for example, to start a T-shirt factory. They manufacture cotton T-shirts with pictures that resemble Mexican symbolic icons (from Mexican historic sites and heroes to wildlife and funny words) and sell them in the Los Angeles market. Los Angeles is the city with the largest population of Mexicans outside of Mexico, second only to Mexico City. In addition to the money they receive from their relatives in the US, recipients of remittances can go to *Nacional Financiera* (Nafinsa – Mexican Development Bank) and obtain funds that can amount up to $1 or 2 million (after providing a market study and some initial feasibility studies). This Nafinsa project offers to migrants and their relatives possibilities to transform remittances into productive resources to create new enterprises. Funds to support these projects range from $9,000 to $2 million. With this approach, Mexican migrants and their relatives can become business entrepreneurs. Some other successful new venture creations have been seen in the food sector, such as spicy powder that mixes with water to produce Mexican salsas and organic food exported to the US.

In addition to Nafinsa, some other areas in central Mexico have the three-to-one formula. For every dollar of remittances people receive in Mexico, the federal, state and municipal governments offer one dollar each in order to start new business. This is the case in the state of Zacatecas. New emerging trends are very promising and are expected to grow in the years to come.

Conclusions

SMEs represent a sector of great importance in Mexico. They signify 99 per cent of the total number of Mexican companies; concentrate 64 per cent of the labour force and 40 per cent of gross domestic product.

A number of programmes and strategies to assist and support SMEs have been created. These programmes include managerial and technical assistance, training, financial support, export-oriented processes, clustering, infrastructure and human capital. Assistance is related to pre-production, production and distribution across all geographic regions in Mexico and the US. The largest number of SME companies is located in areas of high population density, large number of suppliers and customers, availability of resources and infrastructure and human capital. These areas are the states of Guanajuato, Mexico, Veracruz, Puebla, Jalisco and Distrito Federal.

Several government and non-government agencies have participated in developing policy and tactics to foster and develop SMEs. The most active and known of these include CIPI, SIEM, SE, FUNDES, Observatorio PyMES and university research centres.

The main challenges for SMEs in Mexico are of a different nature and magnitude depending on size, sector, geographic region and orientation. Yet the most evident are: lack of clear industrial policy, labour policy and fiscal policy; insufficient financial support and/or non-competitive interest rates; scale factors related to size of domestic markets in the presence of competition from US and European companies; and lack of quality and prices on public services and infrastructure.

A variety of programmes have been created to assist SMEs, yet 86 per cent of the SMEs say that they do not know about them, 12.65 per cent know of them but do not use them and less than 2 per cent know about them and take advantage of them. Therefore, additional efforts need to be undertaken for SMEs to utilize all of these support packages, incentives and special funds to assure SMEs' competitiveness.

Programmes developed and implemented by *Secretaría de Comercio y Fomento Industrial, Banco Nacional de Comercio Exterior, Secretaría de Hacienda* and other government and non-government agencies have been unified in a more systemic and strategic initiative to cope with the lack of knowledge and use of them by SMEs.

Additional reforms and initiatives need to take place though. In particular, there is a tremendous necessity to remain committed to macroeconomic stability, have more solid and predictable public revenue and expenditure (fiscal reforms), provide more and more effectively used resources for education and training, emphasize strategic thinking and new business vision for SMEs' decision-makers, raise and improve the stock of infrastructure capital, pursue reforms in the labour market and the electricity and telecommunications sector, eliminate corruption, alleviate extreme poverty and ensure that benefits of stronger growth are shared more broadly across population groups and assure the strengthening of legal system and financial/banking institutions.

Finally, new emerging trends based on innovation, value added and design are increasingly growing as alliances between CONACYT, *Secretaría de Economía* and leading business schools in Mexico. More than 150 technology-based new venture-creation projects are already on their way to incubators or accelerators. Business schools are contributing with the business models and plans to enable these projects to materialize. These trends include: a) innovation-driven positioning and differentiation, b) technology-based new venture creation, c) SMEs from Mexico and other countries that also have (or soon will have) FTAs with the US and e) use of remittances (money sent back to Mexico by people who migrated to the US and work there) to start new companies. Very promising results, but not yet conclusive, are starting to appear, in particular in the areas of: information technology, biotechnology (food), healthcare, mechatronics and environmental.

Mexican SMEs have problems related to competitiveness, lack of proper government policies and managerial vision. However, with the current and expected reforms (once the new government administration is in place), the extensive use of current assistance programmes and funds, the new emerging trends involving government agencies, universities and business schools, and, in particular, with the new, younger generations that will be succeeding current decision-makers, economic growth exceeding 2 or 3 percentage points will allow Mexico to enjoy the same levels of SME productivity and GDP per capita that the other OECD countries have. Mexico is betting on these efforts and it is expected that results will be produced in the years to come.

Notes

1. This chapter considers micro and small (micro and *pequeña*) companies as one single category: small companies.
2. Palomo, 2005.
3. Arthur D. Little, *Innovation Excellence Study*, 2005.
4. Mexico has had a Free Trade Agreement (FTA) with the US and Canada since 1994. Current exports (2004) to the US and Canada are around US$110 billion and US$10 billion respectively. Mexico has 46 active FTAs around the world.
5. A lot of the data on this section was taken from a study made by the Consejo Nacional de Población at the census office in the Secretaría de Gobernación.

References

Arthur D. Little (2005), *Innovation Excellence Study*, Arthur D. Little, Rotterdam.
Austin, J. (1990), *Managing in Developing Countries*, Free Press, New York.
Cutierrez, R. et al (1998), 'Challenges for the New Millennium in Latin America,' Corporación Andina de Fomento, Caracas, Venezuela.
Chase, R., Aquilano, N. and Jacobs, F. (1998), *Production and Operations Management. Manufacturing and Services*, McGraw-Hill, Boston.
CIPI (2001), Comisión Intersecretarial de Política Industrial, at http://www.cipi.gob.mx/html/principal.html
Cuarto informe de labores, Secretaría de Economía (2004), http://www.economia.gob.mx/pics/p/p1376/CuartoInformedeLaboures.pdf
Conference Board, Report 1231- 99 – CH.
Crawford, R. (1991), *In the Era of Human Capital*, Harper Business, New York.
Dávila, T., Epstein, M. and Shelton, R. (2006), *Making Innovation Work*, Wharton School Publishing, Upper Saddle River, NJ.
De Kluyver, C. and Pearce, J. (2003), *Strategy: A View from the Top*, Prentice Hall, Upper Saddle River, NJ.
Diagnóstico de las PyMEs, CIPI (2002), at http://www.cipi.gob.mx/html/..%5CDiag_Desem_Mpymes.pdf
Diagnóstico sobre el impacto del fraude y la corrupción en las PyMEs (2005), at http://www.radioformula.com.mx/rf2001.asp?ID2=31956
'El Gran Libro de la PyMes' (2006), Casa Editorial El Tiempo SA, Colombia.
Feinstein, J. (2006), *The Nature of Creative Development*, Stanford Business Books, Palo Alto, CA.
Flaherty, M. (1996), *Global Operations Management*, McGraw-Hill, New York.
Hamel, G. (2002), *Leading the Revolution: How to Thrive in Turbulent Times by Making Innovation a Way of Life*, Plume, New York.
IDC de México, at http://www.idclatin.com/mexico/
InfoChannel (2005), *IDC define escenarios de crecimiento*, at http://www.infochannel.com.mx/mundos33.asp?id_nota=13281&industria=3

Jones, O. (2003), *Competitive Advantage in SMEs: Organizing for Innovation and Change*, John Wiley, England.

Kauffman, S. (2001), 'El desarrollo de las PyMEs: Un reto para la economía mexicana', Revista Ciencia Administrative, 1, at http://www.uv.mx/iiesca/revista2001-1/empresas.htm

Leifer, L. et al. (2000), *'Radical Innovation,'* Harvard Business School Press, Boston.

Levy, M. and Powel, P. (2004), *Strategies for Growth in SMEs: The Role of Information and Information Systems*, Butterworth-Heinemann, Oxford, UK.

Miller, D. and Le Breton-Miller, I. (2005), *'Managing for the Long Run,'* Harvard Business School.

Observatorio PyME México (2003), *Primer Reporte de Resultados 2002*, CIPI, SE 2003, at http://www.cipi.gob.mx/html/reporteanalitico.pdf

Palomo, M. (2005), 'Los procesos de gestión y la problemática de las PyMEs', at http://ingenierias.uanl.mx/28/28_los_procesos_gestion.pdf

Prahalad, C.K. (2005), *The Fortune at the Bottom of the Pyramid: Eradicating Poverty through Profits*, Wharton School Publishing, Upper Saddle River, NJ.

Presidencia de la República(200),. 'Detona el sexenio impulso a PyMES', at http://www.presidencia.gob.mx/buenasnoticias/?contenido=19948&pagina=56

PyMeS, Guía de Promoción, 5a. edición (2005–6), LEGIS Publicaciones especializadas, Bogotá, Colombia.

SIEM (2005), at http://www.siem.gob.mx/portalsiem/

6
Italian SMEs and Industrial Districts on the Move: Where are they Going?

*Anna Carabelli, Giovanna Hirsch and Roberta Rabellotti**

Since the second half of the 1990s the Italian economy has experienced significant slow-down in the rate of economic growth. Although the other advanced countries have also suffered some slow-down in their economies, macroeconomic indicators show the Italian slow-down to be more marked. Italy has lost ground essentially because its economic growth rate has weakened relative not only to its own past performance, but also to that of most other advanced countries (OECD, 2005a).

The main reason for Italy's poor performance is the decline in labour productivity. Daveri and Jona-Lasinio (2005) have demonstrated convincingly that this labour productivity slow-down is due to a sharp decline in total factor productivity (TFP), especially in the manufacturing sector, rather than to a decline in capital deepening. Daveri and Jona-Lasinio show that this decline has been particularly striking in the 'Made in Italy' industries, such as textiles and clothing, leather and footwear, and wood products, suggesting decreased dynamism and innovation capacity in the Italian economy (ICE, 2005; Brandolini and Cipollone, 2003).

There has been wide-ranging debate among scholars and policy-makers about the main causes of this slowed growth. One of the main issues in this debate is the relationship between some peculiarities of the Italian manufacturing system, which is dominated by very small firms and very traditional sectors (such as textile and clothing, leather and shoes, ceramic tiles), and its decreasing competitiveness in the international market.

---

* Corresponding author: rabellotti@eco.unipmn.it

The deep transformations that are occurring in the international production system are changing the relative positions of the advanced countries in terms of export performance. Within this framework of global changes, the EU area has experienced a decline in its export share over the last ten years, based on the introduction of the euro and its appreciation against the US dollar and the emergence of highly competitive Asian economies, especially China and India. Italy seems to have suffered most from these structural changes precisely because of its low-tech model of specialization and the 'dwarfism' of its manufacturing system.

Since the 1980s, the peculiarities of Italian industry have been recognized internationally as key components of a successful pattern of industrial development, which is based on 'flexible specialization' and has been seen as an alternative to large, mass-scale production (Piore and Sabel, 1984; Pyke, Becattini and Sengenberger, 1990; Pyke and Sengenberger, 1992). Industrial districts have been acclaimed internationally as key to Italy's manufacturing growth. The literature on industrial districts is immense; their definitions are many.[1] According to the generally accepted definition, an industrial district is a cluster of mainly small and medium-sized, spatially concentrated firms, specialized both in one sector and often in one or a few phases of the production process, characterized by a strong, relatively homogeneous, social and cultural background and embedded in a favourable institutional context (Rabellotti, 1997).

Up to the early 1990s, Italian industrial districts displayed a remarkable economic dynamism, based on their positive performance in terms of sales, exports, employment and profits, and certainly were the central players in the Italian manufacturing system (Signorini, 2001; Brusco and Paba, 1997).

In the most recent years of zero or very little growth, and continuously reduced international competitiveness, industrial districts have continued to be at the centre of the economic debate in Italy; however, the widespread enthusiasm of past decades is being replaced by increasing criticism and they are being held responsible for Italy's 'industrial decline'. According to these critics, the very small scale of these manufacturing firms and their specialization in traditional sectors represent a major structural weakness in the Italian industrial system, which is unable to respond to the challenges of globalization and innovation (De Cecco, 2004; Gallino, 2003; Onida, 2004; Nardozzi, 2004). Italy's 'industrial decline' has combined with the loss of confidence in the industrial district model, considered to be an Italian anomaly, which in the changing international context, has gone from being a strength to becoming a drawback.[2]

Alongside these critical views, is a vast and flourishing literature on how industrial districts and their firms are evolving in terms of sectoral transformation (new sectoral specialization), international strategies (outsourcing, FDI and participation in global value chains), innovation strategies (ICT diffusion, process and product innovations) and the emergence of new forms of enterprise organization (verticalization and hierarchization, business groups; appearance of leading medium-size companies).

In this chapter, we aim to contribute to the ongoing debate with a survey of this literature, addressing the question of how industrial districts and their firms are reacting and adapting to the era of globalization. Among and within industrial districts, many different behaviours can be identified and our objective is to present some of the available evidence of such heterogeneity.

The chapter is structured as follows. The first section presents some stylized facts characterizing the manufacturing system, namely the predominance of small and medium enterprises (SMEs) and their organization in industrial districts, specialization in the so-called traditional sectors and the international pattern of specialization. The second section presents a review of some of the most recent and more interesting studies analysing the main changes that are occurring in industrial districts: the shift in production specialization, the international strategies of firms and districts, their innovation capacity and the emergence of new forms of enterprise organization. The third section concludes the chapter.

Some stylized facts on the Italian manufacturing system

The Italian manufacturing system is characterized by three main, and interconnected, features, which differentiate it from the systems in most other advanced countries: first, the predominance of SMEs, second, specialization in the so-called traditional sectors and, third, the organization of firms in industrial districts (Fortis, 2006). These peculiarities influence Italy's international pattern of specialization. In this section, these stylized facts are investigated in some detail.

The predominance of SMEs

Firms with less than 50 workers are responsible for about half of total manufacturing employment in Italy, while in France and the United Kingdom this share is some 30 per cent and in Germany only 20 per cent (Figure 6.1). Firms employing more than 250 workers account for

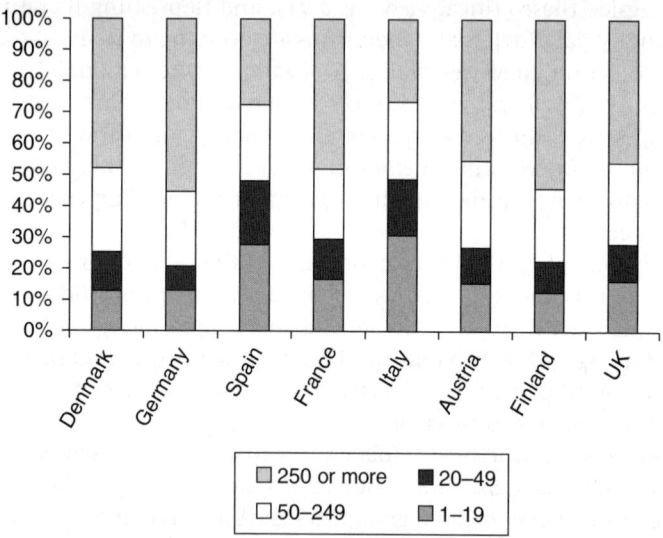

Figure 6.1 The manufacturing sector by employment size classes in selected EU countries (percentage of each class over total manufacturing employment), 2002

Source: Eurostat, 2006.

about 26 per cent of the Italian manufacturing labour force,[3] compared with 55 per cent in Germany and 48 per cent and 45 per cent respectively in France and the United Kingdom. The only other country with a predominance of SMEs in the manufacturing sector is Spain, but here the average size of manufacturing firms is higher than in Italy: 11 versus 7.5 employees (35 in Germany, 21 in the UK and 14 in France).

Historically, SMEs have been at the heart of the Italian 'family based capitalism', another distinguishing feature of the Italian productive model (Pagano and Trento, 2002) according to which the separation between ownership and control of firms is very small.[4] This governance system is also traditionally characterized by limited involvement of banks and financial institutions. The very small number (compared to other advanced countries) of companies listed on the Italian stock exchange is further evidence of this structure (Battagion and Tajoli, 2000).

For many years, the predominance of small-sized firms was considered to be an asset, allowing dynamism and flexibility in the Italian manufacturing system. However, recently the limited dimension of firms and the weaknesses related to their specific form of corporate governance have been seen by many observers as among the structural failings of the Italian economic system (Gallino, 2003; De Cecco, 2004; Onida, 2004, Nardozzi, 2004). In a recent study, Foresti, Guelfa and Trenti, (2005) identify the small size of firms as the most important cause of low labour productivity in Italy. Using a simulation, they found that Italian labour productivity would increase by about 21 per cent if Italy had a similar industrial structural composition and average dimension of firms to France, Germany or the UK.

The small size of firms is also seen as inhibiting innovation and internationalization (ICE, 2005; Onida, 2004). At the same time, it has been argued that many Italian SMEs have an inner capacity, often informal and not easy to detect using standard international benchmarking indicators, to undertake substantial process and product innovation, as will be discussed in more detail in the second section (Fortis, 2006; Centro Studi Confindustria, 2002).

Finally, it should be mentioned that there are signs of the increasing importance of medium-sized enterprises and business groups within the Italian manufacturing structure, which challenges the traditional view of a system strongly polarized between many small firms and a very few large enterprises (Unioncamere and Istituto Tagliacarne, 2005; Mediobanca and Unioncamere, 2005).

The specialization pattern

The second characteristic of the Italian manufacturing sector that is perceived as problematic is its specialization pattern. Historically, Italy has had a specific pattern of production and export specialization very different from that in other advanced countries (De Nardis, 1997; De Nardis and Pensa, 2004). It is specialized in highly labour-intensive sectors and upgrading to higher technology sectors has been slower than in other industrialized countries, including Spain (Amighini and Chiarlone, 2003). In considering the share of high-tech manufacturing[5] value added to total gross value added, the Italian share (1.9 per cent) is lower than the European and OECD averages (respectively 2.2 per cent and 2.6 per cent) (OECD, 2005b). Although Italy is in a good position in certain high-tech sectors (such as the aerospace industry, yacht and cruise shipbuilding, luxury cars and medical equipment), the bulk of its manufacturing production and exports is in low-tech, highly labour-intensive sectors. Since the 1980s, the typical Italian sectors of specialization have been often referred to as 'Made in Italy', which includes personal consumer goods (textiles, garments, leather, shoes, jewelry, spectacles), furnishing products (furniture, ceramic tiles, lights), food products and mechanical equipment.

Italian manufacturing employment data shows that the traditional manufacturing sectors absorb a significant percentage of total manufacturing employment: sectors such as food, textiles, wood and leather – considered the pillars of Made in Italy production – accounted for about 30 per cent of total manufacturing employment in 2001. If we also include the mechanical goods and equipment sector, this share grows to more than 40 per cent of total manufacturing employment. Another relevant sector in terms of employment is the electrical and optical equipment industry, which employs about 9.4 per cent of total manufacturing workers. It should be noted that within this sector, the high-tech sub-sector – office, accounting and computing machinery – accounts for just 0.4 per cent of total manufacturing employment, again highlighting the low-tech specialization of the Italian system (ISTAT, 2001).

In the context of our analysis it is interesting to investigate the transformations that have occurred in the manufacturing sector since the beginning of the 1990s. Between 1991 and 2001, the composition of employment in the Italian industrial structure has seen some significant changes. While the overall economy has increased by about 1 million employees, mainly due to an increase in the service sector (reflecting a common trend in the most advanced countries), total manufacturing employment has decreased by about 366,000 employees. Within the manufacturing sector, the most significant changes have been in the traditional sectors, such as: textiles and clothing, which decreased by more than 26 per cent between 1991 and 2001 (with the loss of some 216,000 workers); leather and shoes, which decreased by about 15 per cent (with the loss of 37,000 jobs); food, which decreased by 6 per cent; and wood and paper, shrinking respectively by 4 per cent and 9 per cent (ISTAT, 2001).

As Murat and Paba (2005) highlight in their analysis, these trends in part reflect the recent reduction in export trends (discussed later in this section) and are evidence of a competitiveness problem in the Italian traditional sectors.

The industrial districts

A third feature of the Italian manufacturing system is the major presence of industrial districts (IDs), which are spread across the national territory. This feature is closely linked to the first two characteristics discussed above in that IDs mainly comprise SMEs and are typically specialized in traditional industries.

One of the main problems that arise in the measurement and the analysis of the economic role of industrial districts is finding a way to match the definition of IDs with the available statistics. In the 1990s the Italian Statistical Institute (ISTAT), using a rather complex algorithm, identified 199 industrial districts as 'socio-territorial entities where a community of people and a population of industrial firms are reciprocally integrated'[6] and began to collect statistical information at district level (ISTAT, 1997). On the basis of the results of the 2001 Manufacturing Census, ISTAT reduced the number of districts to 156, which account for 25.4 per cent of total Italian employment and 39 per cent of manufacturing employment (Figure 6.2).[7]

Although IDs are spread across the Italian territory, they are historically more common in certain regions. The centre of Italy and the North East are the geographical areas where IDs are concentrated.

As can be seen from Figure 6.3, IDs are traditionally specialized in the Made in Italy sectors; more than 40 per cent of them are specialized in the textiles, garments, leather and shoes sectors, 24 per cent in mechanical products and around 20 per cent in housing-related goods sector. In terms of employment, the textile and garment, mechanical products and housing-related goods sectors account for more than 78 per cent.

Analysis of the trends in manufacturing employment in IDs since the mid-1990s is not straightforward. Taking IDs as unique entities, ISTAT (2005) compares employment in the 199 IDs identified in 1991

	156 industrial districts	Italy	ID (percentage)
Number of units	1,180,042	4,755,636	24.8
Number of employees	4,929,721	19,410,556	25.4
Number of manufacturing plants	212,410	590,773	36.0
Number of employees in manufacturing plants	1,928,602	4,906,315	39.3
Area (sq km)	62,113.83	301,328.45	20.6
Population	12,591,475	56,995,744	22.1

Figure 6.2 Industrial districts: main indicators, 2001
Source: ISTAT, 2005.

Main sector	Number of districts	Number of plants	Number of employees
Textile and garment	28.8	30.1	27.9
Mechanical products	24.4	26.7	30.5
Housing-related goods	20.5	19.9	19.8
Leather and shoes	12.8	11.0	9.7
Food products	4.5	1.8	1.7
Jewellery	3.8	6.1	6.1
Paper products	2.6	2.0	1.9
Rubber and plastic products	2.6	2.2	2.5
Italy	**100**	**100**	**100**

Figure 6.3 Industrial districts: sectors of specialization (per cent)
Source: ISTAT, 2005.

with employment in the 156 IDs defined 2001, and concludes that there has been a greater decline (−13 per cent) than the average for the manufacturing sector at national level (−6 per cent). In a recent study, Murat and Paba (2005) compared the employment performance of the 199 IDs identified in the 1991 Census and argue that IDs seem to be more resilient and reactive (with a variation of only −0.9 per cent) than the total manufacturing sector. The different conclusions reached by these studies show that where reference groups are not the same interpretations will differ.

Following a brief analysis of the Italian international specialization model and Italy's competitive position in terms of exports, the second part of this paper will discuss the evolving structure and organization of Italian IDs in terms of their capacity and propensity for innovation and engagement in the processes of internationalization, as well as their ability to change their internal organization. Much of the Italian economy still depends on the flexibility of IDs and on the evolution of ID firms' production and organization.

The international pattern of specialization

A country's pattern of specialization is based on longstanding historical and structural factors – such as relative factor endowments, technology and institutions, which affect its comparative and competitive advantages.[8] Unlike most of the advanced countries, Italy's specialization model is based mainly on the production and export of highly labour-intensive goods. Two main concerns have been voiced about the anomalies of this model of specialization: first, the risk of exposing Italian manufacturing industry to competition from low-cost producers, especially those located in the emerging economies; second, the risk that Italy will begin to lag behind the other industrialized countries in the production and export of more dynamic goods such as high-tech and ICT products.

Analysis of Italian export shares in the total world exports confirms the decreasingly competitive position of Italy over the last ten years. The export share of Italy has declined from some 5 per cent of total world exports in 1990 to about 3.9 per cent in 2004 in terms of value (UNCTAD, 2006). Moreover, within the euro area and in the markets of North and South America, Italian export share has decreased from 6.7 per cent in 1997 to 5.6 per cent in 2004, and has maintained its weak position (1.4 on average between 1997 and 2004) in the dynamic markets of East Asia, despite increased exports towards China (ICE, 2005). This reduction in export share is even more significant if we take into account the fact that it occurred in a period of constant growth in international trade, firm evidence of the difficulties experienced by the Italian economy in terms of international competitiveness (Murat and Paba, 2005). Problems first arose in the mid-1990s, when the effects of the euro began to be felt, and Italy could no longer rely on devaluation to defend its export capacity.

If we widen the scope of our investigation and look at the export shares of other countries, we can see that most of the advanced countries lost share in the international market in the last ten years. On aggregate, the export share of the advanced countries in total world exports decreased from 80 per cent to 70 per cent between 1993 and 2004 in favour of some of the emerging economies (ICE, 2005). China and some other South East Asian economies, along with India, Mexico, Brazil and some Central European countries, have significantly increased their share in the international market.

The recent integration into the global market of these fast-developing economies – especially China and India – has had a strong negative impact on the middle- and high-income countries specializing in labour-intensive goods. Italy has been a particular victim of this competition, although some scholars will argue that Italian specialization and industrial output and export composition have evolved in terms of quality upgrading, better services to customers and greater product innovation, protecting it from competition from low–labour-cost countries. In a recent paper, De Nardis and Pensa (2004) showed that traditional Italian exports have not been displaced by the same goods from less developed countries because of a vertical shift within sectors towards more advanced segments of production characterized by better quality. They assessed the intensity of competition from foreign competitors in traditional industries such as textiles, clothing, leather goods, ceramics and wooden furniture, evaluating the market power of Italian exporting firms in their major destination markets. Their conclusion is that during the 1980s and 1990s Italian exporters were able to apply mark-ups over marginal costs for most of the products analysed and in most destination markets. In other words, according to their analysis, Italian exporters of traditional products were not generally at the mercy of foreign competitors, not even those located in low-cost countries. Consistent with these findings, Monti (2005) found evidence of quality upgrading in Italy's exports in the 1990s and shows that, as they were on average of better quality, only a small share of exports was in direct competition with goods from emerging countries. The quality upgrading of Italian exports is also confirmed if we look at shares in value, which, after a decline at the end of the 1990s, have remained stable at about 4 per cent notwithstanding the continuous decline in terms of volume (ICE, 2005).

One possible explanation for this could be the reallocation of Italian exports towards higher-quality goods and a shift towards exports of higher unit price goods. In the light of the recent problems in the Italian economy, this has been interpreted as a reaction to the challenges from the emerging economies (Coltorti, 2006; De Nardis and Pensa, 2004).

Market power, in the form of firms' price strategies, taking advantage of more dynamic foreign demand, in a context of euro appreciation, could produce an increase in the unit value of exports. However, such an increase could also result from product upgrading aimed at shifting production towards higher-quality goods and towards sectors less exposed to competition from low labour-cost countries (ICE, 2005). However, higher prices might simply reflect a strategy of translating higher costs into higher prices abroad, at the expense of lower market share and less sustainable competitive position in the long run. This ambiguity affects the interpretation of recent data on the value of exports in the first six months of 2006, which have increased by about 10 per cent over the same period in 2005. It is very difficult to say whether this is a sign of a sustainable recovery or a short period drag effect of the increase in the world demand.

In addition, although there are some definite signs of quality upgrading among Italian producers, emerging countries are progressively and rapidly extending their competition from low-tech to medium-tech goods and are increasing the quality of their exports. Monti (2005) empirically illustrates that the direct competition between Italian exports and those from emerging countries has increased during the last few years. Amighini and Chiarlone (2003) reached a similar conclusion in their study, which compares the Italian and Chinese international specialization structure (over OECD markets) and shows that these two countries exhibit very similar patterns and that during the last decade the overlap has increased and the quality gap has narrowed.

This competitive pressure on the Made in Italy sectors is confirmed by analysis of the export shares by sector (Figure 6.4). The Italian export market, with some specific exceptions, has experienced a significant loss of quota precisely in the final products typical of Made in Italy. Between 1997 and 2004, in particular the textile, leather and food industries, and the other non-metallic mineral products sector (which includes the tile and ceramic industry), experienced a huge reduction. On the other hand, non-traditional sectors, such as the basic metals and fabricated metal products industry and fuel products, experienced an increase in their world market share in the same period, and particularly after 2000.

The mechanical products and equipment sector is particularly interesting; it is one of the most dynamic sectors in the Italian manufacturing industry (Murat and Paba, 2005). Since 2000, this industry regained position, after declining in the three previous years, and is at a level of around 10 per cent of world exports. Italy was the fourth largest world exporter in the mechanical products sector in 2003.[9] The key role of the mechanical products industry is confirmed by Coltorti (2006), who analysed export performance from 2000–5 by province: seven out of the eight best-performing provinces in terms of exports are specialized in mechanical products, which is also the main exporter.

Despite Italy's competitive advantage in the top-quality traditional sectors, which is being supported by continuous product and process innovations, its pattern of output specialization is becoming increasingly inadequate to ensure the creation and training of high-skill employment and investment in R&D-based innovation. It is rendering Italy more exposed to competition from the low-cost countries in their catching-up development process (Onida, 2004).

	1997	1998	1999	2000	2001	2002	2003	2004
Sectors				%				
Total manufacturing industry	5.1	5.2	4.8	4.5	4.7	4.7	4.7	4.6
Food products, beverages, tobacco	5.1	5.2	4.8	4.5	4.7	4.7	4.6	4.6
Textile and textile products	8.2	8.3	7.7	7.3	7.7	7.5	7.6	7.2
Leather and leather products	15.9	16.9	15.5	15.4	15.9	15.4	15.6	14.8
Wood and products	2.2	2.5	2.4	2.3	2.4	2.4	2.3	2.1
Pulp, paper, paper products, printing, publishing	3.7	3.8	3.6	3.5	3.7	3.8	3.9	3.8
Coke, refined petroleum products, nuclear fuel	2.9	3.2	2.8	3.1	3.2	3.1	3.5	3.5
Chemicals and chemical products	3.8	3.8	3.8	3.8	3.9	3.8	3.7	3.5
Rubber and plastics products	7.0	7.0	6.7	6.3	6.4	6.4	6.6	6.4
Other non-metallic mineral products	13.4	13.8	13.2	12.4	12.5	12.3	12.1	11.8
Basic metals and fabricated metal products	4.9	5.0	4.9	4.6	4.9	4.9	5.0	5.0
Mechanical products and equipment	10.4	10.5	10.2	9.3	9.9	9.9	10.2	9.8
Electrical and optical equipment	2.1	2.1	1.9	1.7	1.9	1.8	1.8	1.7
Transport equipment	3.5	3.8	3.4	3.5	3.3	3.1	3.3	3.3
Other manufacturing	10.1	11.0	10.5	10.0	9.6	8.5	7.6	6.8

Figure 6.4 Italian manufacturing export shares in world export by sector (1997–2004) (per cent)
Source: ICE, 2005.

The new challenges for the Italian systems of SMEs

The analysis conducted above demonstrates the central role of SMEs and IDs in the Italian industrial system. However, it is also evident that both these features are coming under pressure from globalization.

Therefore, it is clear that IDs still remain a focus of the economic debate in Italy. While an increasing host of critics considers districts to be an inadequate and outdated organizational model, responsible for the recent Italian 'industrial decline' (De Cecco, 2004; Gallino, 2003; Onida, 2004; Nardozzi, 2004), there is an emerging literature looking at whether IDs are in fact reacting to the new challenges from globalization and investigating in which directions they are evolving within the rapidly changing international context. Among the main issues tackled in this growing literature are questions related to the shift in production specialization (quality upgrading, new sectors, the increasing importance of the service sector), with the internationalization strategies of firms and districts (outsourcing, FDI and participation in global value chains), the innovation strategies being adopted in districts (ICT diffusion, process and product innovations), and the emergence of new forms of enterprise organization (verticalization and hierarchization, business groups, appearance of leading medium firms).

Many of these analyses are based on case studies, often on qualitative empirical evidence on particular districts, although quantitative studies are increasingly available thanks to the availability of data at district, province and firm levels. Overall the literature is highly fragmented and the picture that is emerging is mixed; there is evidence of a variety of firm behaviours and performances, and different evolutionary patterns in IDs (Solinas, 2005). In this section, we aim to contribute to this literature by providing a review of some of the most interesting studies and presenting a comprehensive picture of the heterogeneity of behaviours.

The new specializations of districts

Evidence of some of the transformations that are occurring in Italian IDs can be found in the recent exercise undertaken by ISTAT on the basis of the 2001 Industrial Census (ISTAT, 2005). The first striking result is that the number of 'official' districts, identified by ISTAT according to the algorithm already described (see Note 7), has decreased from 199 (identified by the 1991 Industrial Census) to 156, with the addition of some new districts in the South and a significant reduction in the number of districts in the North and the centre of the country, the two geographical areas historically characterized by this organizational pattern (Figure 6.5).

On the basis of the information provided in ISTAT (2005), in some cases the reduction in the number of IDs results from a merger of two previously separate districts. However, the reduction is mostly explained by the disappearance from the list of the areas: Sassuolo in Emilia Romagna, specializing in tile manufacture; Castel Goffredo in Lombardia, specializing in the production of women's tights; Florence, Tuscany,

	Number of IDs		
	1991	2001	Difference 2001–1991
Italy	199	156	−43
North West	59	39	−20
North East	65	42	−23
Centre	60	49	−11
South	15	26	11

Figure 6.5 IDs identified by ISTAT: 1991 and 2001 Industrial Censuses
Source: ISTAT, 2005.

specializing in the production of leather goods; and Carrara and Pietrasanta, specializing in ornamental stones. The reason for excluding such areas from the 'official' list of districts is that they no longer satisfy the statistical criteria for identification as IDs. In some cases this is because the size of firms has increased with the appearance of some lead firms, and the process of hierarchization implies that there is no longer a predominance of SMEs; thus, one of the requirements of the ISTAT algorithm cannot be satisfied (see above on the emergence of leading firms in districts). This is the case in Sassuolo and Castel Goffredo.

In the case of Padova in Veneto and Udine in Friuli Venezia-Giulia, firms no longer specialize in the manufacturing industry because the weight of the service sector in the local economic system has increased. This growing importance of the service sector, and particularly business services, was highlighted in a recent report on the economic and social conditions of the North-Eastern part of Italy (Fondazione Nord Est, 2006). It is described as a new pattern of production organization characterized by an increasing number of functions that are no longer carried out within manufacturing firms, but are being outsourced to service firms. The manufacturing and service sectors are coexisting, with the result that the local systems do not satisfy another requirement of the ISTAT algorithm, that of manufacturing specialization. This same report documents the increasing importance of services to the population such as healthcare, cultural and leisure services, explained by the greater wealth that has resulted from the successful performance of IDs during the past two decades.

Although there is much argument among scholars with respect to the ISTAT definition because of the difficulties of including historical districts in the official list of IDs (Cainelli, 2003) and the evidence of an existing array of many different organizational forms, which are not accounted for by the ISTAT algorithm (Paniccia, 1998; 2006), the new list is a sign that the district form is evolving.

Other studies confirm that some districts have changed their sectoral specialization. Menghinello (2002) analyses data on exports at LLS level (see Note 7 for a definition) and concludes that there are a number of IDs that now specialize in the export of a variety of different goods.[10]

The empirical literature shows the tendency for a shift from specialization in the production of final goods to the production of the machines needed to produce them. An example is the district of Vigevano in Lombardy, once the main shoe-manufacturing area in Italy and now an internationally recognized producer of shoe-making machinery. De Arcangelis and Ferri (2003) demonstrate, using an econometric model, that an increase in the export share of machinery for the Made in Italy sectors is more likely to occur in provinces with a strong presence of IDs.

So far we have reviewed some of the empirical studies that show that IDs are evolving towards new areas of specialization, both within the manufacturing industry and outside it, with increasing emphasis on the services sector. In what follows, we investigate where districts are going and how the district firms are changing, focusing on their strategies for internationalization and integration into the new global production system, on their innovation capacities and on the emergence of leading firms and business groups.

Are districts going global?

The worldwide changes in production systems, distribution channels and financial markets, the spread of information technologies and the adoption of the euro have radically changed the context for Italian firms and challenged the capacity of IDs to sustain growth and penetrate foreign markets (Basile and Giunta, 2004).

Historically, IDs have been very successful exporters, as is extensively documented by Menghinello (2002) based on data at LLS level. On average, the share of exports from the 199 IDs identified by ISTAT is 46 per cent of the total Italian manufacturing exports, which is proportional to their weight in terms of employment (ISTAT, 2002).[11]

A more disaggregated analysis shows that for some products, such as leather (85 per cent), agricultural machinery (85 per cent), musical instruments (82 per cent) and fabrics (74 per cent), the share is much higher. Analysis at district level shows that there are some districts that account for a significant share of the world market. Examples are Sassuolo, which accounts for 27 per cent of world exports of ceramic tiles, Prato, which holds 4 per cent of the textile world market, and Arezzo which accounts for 3.5 per cent of world jewellery sales (Menghinello, 2002).

Several studies have focused on the positive effects of geographical agglomeration on performance of firms and propensity to export, generally showing that district firms have a greater propensity to export than firms located outside districts, when controlling for structural features as size and the level of development locally (Bugamelli and Infante, 2003; Becchetti and Rossi, 2000; Becchetti, de Panizza and Oropallo, 2003).

With the acceleration of globalization, increasing international competitive pressure and the introduction of the euro,[12] there is concern about the capacity of the Italian industrial system, and in particular of IDs and their firms, to re-shape their internationalization strategies.

In a recent empirical study, Basile and Giunta (2004) show that the internationalization pattern typical of ID firms is focused on export activity. Their analysis, based on a large database at firm level, shows that between 1995 and 1997 43 per cent of ID firms had undertaken no other form of internationalization than exporting, while only 1.7 per cent of firms in the sample had made direct investments abroad; the picture for 1998–2000 is essentially the same.

These findings are coherent with the low rate of internationalization, particularly in terms of FDI, that characterizes the Italian economy overall, and contrasts with other advanced countries (Federico, 2003).[13] The lack of internationalization efforts by Italian enterprises has been explained by the small size of firms and the related difficulty to devote organizational, managerial and financial resources to transferring productive capacity to different and distant economic contexts (Barba Navaretti and Castellani, 2004). Also, unlike export activities, these types of internationalization efforts require considerable and regular investment and involve sunk costs (Dunning, 1993), partially explaining the paradoxical situation in Italy of high export capacity and small presence of Italian firms abroad in terms of direct investments (Chiarvesio, Di Maria and Micelli, 2005).

Therefore, in a global, competitive context that requires a direct presence in international markets, some of the characteristics typical of Italian IDs, which in the past have been seen as strengths, are becoming weaknesses and limitations to foreign expansion (Mariotti, Mulinelli and Piscitello, 2004). The competitive advantages of IDs are strongly localized; firms depend on idiosyncratic externalities and their integrated system of customers, subcontractors, services and knowledge is difficult to replicate abroad.

Some recent studies have tried to empirically investigate the degree of internationalization of IDs and the main determinants of FDI. Federico (2003) shows that IDs, which account for 46 per cent of Italian manufacturing exports, account for only 28 per cent of total FDI. Mariotti, Mulinelli and Piscitello, (2004) show that differences in the internationalization processes of ID firms are influenced by the presence of large firms and by the intensity of domestic rivalry, combining to positively influence the likelihood of a district to internationalize.

Bronzini (2003) looked at the capacity of IDs to attract foreign investment, and showed that FDI is generally not influenced by a 'district or agglomeration effect', because districts are perceived by potential foreign investors as closed communities; factors such as strong specialization and availability and efficiency of infrastructure seem to be more relevant in this context.

Most research on FDI activity in IDs acknowledges that it examines only one possible form of internationalization, thereby underestimating the overall involvement of SMEs in international activities; non-equity or intermediate forms of internationalization should also be considered (Bugamelli and Infante, 2003; Federico, 2003).

A recent group of studies shows that in order to analyse the international productive reorganization of IDs, it is necessary to look at how the local value chain is extending at the global level (Rabellotti, 2004; Corò and Volpe, 2003; Corò, Volpe and Bonaldo, 2005). IDs have traditionally based their economic success on deep specialization along the value chain confined within the geographical boundaries of the local system. In the new landscape of global competition, districts have begun to participate in an international reorganization of their value chains (Corò, Volpe and Bonaldo, 2005). The studies by Amighini and Rabellotti (2006), Baldone, Sdogati and Tajoli (2002), Corò and Volpe (2003) and Corò, Volpe and Bonaldo (2005) assess the dimension of international fragmentation of production within IDs based on international trade flows.

Baldone, Sdogati and Tajoli (2002) and Amighini and Rabellotti (2006) use data on outward processing trade as an indicator of the fragmentation of production. Amighini and Rabellotti (2006) find for the footwear sector that districts vary in their outsourcing strategies, depending on their market position. Southern districts, which specialize in the low-price market segments, outsource a higher percentage of intermediate production abroad than districts in Veneto and the Marches, which are net importers of parts from foreign subcontractors.

Corò, Volpe and Bonaldo (2005) calculated an index of internationalization based on bilateral trade flows of intermediate goods between districts and foreign countries for three value chains (textile and apparel, leather and shoes, wood furniture) and then, for each district specializing in these chains, they computed an indicator of 'Induced Foreign Employees'.[14] According to this analysis, the textile and apparel chain is more open to internationalization than the other two; moreover, all three chains are linked mainly to countries in Eastern Europe.

Alongside attempts to quantify the importance of production fragmentation in IDs, there are few studies that analyse the impact of delocalization on the local production systems. The most relevant question here is whether and to what extent this process may impact on local employment, development and growth (Corò, Volpe and Bonardo, 2005). The studies by Barba Navaretti and Castellani (2004) at firm level and Savona and Schiattarella (2004) at local system level (proxied by province) highlight the existence of a positive relationship between the degree of production internationalization and indicators of economic growth and employment. Corò, Volpe and Bonardo (2005), however, are cautious about the interpretation of these results as the direction of the relationship between internationalization and employment is not straightforward. They argue that, in a first phase, delocalization could lead to a loss in terms of local employment due to the displacement of economic activities, while in a second phase, delocalization fostering local competitiveness, could have a positive effect on overall employment performance and in particular on employment composition in terms of skill upgrading.

Mariotti and Piscitello (2005) specifically study changes in employment composition associated with outward FDI in 33 districts located in Veneto. Their results show that internationalization somehow contributes to an upgrading in the skills of domestic employment, and that outward FDI has a positive impact on employment growth in the service sector.

Rather interestingly, Murat and Paba (2004) draw attention to some possible interactions between the international outsourcing of production in IDs and migration flows. They conclude that, although from the point of view of individual firms both employment of immigrants and outsourcing of production can represent useful strategies to cut labour costs, the utilization of unskilled immigrants tends to drive the specialization of the manufacturing industry towards low-skilled sectors with implications for growth in the long run.

There is a wide literature, mainly based on case studies, that makes the point more generally that IDs and their firms have very different internationalization strategies. Solinas (2005) identifies some stylized cases of IDs in terms of their approach to internationalization and its effects on the structure, organization, specialization and competitiveness of districts. First, there are those districts that adopt a defensive strategy of vertical delocalization of production. These districts often specialize in textile, apparel and shoes and their delocalization is directed to Eastern Europe (particularly Romania), North Africa (particularly Tunisia) and, in a few cases, China. This kind of delocalization often results in reduced local employment, as occurred in the shoe-manufacturing district of Barletta (Amighini and Rabellotti, 2006) and in the textile and garment industry in Vicenza (Crestanello and Dalla Libera, 2003). Sometimes, delocalization has a positive impact on the organization of labour internal to the district in terms of skill upgrading, as demonstrated by Mariotti and Piscitello (2005) in the case of some districts in Veneto.

Another interesting outcome is exemplified by Montebelluna, which, by attracting foreign multinationals, has become an international centre of innovation and technology for the winter sports industry (Belussi and Asheim, 2003). Montebelluna has undertaken a substantial delocalization process towards countries in Eastern Europe and Asia, outsourcing the most labour-intensive and unskilled phases but maintaining all the key competencies (and a substantial manufacturing base) within the local system (Solinas, 2005). As a result of the technological and innovation capabilities that are strongly rooted into the local context, Montebelluna has been able to trigger a process of multinational entry into the district. Another example of success is Mirandola, near Modena, where a number of US, Swedish, German and Japanese multinationals have relocated, making it a world-leading centre in the biomedical industry.

In contrast, in Brenta, which is near Venice, the local shoe producers have accepted a functional downgrading, abandoning design and marketing and focusing on production to become part of a top brand global value chain. The recent quite remarkable growth rates in the luxury industry, which is built around global top brands, have allowed local producers in this chain to perform better than those in other chains (Rabellotti, 2004).

To conclude, we can say that SMEs in IDs are becoming increasingly internationalized using a variety of strategies: some delocalization processes can be defined as 'defensive' strategies, aimed at reducing production costs through the outsourcing of low value added activities, and some as 'offensive' strategies aimed at creating new productive units abroad in order to get closer to potential local markets, and allowing a focus on key competencies at home.

IDs and innovation capacity

The lack of innovation and technological capacity compared to other advanced countries is one of the main reasons for Italy's slow growth and loss of competitiveness. This problem is continuously stressed in the press, in the political arena and in the academic literature. Italy is lagging behind major industrialized economies in terms both of funds invested in formal R&D and in innovation outputs, generally measured by numbers of new patents. There is a widely held view that Italy's very modest technological innovation activity is due to the average small size of manufacturing firms and specialization in traditional sectors, and very small presence of SMEs in science-based industries (Daveri, 2006; ICE, 2005; Larch, 2004). In addition, according to Battagion and Tajoli (2000), the specificity of the Italian corporate governance system, weak capital markets, limited separation between ownership and control and ownership concentration, negatively influence the innovation capacity of firms, reducing their capacity for risk and limiting their access to external finance to fund innovative projects.

However, although the Italian industrial system has traditionally been lacking in high-tech, science-based and Schumpeterian firms, which have played a crucial role in the economic growth of the US and some European countries (Lissoni and Malerba, 2002), its system of SMEs has achieved a great deal in the textiles, apparel, leather and footwear sectors in terms of product innovation, and in those parts of the mechanical industry supplying machinery to the Made in Italy sectors (Amighini, 2003).

It has been pointed out that the low level of Italian investment in R&D does not necessarily imply that Italian firms do not undertake significant informal research, aimed at product quality upgrading and incremental process innovation, as has been demonstrated by the ability of the industrial district model to compete in both domestic and international markets for several decades (Centro Studi Confindustria, 2002). Thus, even though IDs may not typically produce R&D-based radical innovations, they represent an appropriate context for the development of incremental, but economically relevant innovations (Belussi and Pilotti, 2002).

From a theoretical point of view, the traditional literature on IDs has, for a long time, stressed that firms in IDs can exploit technological externalities deriving from the synergies and relationships that develop among geographically clustered firms. In particular, much attention has been devoted to the diffusion of 'tacit knowledge', to the transfer of qualitative and quantitative information, to the ease of transmission and exchange of ideas, information and workers from one firm to another, to the intensity of user-supplier links, and to the pressure exerted by a competitive-cooperative relationship among clustered firms (Becattini, 1990; Belussi and Pilotti, 2002). Regional economists (Camagni, 1991; Capello, 1999) have referred to the concept of an *innovative milieu* to account for the learning processes occurring at local and network levels. In this perspective learning is seen as a collective, social process involving people who share strong social and cultural values (Capello and Faggian, 2005).

However, although the above studies have pointed to the importance of networking and informal contacts in spreading knowledge locally, very few provide detailed empirical evidence and an increasing number of contributions is questioning some of the assumptions underlying these studies, such as the widespread belief that local systems consist of undifferentiated communities of firms and individuals where knowledge is freely appropriable. Along these lines, in a recent empirical study Lissoni (2001) explored the mechanisms through which knowledge is produced and exchanged in an Italian industrial district, arguing that 'rather than flowing freely within the cluster boundaries, knowledge circulates within a few smaller "epistemic communities"' (p. 1498). This statement relies on the argument that tacit knowledge is personal and specific, so that it cannot be easily communicated by word of mouth; in other words it is not a public good (Breschi and Lissoni, 2001). The authors conclude that networks, not geographical proximity, are the key vehicles of knowledge transmission.

This opens up the debate concerning the different capacity of firms within districts to trigger and absorb innovation, and raises issues related to the increasing importance for the district of exposure to non-local sources of knowledge (Boschma and Wal, 2005).[15] From this perspective, it has been highlighted that firms within districts are not homogeneous agents as far as knowledge absorption and creation are concerned. A growing number of studies is focusing on the role of leading firms for absorbing external knowledge, and acting as a bridge between non-local knowledge and the majority of small firms, and carrying out independent research activities (Lissoni, 2001; Boschma and Wal, 2005; Aage, 2004). According to this literature, leading firms and business groups can have a major effect on the innovation capacity and the nature of knowledge transfer within districts (see above).

Alongside these more theoretical contributions on the issue of innovation in IDs, there are a number of empirical works investigating the impact of a 'district or agglomeration effect' on innovation at firm level. Cainelli (2003) investigates the possible relationships between agglomeration and innovative activities in a sample of 2,800 Italian manufacturing firms. His econometric analysis shows that firms' membership in IDs, and product innovations, are key factors in explaining firms' economic performance. More recently, Cainelli and Guerrieri (2005) showed that location in an industrial district, and product innovation, are the main reasons for firms' propensity to export.

The case study literature has demonstrated that there is high heterogeneity in terms of forms of learning, innovation capacity and channels of innovation diffusion, within districts and among district firms. A classification proposed by Belussi and Pilotti (2002), which groups IDs according to three different types of learning systems, may help to systematize this heterogeneity. First, the so-called 'weak learning systems' include those districts whose performance is mainly linked to craft-based skills and whose innovation opportunities are very low or even non-existent. Several Italian districts specializing in traditional sectors, such as textiles and clothing, fall into this category and are therefore being very negatively affected by increasingly strong competition by low-labour-cost countries. Second, 'systems characterized by some absorptive capacity from the outside circuits of knowledge' include those districts that have been able to activate a knowledge absorption process, combining internal existing knowledge with new information and ideas external to the district. An example here is the garments and knitting industry in Carpi, which has managed to upgrade the quality and range of products, to diversify sales channels and to enter new foreign markets (Solinas, 2005; Bigarelli and Solinas, 2003). Third, there are the so-called 'dynamic evolutionary systems', which include the few examples of Italian districts organized around very innovative firms. Examples here include the auto-component district around Modena, the packaging machinery district in Bologna, the biomedical instrument system in Mirandola, the ceramic tile district in Sassuolo and the sportswear district in Montebelluna.

The study on Montebelluna by Belussi and Asheim (2003) highlights the role of dynamic evolutionary firms and their capacity to introduce important radical innovations transforming the district into an international technological centre for ski boots, and attracting foreign multinationals. R&D, design and manufacturing of prototypes and test products are the key activities in this district (Aage, 2004) and firms such as Arena, Nike and Prada have established design branches in the district in order to get access to skilled employees and knowledge.

In Sassuolo, the process of innovation in the tile industry is dominated by capital goods producers, which are also concentrated in the cluster. The radical and incremental innovation that has occurred is due to the close interaction between tile manufacturers and producers of technology. However, Meyer-Stamer, Maggi and Seibel, (2004) point out that the existence of very strong user-producer links does not involve exclusive relationships and capital goods manufacturers can sell their products to whoever is most willing and able to pay. According to Meyer-Stamer, Maggi and Seibel, in Sassuolo relationships between capital goods and tile manufacturers are good, despite the fact that the former are very active in creating competitors for the latter.

Another strand of literature on innovation in IDs has investigated the degree of ICT diffusion among SMEs in IDs and the effects of ICT adoption on firms' and districts' performance and patterns of innovation. In the economic literature three factors are identified as major determinants of ICT adoption: first, the sector of specialization (some sectors such as banking and financial sectors use ICT more intensively than others, especially the traditional sectors); second, the size of firms (larger firms have a higher propensity to adopt ICT); third, the availability of human capital and the capacity of labour force to acquire the needed skills (Daveri, 2006). All these factors contribute to the slow rate of ICT adoption among Italian firms (Miglietta, 2004).

In IDs firms mainly share knowledge informally and, therefore, the rate and type of adoption of inter-firm communication technologies may be different from that in firms outside districts. For example, in a recent empirical analysis of three Italian IDs, Belussi (2005) found that the diffusion of technologies for structured communication and data interchange was limited in relation to simpler and more general ICT. According to Belussi (2005: 264), 'They were regarded as not being useful supports for the exchange of intense communication, rich in terms of knowledge, which exists within the districts, where informal relations, and face to face contacts, are the glue of networking.'

A similar result was obtained from econometric testing of a sample of firms located in Biella, an industrial district specialized in medium- to high-quality woolen yarns and textiles (Ciarli and Rabellotti, 2007). Ciarli and Rabellotti's empirical analysis distinguishes between different ICTs and concludes that the peculiarities of production organization, product specificities and the informality of knowledge exchanges in IDs do not induce wide use of communication technologies among final producers.

Furthermore, sectoral specificity influences the adoption and use of ICT. In Biella firms' adoption of IT is higher than their use of communication technologies because interaction with buyers and suppliers is shaped by the need to transfer knowledge that is directly contained in the products, requiring face-to-face interactions. For a sample of Italian SMEs, Lucchetti and Sterlacchini (2004: 164) found that 'the adoption and effective use of ICT among SME depend, firstly, on the types of ICT'.

These findings provide strong evidence that there is a need to take into consideration sectoral and geographical specificity when considering ICT adoption and use; individual sectors or regions may use and adopt ICT in different, idiosyncratic ways, so that differences in adoption rates and patterns of use may not necessarily imply a loss of relative competitiveness.

Towards a 'fourth Italian Capitalism'? Medium firms and business groups in IDs

In the Italian industrial system, significant attention has been devoted to the role of medium sized firms.[16] The first industrial medium-sized firms were established during the 'boom' of the 1950s and 1960s and were followed by more, first in the 1980s (Colli, 2005). Nevertheless, although the so-called Italian 'fourth capitalism'[17] (the first being the large private firms, the second public enterprises and the third small firms in IDs) cannot be considered a new phenomenon, a hard core of innovative, well-performing medium-sized firms has recently attracted the attention of scholars and policy-makers searching for new growth strategies to challenge the threat of industrial decline in the Italian economic system, and at the same time challenging the traditional perspective of an industrial system polarized between many small and a few large firms (Colli, 2005; Coltorti, 2006).

Between 1995 and 2003, medium-scale firms experienced average value-added annual growth of about 2.9 per cent, slightly outperforming small enterprises (2.7 per cent) and significantly outperforming large firms (1 per cent). In addition, their share in total manufacturing value added increased (plus 1.1 per cent relative to 1995), while larger firms lost ground (minus 2.8 per cent relative to 1995) (Unioncamere and Istituto Tagliacarne, 2006). The results for medium-sized firms in terms of profits, employment creation, and integration into world markets have also been very positive (Mediobanca and Unioncamere, 2005).

The medium-sized enterprise world is very differentiated: many are specialized in typical Made in Italy sectors; the best-known examples being Benetton in the clothing sector, Tod's in the shoe sector, Luxottica in the optical industry, Merloni for white goods and Marazzi, Iris, Ricchetti and Ragno in the ceramic tile industry. Aprilia and Piaggio, which specialize in scooters and motorbikes, and Riello for heating equipment, are also important examples from the mechanical products sector.

These successful medium-sized firms originated and still continue to be located in IDs. Accordingly, Coltorti (2004) argues that medium-sized enterprises are a consequence of the patterns of growth in IDs, rather than the decline of large firms. Moreover, many Italian medium-sized firms are still family run and find IDs to be a natural and profitable development environment (Colli, 2005). Unfortunately, the information available on medium-sized firms is scant and more empirical research is needed; an interesting starting point for future research would be to analyse the extent to which medium-sized firms are the result of a Darwinian process of selection within IDs.

A rich strand of research has examined patterns of growth in firms, focusing on the formation and development of business groups, that is, groups of firms legally independent, but under the same ownership (Barca *et al.*, 1994; Brioschi and Cainelli, 2001; Cainelli, Iacobucci and Morgante, 2004; Cainelli and Iacobucci, 2005; Iacobucci and Rosa, 2005). The economic reasons for growth through groups rather than through internal processes have been widely analysed in transaction cost theory (Williamson, 1975). However, some of the Italian studies on SME groups make the point that there are other reasons than the minimization of transaction costs (ISAE, 2005). The creation of a group can be motivated by the desire to achieve a reduction in disinvestment costs in very competitive sectors, by the need to resolve conflicts within the family, which often arise when there is a generation change, and by the desire to absorb new human resources without losing ownership control, thereby creating new linked enterprises, often owned by former employees of the group leader (Cainelli and Iacobucci, 2005). Finally, groups may be created to decrease transparency, very often for fiscal reasons; complex groups are more conducive to tax evasion. It may be useful to add that, until 2003, there were no laws in Italy specifically related to groups and it is too early to evaluate the effects of the regulations that have been introduced (ISAE, 2004).

The increasing number of business groups is forcing a reconsideration of the average dimension of Italian firms. On the basis of a database made available by ISTAT, Cainelli and Iacobucci (2005) argue that if we consider business groups as the economic unit of analysis,[18] the average size of Italian firms increases from 43.5 employees to 156.3.[19] The phenomenon of groups is particularly relevant in IDs among medium-sized firms and it can be considered to be an organizational strategy that many enterprises adopt in their processes of growth, expansion and diversification of economic activities. Cainelli, Iacobucci and Morgante (2004) showed empirically that groups are more widespread in IDs than in non-district areas; moreover groups in IDs are less diversified than groups outside districts.[20]

In addition, there are a number of studies that have analysed the importance and characteristics of business groups in IDs, which refer to specific regions or districts (Dei Ottati, 1996; Balloni and Iacobucci, 2004; Brioschi and Cainelli, 2001; Iacobucci, 2002). Cainelli and Iacobucci (2005) summarize the findings of this rich empirical literature, suggesting that business groups in IDs adopt two main strategic options: a vertical integration strategy and a horizontal diversification strategy. Firms located in IDs specializing in traditional sectors, for example, the knitwear district of Carpi or the shoe cluster in San Mauro Pascoli, have often adopted a strategy of vertical integration aimed at acquiring key suppliers to upgrade the quality of products, in order to resist the pressure of international low-cost competition. The acquisition of suppliers increases control over quality and delivery times. On the other hand, in IDs specializing in the mechanical sector (such as the area of Bologna), or in the cases of the ceramic tile district of Sassuolo and the biomedical district of Mirandola, firms tend to adopt a strategy of horizontal differentiation. In such cases, firms have reacted to the new global challenges by widening the range of their production and acquiring firms in the same market segment.

What has been said so far provides evidence of an important phenomenon of evolution of IDs within which medium-sized firms, very often organized in business groups, are increasingly appearing as key actors with the potential to overcome some of the constraints suffered by small firms in terms of internationalization and innovation strategies, which were discussed in the previous two sections. Nevertheless, further empirical evidence is needed to understand the magnitude of this phenomenon and to assess its impact in real terms on the competitiveness of the Italian manufacturing system.

Conclusions

Is Italy facing the risk of 'industrial decline'? Are SMEs and IDs the major culprits in this decline? Since 2004, these questions have been at the top of the agendas of Italian scholars and policy-makers. Recent data on exports and sales have been interpreted as the first positive signs of a recovery. But it is still not clear whether these improvements are mainly, or even completely, due to a more favourable international economic environment or whether something is really changing in the Italian manufacturing system.

In this chapter, we do not attempt to provide answers to these questions, or to enter the debate between the detractors of the Made in Italy model of industrialization and the supporters of IDs. Our aim, more modestly, is to provide a review of the very rich, although fragmented and scattered literature available (very often only accessible to Italian readers) on what is happening in IDs and in some district firms.

Overall, our conclusion is that IDs are moving towards a much greater degree of heterogeneity than before. Districts are losing their specialization and becoming more diversified, with an increasing weight of the mechanical sector, which, during the last five years of very slow growth has been the most dynamic industry in terms of export, and with a greater emphasis on the service sector. Therefore, one of the main features of the general definition of an industrial district is disappearing, that is, specialization in one manufacturing value chain.

Second, and very importantly, the main architects of structural changes in IDs are medium-sized companies. Various pieces of empirical research indicate that medium-sized companies are the most dynamic economic actors currently in the Italian manufacturing industry. Moreover, some studies have provided preliminary evidence that medium-sized firms have grown within IDs and are the result of a process of Darwinian selection.

The empirical evidence available on medium-sized firms and business groups does not allow us to quantify the significance of this transformation that is occurring in the Italian manufacturing system. Nevertheless, the studies available allow us to draw some conclusions about the capability of these medium-sized firms to face the challenges of internationalization and innovation. A major constraint, underlined in many of the studies reviewed, is the small scale of foreign investment by Italian firms through FDI, of participation in global value chains, of successful outsourcing, of innovation and of adoption and use of ICT. Therefore, the growing importance of medium-sized firms can be interpreted as a positive sign of increasing potential in the Italian manufacturing system to undertake new efforts in terms of more innovation and internationalization.

To conclude, Italian districts, and especially some of their firms, are making positive progress, but it is not clear whether the changes that are occurring will be significant and rapid enough to avoid industrial decline in the country.

Notes

1. For a recent and very accurate review see Paniccia (2002).
2. This opinion has recently reached a wide international audience thanks to a special issue on Italy that appeared in *The Economist* (2005).
3. Only 16 per cent of the total manufacturing labour force is accounted for by enterprises with more than 500 employees (ISTAT, 2001).
4. It should be said that, family-based capitalism is widespread among SMEs, but it also characterizes large firms in Italy. A good example is Fiat, the largest Italian privately owned company (Pagano and Trento, 2002).
5. The definition of high-tech industries is based on the OECD classification of manufacturing industries as high-tech, medium high-tech, medium low-tech and low-tech according to their technological and R&D intensity. Using the ISIC Rev3 breakdown of activities, high-tech industry includes: aircraft and spacecraft; pharmaceuticals; office, accounting and computing machinery; radio, TV and communication equipment; medical, precision and optical instruments (OECD, 2005b).
6. The unit of analysis is the local labour system (LLS), defined on the basis of information about commuting from the 1991 Population Census. First, 784 LLSs are identified on the basis of the degree of commuting that characterizes each Italian municipality. These LLSs are groups of contiguous municipalities characterized by a certain level of commuting to work. Second, industrial districts are identified among LLSs when they satisfy the following requirements: (i) in the LLS the percentage of manufacturing employees compared to the total non-agricultural employment must be higher than the national average; (ii) the LLS is specialized in one particular manufacturing industry; (iii) in the LLS the percentage of employees working in firms with less than 250 employees must be higher than the national average. This identifies 199 industrial districts (ISTAT, 1997).
7. As above, some of the LLSs originally identified as industrial districts are no longer considered as such, either because their manufacturing system is now more diversified or because there is no longer a predominance of small firms.
8. There has been extensive debate among international trade economists rejecting the notion of 'competitiveness' as essentially incorrect and misleading compared to the clear concept of 'comparative advantage' (Krugman, 1996). In this latter context, all economies benefit from *any* international specialization, provided that it is consistent with their pattern of comparative advantage. However, insofar as we admit the possibility of inter-firm (intra-sector) differentials (for example, related to market imperfections, information asymmetries, firm-specific learning and capabilities), which are ruled out by (macro) theories of comparative advantage, then competitiveness becomes a meaningful, and indeed relevant, concept (Lall, 2001).
9. The performance of the mechanical products sector has been generally good; results are more mixed if more disaggregated data are considered. In particular, exports have declined for equipment directed to the final sectors that experienced a strong decline in the world markets, such as machinery for producing tiles (included in machines for specialized industries) or for the textile sector, while sub-sectors such as agricultural machinery, non-electrical machinery, mechanical handling equipment, pumps and paper-milling

machines have increased their share in the last decade (Murat and Paba, 2005).
10. Districts are considered to be specialized in one sector if the location coefficient is greater than three (Menghinello, 2002).
11. Data refer to 1996. More recent data on exports of the 156 newly defined districts are not yet available.
12. In the past, Italy has frequently used competitive devaluations to boost exports.
13. Italy is also lagging behind with respect to other advanced countries in terms of FDI inflows. During the period 1990–2000, Italy slipped from eighth to the ninth place (in favour of Ireland) in the EU15 ranking in terms of FDI attraction (ICE, 2005). This can be explained by historical deficiencies in terms of infrastructure, human capital and bureaucracy and inefficiency in the public sector.
14. This indicator is the number of foreign workers involved (directly and indirectly) in the supply chain governed by the Italian local system of production and is estimated on the basis of the value of production outsourced abroad and the average labour productivity of Italian FDI in the same sectors.
15. In a study on the footwear-producing district of Barletta, Boschma and Wal (2005), using social network analysis, show that most local firms that are suffering from competition from low-cost countries are not engaged in local knowledge activities despite their geographical proximity. Some firms do belong to the local knowledge network and this positively influences their innovation capacity, and those few firms that are connected to non-local actors are even more innovative.
16. Medium-sized firms are defined as companies with 50–499 employees and a turnover of €13–260 million (Mediobanca and Unioncamere, 2005).
17. The expression 'fourth capitalism' was first coined by Turani (1996).
18. The authors exclude 'pseudo-groups', in other words groups created for purely fiscal reasons.
19. The database includes only companies, and excludes individual firms.
20. This latter finding is verified only for groups specializing in the textiles and clothing sector, confirming the literature on industrial districts, which suggests that agglomerative forces play a more intense role in traditional clusters.

References

Aage, T. (2004), 'Acquisition of External Information by Industrial Districts: A Case Study of the Leisure and Sportswear Industry in the Industrial District of Montebelluna, NE Italy', DRUID Winter Conference on Innovation, Growth and Industrial Dynamics, January, Allborg.

Amighini, A. (2003), 'Innovazione e competitività: un confronto settoriale tra l'Italia gli altri Paesi europei', paper presented at the Conference Innovare per competere. Come finanziare l'innovazione?, May, Università del Piemonte Orientale, Novara.

Amighini, A. and Chiarlone, S. (2003), 'Rischi e opportunità dell'integrazione commerciale cinese per la competitività internazionale dell'Italia', CESPRI Working Papers, 149.

Amighini, A. and Rabellotti, R. (2006), 'The Effects of Globalization on Italian Industrial Districts: Evidence from the Footwear Sector', *European Planning Studies*, 14(4), pp. 485–502.

Baldone, S., Sdogati, T. and Tajoli, L. (2002), 'Moving to the Central-Eastern Europe: Fragmentation of Production and Competitiveness of the European Textile and Apparel Industry', *Rivista di Politica Economica*.

Balloni, V. and Iacobucci D. (2004), 'The Role of Medium-sized and Large Firms in the Evolution of Industrial Districts. The Case of Marche', in G. Cainelli and R. Zoboli (eds), *The Evolution of Industrial Districts*, Physica-Verlag, Heidelberg, pp. 175–97.

Barba Navaretti, G.and Castellani, D. (2004), 'Does Investing Abroad Affect Performance at Home? Comparing Italian Multinational and National Enterprises', CEPR Discussion Papers, 03/ 2004.

Barca, F., Bianco, M., Cannari, L., Cesari, R., Gola, C., Manitta, G., Salvo, G. and Signorini, L. (1994), *Assetti proprietari e mercato delle imprese. Proprietà, modelli di controllo e riallocazione delle imprese industriali italiane*, Vol.I, Il Mulino, Bologna:.

Basile, R. and Giunta, A. (2003, revised 2004), 'Things Change. Foreign Market Penetration and Firms' Behaviour in Industrial Disctricts: An Empirical Analysis', paper presented at the Conference on Clusters, Industrial Districts and Firms: the Challenge of Globalization. Conference in honour of Professor Sebastiano Brusco. September, Università di Modena, Modena.

Battagion, M. and Tajoli, L. (2000), 'Ownership Structure, Innovation Process and Competitive Performance: The Case of Italy', CESPRI Working Paper, 120.

Becattini, G. (1990), 'The Marshallian Industrial District as a Socio-economic Notion', in F. Pyke, G. Becattini and W. Sengenberger (eds), *Industrial Districts and Inter-Firm Cooperation in Italy*, ILO, Geneva, pp. 37–51.

Becchetti, L. and Rossi S. (2000), 'The Positive Effect of Industrial District on the Export Performance of Firms', *Review of Industrial Organisation*, 16(1).

Becchetti L., de Panizza, A. and Oropallo, F. (2003), 'Forma giuridica, export e performance dei distretti industriali: Un'analisi empirica sull'universo delle imprese italiane', *Rivista Italiana degli Economisti*, 8(2), pp. 185–217.

Belussi, F. (2005), 'Are Industrial Districts Formed by Networks without Technologies?', *European Urban and Regional Studies*, 12(3).

Belussi, F. and Pilotti, L. (2002), 'Knowledge Creation, Learning and Innovation in Italian Industrial Districts', *Geografiska Annaler*, 84B(2).

Belussi, F. and Asheim, B. (2003), 'Industrial Districts and Globalisation: Learning and Innovation in Local and Global Production Systems', paper presented at the Conference on Clusters, Industrial Districts and Firms: the Challenge of Globalization'. Conference in honour of Professor Sebastiano Brusco, September, Università di Modena, Modena.

Bigarelli, D. and Solinas, G. (2003), 'Different Routes of Globalization: The Case of Carpi', paper presented at the at the Conference on Clusters, Industrial Districts and Firms: the Challenge of Globalization, University of Modena, Modena.

Boschma, R. and Wal., L. (2005), 'Knowledge Networks and Innovative Performance in an Industrial District: The Case of a Footwear District in the South of Italy', Utrecht University Papers in Evolutionary Economic Geography, 06/01.

Brandolini A. and Cipollone P. (2003), 'Una nuova economia in Italia', in S. Rossi (ed.), *La Nuova Economia. I fatti dietro il mito*, Il Mulino, Bologna.
Breschi, S. and Lissoni, F. (2001), 'Knowledge Spillovers and Local Innovation Systems: A Critical Survey', *Industrial and Corporate Change*, 10(4), pp. 975–1005.
Brioschi, F. and Cainelli, G. (2001), *Diffusione e caratteristiche dei gruppi di piccole e medie imprese nelle aree distrettuali*, Giuffrè, Milan.
Bronzini, R. (2003), 'Distretti industriali, economie di agglomerazione e investimenti esteri in Italia', paper presented at the Conference Economie locali, modelli di agglomerazione e apertura internazionale, Banca d'Italia, Rome.
Brusco, S. and Paba, S. (1997), 'Per una storia dei distretti industriali italiani dal secondo dopoguerra agli anni novanta', in F. Barca (ed.), *Storia del capitalismo italiano dal dopoguerra ad oggi*, Donzelli, Rome:.
Bugamelli, M. and Infante, L. (2003), 'I costi irrecuperabili per l'accesso ai mercati esteri: un ruolo per i distretti industriali?', in Banca d'Italia, *Economie locali, modelli di agglomerazione e apertura internazionale. Nuove ricerche della Banca d'Italia sullo sviluppo territoriale*, at http://www.bancaditalia.it/ricerca/statist/ecoloc/Bugamelli_Infante.pdf
Cainelli, G. (2003), 'Agglomeration, Technological Innovation, and Productivity. Evidence from the Italian Industrial Districts', PRIN Capabilities dinamiche tra organizzazione di impresa e sistemi locali di produzione, Working Paper 2/2003.
Cainelli, G. and Guerrieri, A. (2005), 'Agglomeration, Innovation and Export Behaviour at the Firm Level. Evidence from Italian Industrial Districts', Working Paper PRIN Capabilities Dinamiche tra Organizzazione d'Impresa e Sistemi Locali di Produzione, 4, Università di Bologna, Bologna.
Cainelli, G. and Iacobucci, D. (2005), 'I gruppi d'impresa e le nuove forme organizzative del capitalismo locale italiano', *L'Industria*, 2, April–June.
Cainelli, G., Iacobucci, D. and Morgante, E. (2004), 'Spatial Agglomeration and Business Groups: New Evidence from Italian Industrial Districts', Working Paper PRIN Capabilities Dinamiche tra Organizzazione d'Impresa e Sistemi Locali di Produzione,1, Università di Bologna, Bologna.
Camagni, R. (1991), 'Local Milieu, Uncertainty and Innovation Networks: Towards a New Dynamic Theory of Economic Space', in R. Camagni (ed.), *Innovation Networks: Spatial Perspectives*, Belhaven-Pinter, London, pp. 121–44.
Capello, R. (1999), 'Spatial Transfer of Knowledge in High Technology Milieux: Learning Versus Collective Learning Processes', *Regional Studies*, 33(4): pp. 353–65.
Capello, R. and Faggian, A. (2005), 'Collective Learning and Relational Capital in Local Innovation Processes', *Regional Studies*, 39(1), pp. 75–87.
Centro Studi Confindustria (2002), *La Competitività dell'Italia*, Ricerca del Centro studi Confindustria.
Chiaravesio, M., Di Maria, E. and Micelli, S. (2005), 'Internationalisation of Clusters and Competitiveness of Small Firms', paper presented at the Academy of Management 2005 Annual Meeting, August, Hawaii.
Ciarli, T. and Rabellotti, R. (2007), 'ICTs in Industrial Districts: An Empirical Analysis on Adoption, Use and Impact in the Biella Textile District', *Industry & Innovation*, 14(3), pp. 277–203.
Colli, A. (2005), 'Il quarto capitalismo', *L'Industria*, 2, April–June.

Coltorti, F. (2006), 'Il mal d'Africa e la competitività italiana', Annex to Unioncamere Annual Report 2006.
Coltorti, F. (2004), 'Le medie imprese italiane: nuovi aspetti economici e finanziari', *Economia e Politica Industriale*, 121, pp. 5–26.
Corò, G. and Volpe, M. (2003), 'Frammentazione produttiva e aperture internazionale nei sistemi di piccola e media impresa', *Economia e Società Regionale*, 1.
Corò, G., Volpe, M. and Bonaldo, S. (2005), 'Local Production Systems in Italy between Fragmentation and International Integration', paper presented at the CNR Working Group Meeting, Università di Urbino, Urbino.
Crestanello, P. and Dalla Libera, E. (2003), 'International Delocalization of Production: The Case of the Fashion Industry of Vicenza', paper presented at the Conference on Clusters, Industrial Districts and Firms: the Challenge of Globalization, September, Università di Modena, Modena.
Daveri, F. (2006), *Innovazione cercasi: il problema italiano*, Editori Laterza, Rome-Bari.
Daveri, F. and Jona-Lasinio, C. (2005), 'Italy's decline: Getting the facts right', *Giornale degli Economisti e Annali di Economia* (EGEA) (December), pp. 365–410.
De Arcangelis, G. and Ferri, G. (2003), 'La specializzazione dei distretti: dai beni finali ai macchinari del Made in Italy?', Università di Bari, Bari (Mimeo).
De Cecco, M. (2004), 'Il declino della grande impresa', in G. Toniolo and V. Visco, *Il declino economico dell'Italia*, Bruno Mondatori, Milan.
De Nardis, S. (1997), 'Persistenza e cambiamento delle specializzazioni manifatturiere: l'industria Italiana nel confronto con i principali paesi', *Rivista di Politica Economica*, 137(1).
De Nardis, S. and Pensa, C. (2004), 'How Intense is Competition in International Markets of Traditional Goods? The Case of Italian Exporters', ISAE Working Papers, 44.
Dei Ottati, G. (1996), 'La recente evoluzione economica dei distretti industriali toscani', *Sviluppo Locale*, 2–3, pp. 92–124.
Dunning, J. (1993), *Multinational Enterprise and the Global Economy*, Addison-Wesley, Reading.
Federico, S. (2003), 'L'internazionalizzazione produttiva italiana e i distretti industriali: un'analisi degli investimenti diretti all'estero', paper presented at the Conference Economie locali, modelli di agglomerazione e apertura internazionale, Banca d'Italia, Rome.
Fondazione Nord Est (2006), *Rapporto sulla Società e l'Economia*, Marsilio, Venice.
Foresti, G., Guelfa, F. and Trenti, S. (2005), 'Struttura settoriale e dimensionale dell'industria italiana: effetti sull'evoluzione della produttività del lavoro', Studi e Ricerche Banca Intesa, Collana Ricerche (December).
Fortis, M. (2006), 'I distretti industriali e la loro rilevanza nell'economia italiana: alcuni profili di analisi', in A. Quadrio Curzio and M. Fortis (eds), *Società, Stato e Mercato in Italia. Sussidiarietà, Laboratori, Distretti*, Il Mulino, Bologna.
Gallino, L. (2003), *La scomparsa dell'Italia industriale*, Einaudi, Torino.
Iacobucci, D. (2002), 'Explaining Business Groups Started by Habitual Entrepreneurs in the Italian Manufacturing Sector', *Entrepreneurship and Regional Development*, 14(1), pp. 31–48.
Iacobucci, D. and Rosa, P. (2005), 'Growth, Diversification and Business Group Formation in Entrepreneurial Firms', *Small Business Economics*, 25, pp. 65–82.

ICE (2005), 'La posizione competitiva dell'Italia nell'economia internazionale', report presented at the second National Conference on Italian International Trade, Istituto per il Commercio Estero, Rome.

ISAE (2004 and 2005), *Priorità nazionali: dimensione aziendali, competitività, regolamentazione*, Rapporto ISAE – Seconda Parte and Terza Parte, Istituto di Analisi Economica, Rome.

ISTAT (2005), 'Struttura e competitività del sistema delle imprese industriali e dei servizi', Istituto nazionale di Statistica, Rome.

ISTAT (2002), 'Le esportazioni dei sistemi locali del lavoro', Collana Argomenti, 22, Istituto nazionale di Statistica, Rome.

ISTAT (2001), *Ottavo Censimento Generale dell'Industria e dei Servizi*, Istituto nazionale di Statistica, Rome.

ISTAT (1997), *I Sistemi Locali del Lavoro 1991*, Istituto nazionale di Statistica, Rome.

Krugman, P. (1996), 'Making Sense of the Competitiveness Debate', *Oxford Review of Economic Policy*, 12(3), pp. 17–25.

Lall, S. (2001), 'Competitiveness Indices and Developing Countries: An Economic Evaluation of the Global Competitiveness Report', *World Development*, 29(9), pp. 1501–525.

Larch, M. (2004), 'Relegated to the League of Laggards? Roots of Italy's Slow Potential Growth', economic analysis from the European Commission's Directorate-General for Economic and Financial Affairs, *ECFIN Country Focus*, 1(8).

Lissoni, F. (2001), 'Knowledge Codification and the Geography of Innovation: The Case of Brescia Mechanical Cluster', *Research Policy*, 30, pp. 1479–500.

Lissoni, F. and Malerba, F. (2002), 'Le caratteristiche fondamentali del sistema innovativo italiano', in A. Quadro Curzio, A. Fortis and G. Galli (eds), *La Competitività dell'Italia*, vol. I, (Scienza, ricerca e Innovazione), Il Sole 24ORE.

Lucchetti, R. and Sterlacchini, A. (2004), 'The Adoption of ICT among SMEs: Evidence from an Italian Survey', *Small Business Economics*, 2, pp. 151–68.

Mariotti, S., Mulinelli, M. and Piscitello, L. (2004), 'L'internazionalizzazione produttiva dei distretti industriali. Un'analisi degli ostacoli e dei fattori abilitanti', paper presented at the Conference XXV Conferenza Italiana di Scienze Regionali, Università del Piemonte Orientale, Novara.

Mariotti, S. and Piscitello, L. (2005), 'The Impact of Outward FDI on Local Employment: The Case of Italian Industrial Districts', at http://www.fcee.urv.es/departaments/economia/recerca/grit/Catala/web/papers/

Mediobanca and Unioncamere (2005), *Le Medie Imprese Industriali (1996–2002)*, Ufficio Studi Mediobanca and Centro Studi Unioncamere, Milano.

Menghinello, S. (2002), 'Le esportazioni dei sistemi locali del lavoro', ISTAT, Collana Argomenti, n.100.

Meyer-Stamer, J., Maggi, C. and Seibel, S. (2004), 'Upgrading in the Tile Industry of Italy, Spain and Brazil: Insights from Cluster and Value Chains Analysis', in H. Schmitz (ed.), *Local Enterprises in the Global Economy: Issues of Governance and Upgrading*, Edward Elgar, UK, pp. 174–99.

Miglietta, A. (2004), 'Some Theoretical Topics on the Diffusion of Innovation within Industrial Districts: The Case of ICT', Ceris-CNR Working Papers, 8/2004.

Monti, P. (2005), 'Caratteristiche e Mutamenti delle Specializzazione delle Esportazioni Italiane', Temi e Discussioni, 559, Banca d'Italia, Rome.
Murat, M. and Paba, S (2005), 'I distretti industriali italiani tra globalizzazione e riorganizzazione', Università di Modena, Modena (Mimeo).
Murat, M. and Paba, S. (2004), 'International migration, outsourcing and Italian industrial districts', paper presented at the 19th National Conference of Labour Economics, Univeristà di Modena.
Nardozzi, G. (2004), *Miracolo e declino. L'Italia tra concorrenza e protezione*, Editori Laterza, Rome-Bari.
OECD (2005a), *Italy Country Report*, OECD Economic Surveys, OECD, Paris.
OECD (2005b), *Science, Technology and Industry Scoreboard*, OECD, Paris.
Onida, F. (2004), *Se il piccolo non cresce. Piccole e medie imprese italiane in affanno*, Il Mulino, Bologna.
Pagano, U. and Trento, S. (2002), 'Continuità and change in Italian Corporate Governance: The Institutional Stability of One Variety of Capitalism', Quaderni Università degli Studi di Siena, 366.
Paniccia, I. (2006), 'Cutting through Chaos: Towards a New Typolgy of Industrial Districts and Clusters', in B. Asheim, P. Cooke and R. Martin (eds), *Clusters in Regional Development. Critical Reflections and Explorations*, Routledge, London.
Paniccia, I. (2002), *Industrial Districts: Evolution and Competitiveness in Italian Firms*, Edward Elgar, Cheltenham.
Paniccia, I. (1998), 'One, a Hundred, Thousands Industrial Districts, Organizational Variety in Local Networks of Small and Medium Size Enterprises', *Organization Studies*, 19(4), pp. 667–99.
Piore, M. and Sabel, C. (1984), *The Second Industrial Divide. Possibilities for Prosperity*, Basic Books, New York.
Pyke, F. and Sengenberger, W. (eds) (1992), *Industrial Districts and Local Economic Regeneration*, International Institute for Labour Studies, Geneva.
Pyke, F., Becattini, G. and Sengenberger, W. (eds) (1990), *Industrial Districts and Inter-Firm Co-operation in Italy*, International Institute for Labour Studies, Geneva.
Rabellotti, R. (2004), 'How Globalisation Affects Italian Industrial Districts: The Case of Brenta', in H. Schmitz (ed.), *Local Enterprises in the Global Economy: Issues of Governance and Upgrading*, Edward Elgar, UK, pp. 140–73.
Rabellotti, R. (1997), *External Economies and Cooperation in Industrial Districts*, Macmillan, Basingstoke.
Savona, M., and Schiattarella, R. (2004), 'International Relocation of Production and the Growth of Services: The Case of the "Made in Italy" Industries', *Transnational Corporations*, 13(2).
Signorini, F. (2001), 'L'effetto distretto: motivazioni e risultati di un progetto di ricerca', in *Lo sviluppo locale: Un'indagine della Banca d'Italia sui distretti italiani*, Meridiana Libri, Rome.
Solinas, G. (2005), 'Integrazione dei mercati e riaggiustamento nei distretti industriali', Sinergie, at http://www.economia.unimore.it/fiorani_giuseppe/Lettura_02%20Strategie%20di%20riaggiustamento_Solinas.pdf
The Economist (2005), '"Addio, Dolce Vita": A survey of Italy', 26 November.
Turani, G. (1996), *I sogni del grande Nord*, Il Mulino, Bologna.
UNCTAD (2006), International Merchandise Trade, UNCTAD Handbook of Statistics online, http://www.unctad.org/Templates/Page.asp?intItemID=1890&lang=1

Unioncamere and Istituto Tagliacarne (2006), *Rapporto Piccole e Medie Imprese 2005*, Unioncamere – Centro Studi.
Unioncamere and Istituto Tagliacarne (2005), *Le piccole e medie imprese nell'economia italiana. Rapporto 2004*, Unioncamere – Centro Studi.
Williamson, O. (1975), *Markets and Hierarchies: Analysis and Antitrust Implications*, Free Press, New York.

7
Globalization and Spain's SMEs*
Guillermo Cardoza and Gastón Fornes

Spain and SMEs

Spain began the opening of its economy with the death of dictator Franco in 1975 after more than 50 years of living in a closed economy. The accession to the then European Community (now European Union) in 1986 was a major milestone in this liberalization process. Since then, the Spanish economy has been gaining importance in the world stage and its companies are continuously improving their competitiveness, fuelled mainly by important flows of direct investments from neighbouring countries in Europe. The late 1990s marked two other significant milestones in recent Spanish economic history: in 1997 Spain became a net exporter of capital for the first time (Arahuetes and Casilda, 2004), and in 1999 it took part in the first group of countries launching the euro.

In spite of all these achievements, Spanish productivity is 20 per cent lower than that in the EU and the number of hours worked in Spain is higher than the European average (Proudfoot Consulting, 2005). The main factor explaining this situation is the low level of development of the country's innovation system due mainly to low corporate investments in R&D+I (research and development and investment); weak linkages among universities, businesses and public entities; and low qualification of human resources. Under these conditions, international competition and globalization represent huge challenges for a country where more than 99 per cent of its companies are small and medium-sized enterprises.

---

* The authors wish to thank Ms Paola Forero for her comments and help.

This chapter is set out as follows. The first section will provide an overview of the Spanish economy and its prospects along with a description of the SME sector in Spain and the challenges that these companies are facing in the global markets. In the second part, the chapter will describe the most important policies and incentives available for promoting the development of SMEs in Spain. Particular attention is given to the dynamics of cluster formation, the industrialization of regions and the roles that business associations, universities and business schools are playing in the process of creation and consolidation of companies.

The Spanish economy

For most of the second half of the twentieth century, the Spanish economy has played catch-up with those of other Western European nations. Since joining the EU in 1986, Spain has averaged 5 per cent annual growth until 1990. After the EU's recession at the beginning of the 1990s, Spain resumed growth in 1994 but at lower rates, positioning its economy at 80 per cent of the four largest West European countries on a GDP per capita basis. The Spanish economy grew 2.5 per cent in 2003, 2.6 per cent in 2004 and 3.3 per cent in 2005, a satisfactory performance given the 1.7 per cent growth posted by the EU in 2005. Spain's main export partners are France (19.3 per cent), Germany (11.7 per cent), Portugal (9.6 per cent), the UK (9 per cent), Italy (9 per cent) and the US (4 per cent). On the other hand, the country's main import partners are Germany (16.6 per cent), France (15.8 per cent), Italy (8.9 per cent), the UK (6.3 per cent) and the Netherlands (4.8 per cent) (CIA, 2005). Figure 7.1 below shows Spain's main economic indicators in comparison with those from other European countries.

There is a debate over the current economic situation in Spain at different levels, one side claiming that the situation and the prospects are good for the Spanish economy, the other side more pessimistic and even negative on the prospects. This debate is not new and is common in many countries; however, many indicators show reasons for concern. In this context, it is worth highlighting that Spain has gradually lost competitiveness against the Eurozone since the beginning of Monetary Union in 1999, as a consequence of higher inflation rates than those in the Eurozone by more than 1 per cent on average each year. In fact, in 2005, this gap widened to 1.5 per cent. The problem with this gap is that 'if this were to go on for another seven years, there would hardly be a Spanish export industry left' (Munchau, 2006).

This loss of competitiveness is reflected in at least three key indicators. First, an increasing current account deficit of nearly 8 per cent of GDP,

	France	Germany	Ireland	Italy	Poland	Spain	UK
Population growth rate	0.37%	0.00%	1.16%	0.07%	0.03%	0.15%	0.28%
Population, total (millions)	60,656	82,431	4,015	58,103	38,635	40,341	60,441
GDP (Official Exchange Rate in billions US$ 2005)	2,118	2,830	194	1,733	249	1,046	2,275
GDP per capita PPP 2005 est in US$	29,900	29,700	34,100	28,300	12,700	25,100	30,900
GDP growth (annual %) 2005 est	1.50%	0.80%	4.90%	0.00%	3.30%	3.30%	1.80%
Current account balance (% of GDP)	−0.01%	4.23%	−2.67%	−1.59%	−1.67%	−6.18%	−1.69%
Exports (% of GDP)	20.93%	35.90%	52.52%	21.46%	37.24%	18.58%	16.38%
Imports (% of GDP)	22.35%	28.30%	33.71%	21.30%	38.42%	25.98%	21.26%

Figure 7.1 Economic indicators in selected European countries, 2005
Source: CIA, 2005

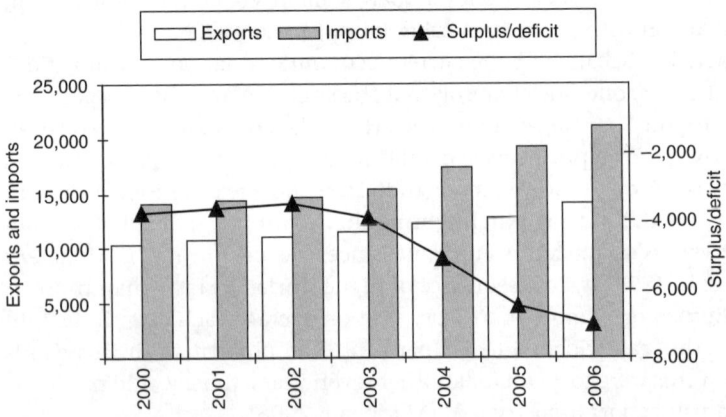

Figure 7.2 Exports, imports and trade surplus/deficit (in millions of euros)
Source: Ministerio de Economía y Hacienda, 2006.

a similar level to that of the US (Ministerio de Economía y Hacienda, 2006). Second, a sustained relative decrease of exports (see Figure 7.2). Third, the fact that during the last three to four years the engines of the Spanish economy have been construction and domestic consumption (Ministerio de Economía y Hacienda, 2006), two sectors fueled mainly by the low interest rates in the Eurozone (and in the rest of the world) but with a question mark about their future in the likely event of higher interest rates.[1]

SMEs in Spain: an overview

Spain is home to 2,809,385 small and medium-sized companies[2] (SMEs), which represent 99.87 per cent of the total of 2,813,120 companies in the country, excluding agriculture and fishing. This figure means that there are '6.7 SMEs per 100 inhabitants, and 5.6 SMEs per km$^{2'}$ (DGPYME, 2005: 16). The evolution of SMEs in nominal terms and by sector for the last years can be seen in Figure 7.3. In this figure it is possible to see that, even being an important sector, SMEs are losing relative importance in the Spanish economy; they have grown only 22.2 per cent in the period between 1995 and 2003, when the country's economy grew 29.31 per cent (World Bank, 2005). Conversely, big companies

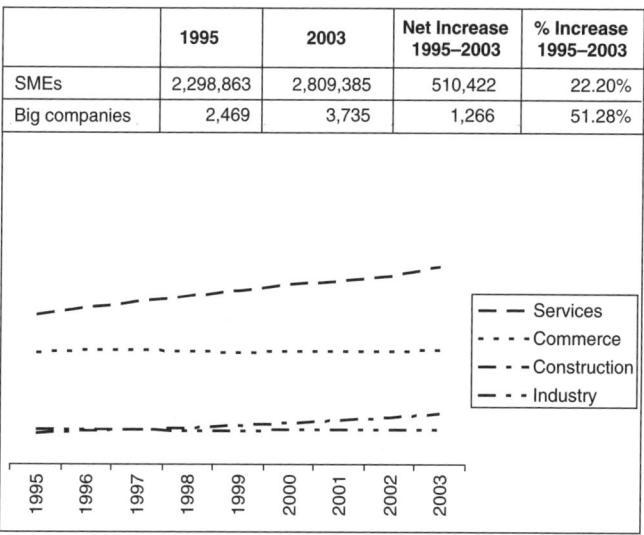

	1995	2003	Net Increase 1995–2003	% Increase 1995–2003
SMEs	2,298,863	2,809,385	510,422	22.20%
Big companies	2,469	3,735	1,266	51.28%

Figure 7.3 SMEs' nominal and sectorial evolution in Spain, 1995–2003
Source: DGPYME, 2005.

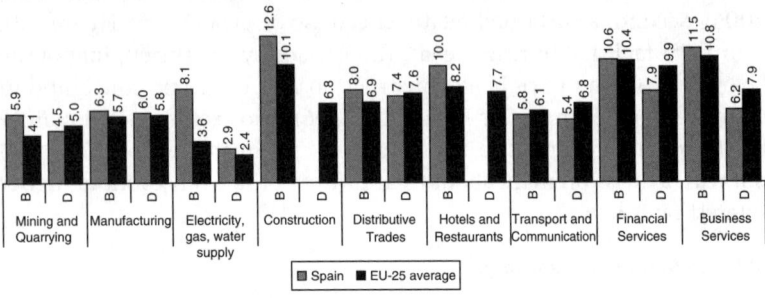

Figure 7.4 Birth and death rates by sector (Spain and the EU in per cent, 2001–2)
Source: Eurostat, 2006.

have gained relative weight by growing 51.28 per cent during the same period.

Despite their loss in relative domestic importance, the evolution of Spanish SMEs has outperformed that of the EU-25 (on average). This comparison is shown in Figure 7.4, which shows the birth and death rates of SMEs[3] in Spain, and the EU-25. As can be seen, Spain presents positive results against the EU's average in all the categories. Business services presents the highest difference, followed by electricity, gas and water supply.[4] An analysis country by country (that is, not against the EU's average) shows that Spain also presents an overall better performance than Italy, one of the largest European economies; however, its performance is not as good as that of the UK.[5] This difference has implications for the policies and incentives designed at the European level, which will be described in the following sections.

Finally, it is important to mention how the Spanish SME sector is constituted. Most SMEs in the country (98.46 per cent) have an annual income of €3 million or less, and the category 'distributive trades'[6] represents the largest sector of this total (28.17 per cent). The category with the second highest number of SMEs is 'business services', with less than €3 million in revenues, representing 18.74 per cent. Figure 7.5 shows the concentration of SMEs by volume of income in millions of euros. This information is relevant for many of the analyses and policies that will be shown later in the chapter, such as investments in R&D, export activities, fiscal incentives, etc., as the companies' relatively small turnover (and therefore their limited capacity to generate internal resources) restricts their available options in these matters to a certain extent.

	Less than 3	3–7.51	7.51–37.56	More than 37.56	Total
Mining and Quarrying	2,716	155	76	3	2,950
Manufacturing	227,969	7,505	4,230	497	240,201
Electricity, gas and water supply	3,240	169	85	14	3,508
Construction	355,353	2,976	1,009	60	359,398
Distributive Trades	791,604	11,312	5,245	670	808,831
Hotels and Restaurants	270,640	761	176	3	271,580
Transport and Communications	226,561	1,739	683	84	229,067
Financial Services	47,358	196	226	110	47,890
Business Services	526,664	2,906	961	119	530,650
Education	50,091	146	34	4	50,275
Sanitary and Veterinary activities	106,630	153	65	3	106,851
Other Services to the Community	157,391	549	219	25	158,184
	2,766,217	28,567	13,009	1,592	2,809,385

Figure 7.5 Number of SMEs by volume of income (in millions of euros, 1 January 2003)
Source: INE, 2003.

Globalization and SMEs in Spain

As part of the EU, Spain adheres to the Lisbon Agenda (the EU's economic reform agenda from 2000), originally designed to make 'the EU the world's most dynamic and competitive economy' by 2010 and, as a consequence, helps the Union to cope with the challenges of globalization. In February 2005, Commission President Barroso recognized that 'five years after its launch, the Lisbon Strategy is not on track to deliver the expected results' and, therefore, the Commission presented policy recommendations aimed at putting the Agenda back in the right direction. In this context, the EU declared that it is 'faced with the challenge of ageing societies' and 'intensifying international competition from countries such as India and China'. It also said that Europe 'needs to raise its productivity growth and employ more people' (European Commission, 2006). The recommended policies consider SMEs, innovation and their interaction, as fundamental pillars for the future development of the EU. For example, it highlights creating an SME-friendly business environment, reaching a 3 per cent GDP target for R&D expenditure, promoting the uptake of information and communication technologies (ICT) and promoting the development of innovation poles linking regional centres, universities and businesses (European Commission, 2006).

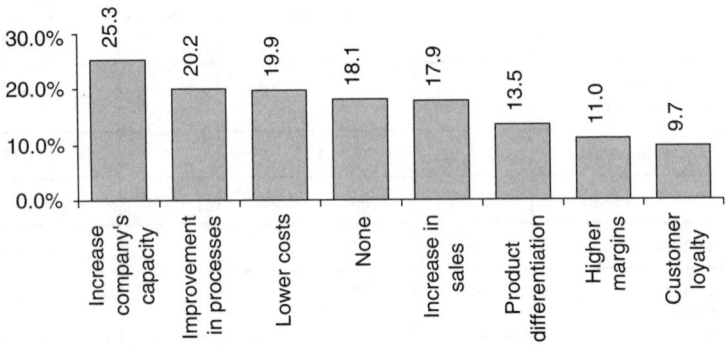

Figure 7.6 Perceived benefits of innovation by SMEs, 2003
Source: Institut Cerdà, 2003, in MEPIMED and Institut Cerdà, 2004.

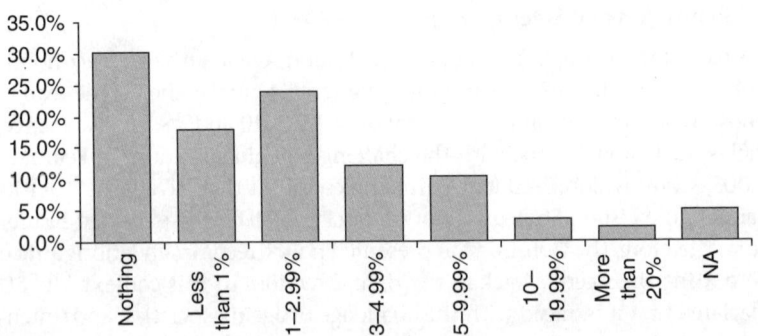

Figure 7.7 Percentage of income invested in R&D in Spanish SMEs
Source: Institut Cerdà, 2003, in MEPIMED, and Institut Cerdà, 2004.

Spain is also working with its companies in the development of capabilities to face the challenges posed by globalization. The government stated that this scenario,

> involves new challenges for both companies and public administration. From now on, a business must compete on the cost and the quality of their products and services. Currently, Spain invests an important amount of funds on technology and R&D, but there is still a great effort to be to match the activities carried out from competitor countries. All entrepreneurial initiatives that create more and better jobs will get the total support from the Spanish Ministry of Industry and Energy. (Ministerio de Industria, 2006)

However, it will still take some time and effort for the country to reach the forefront of international competition. This is mainly because major Spanish exports still do not show a clear detachment from traditional industries.[7] Nevertheless, Spain's international leadership in some sectors is a successful story of collabouration among government agencies (European, national and local), SMEs and universities.

As mentioned above, international competition is not a new challenge for Spanish companies. However, the question now is how well prepared these companies are to face the competition from emerging countries such as China, India and Brazil, or even the competition in the service markets from the UK, France, Singapore, or Hong Kong.

A recent study (MEPIMED and Institut Cerdà, 2004) attempted to answer these questions by analysing three key factors identified by the literature as necessary and relevant to successfully compete in international markets: innovation and R&D, internationalization and cooperation. Some of the conclusions can be seen below:

In the area of innovation, the previous figures, 7.6 and 7.7, show that, in general, SMEs in Spain perceive investments in R&D as potentially beneficial; however, more than 30 per cent of these companies do not have a research budget, and around 39 per cent invest less than 3 per cent of their income. A previous study carried out in 1997 by the OECD showed that, in the case of Spanish SMEs, 'the higher the expenditure on R&D or the proportion of staff allocated to technological development, the greater the export propensity' (OECD, 1997). Therefore, if the results showed in the figures above are kept constant or eventually turn into a downward trend of investments in R&D, the future competitiveness of SMEs in Spain will be under question.

As for internationalization, the situation can be seen in the figures below:

The previous figures show that less than 10 per cent of SMEs in Spain were exporting in 2003, and that the exports represent less than 10 per cent of their sales in 3.9 per cent of the cases and less than 30 per cent in 3.4 per cent of the cases. On the other hand, the largest companies within the SMEs classification (50–249 employees)

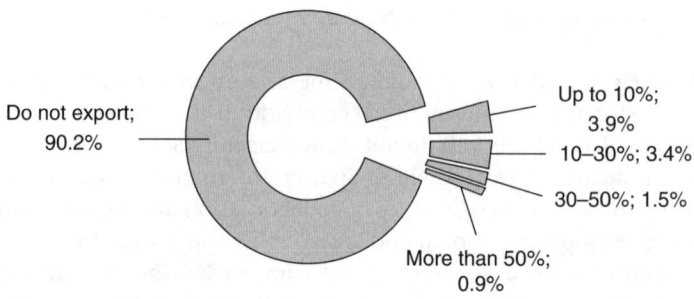

Figure 7.8 SMEs' exports as a percentage of their income, 2003
Source: Institut Cerdà, 2003, in MEPIMED and Institut Cerdà, 2004.

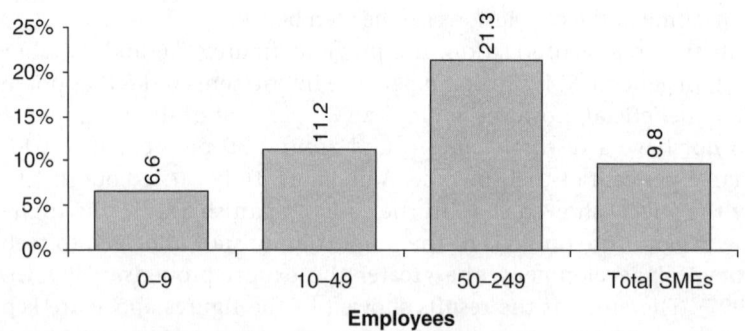

Figure 7.9 Exporting companies per number of employees
Source: Institut Cerdà, 2003, in MEPIMED and Institut Cerdà, 2004.

are the ones with more involvement in some kind of export activity (21.3 per cent). It is difficult to compare these figures with those from the previous OECD study, as the categories (number of employees) are different. However, it seems that the situation within the SME sector has deteriorated, as only 2.4 per cent of companies export more than 30 per cent of their sales in 2003, whereas the same ratio before 1997 was 3.3 per cent for companies with less than 20 employees and 17.1 per cent for companies between 201 and 500 employees (OECD, 1997). Having said that, one of the OECD's hypotheses (larger companies have a higher export propensity) seems to continue holding true as the 50–249 employees category shows the highest number of exporting SMEs.

In terms of cooperation, the results of the study can be seen below:

As can be seen in Figure 7.10, most SMEs perceive cooperation positively. These results are in line with what was presented in the previous OECD study, where SMEs were expected to 'increase co-operation in distribution networks and R&D' (OECD, 1997). Nevertheless, it is worth highlighting that less than 50 per cent of the SMEs perceive cooperation opportunities in R&D and exports. This figure seems to support the notion that the higher the investments in R&D, the greater the export propensity. One may surmise that perhaps these SMEs are not investing in R&D because they do not perceive opportunities in this area. If this suggestion can be confirmed, it will have important implications for policy-makers and training providers. The available data is

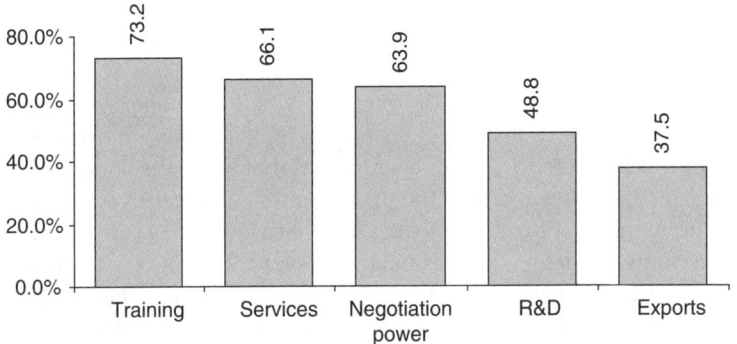

Figure 7.10 Perceived opportunities of cooperation by SMEs, 2003
Source: Institut Cerdà, 2003, in MEPIMED and Institut Cerdà, 2004.

not conclusive and, therefore, a further study is needed to verify this proposition.

The current situation of the Spanish economy, along with the low investments in R&D shown in Figure 7.7 and the low per centage of exports presented in Figure 7.8, considered in the context of the Spanish economy where 99.87 per cent are companies with less than 249 employees, suggest that SMEs in this country have been losing ground to build competitive advantages.

From an economic perspective, this could be explained by saying that the Spanish companies have not been successful in improving (decreasing) their cost per unit of output relative to the Eurozone. Within the EU, this is a situation shared also by Italy. However, Germany has much lower costs than it had in 1999 and France has also managed to hold down its costs (McRae, 2006).

The next section will present the most important policy instruments and incentive programmes, designed and implemented in Spain, to offer support to SMEs. It will attempt to show that, due to the importance of SMEs in Spain, the policies and incentives to enhance their competitiveness should be designed to act at the local level. In addition, due to the nature of the Spanish SMEs, joint initiatives between the public and private sectors are required to help SMEs improve their productivity and internationalization. In this context, collabourative organizational structures, like clusters, have been the leading model in the policy development at regional level in Spain (Porter, 2005).

Policies and systems of incentives for SMEs in Spain

The analysis of policies and systems of incentives for SMEs in the country must be studied at the regional and national levels, as Spain is constituted by 17 Autonomous Communities, where each one legislates and manages its own industrial development policies. Also, since joining the European Union in 1986, a supra-national level was added, giving Spanish companies access to the programmes and incentives of the EU. Furthermore, as a member of the OECD, Spanish SMEs can use OECD frameworks to design and evaluate policies.[8] The next sections will describe the Agency for Small and Medium Companies, the Centre for Industrial Technological Development and the financing and fiscal incentives for SMEs in Spain. Then, this section will discuss the role of universities and business schools in the creation of new companies and the dynamics of cluster formation in the process of regional industrialization.

Finally, this section will present examples of Spanish SMEs competing successfully in international markets.

The Agency for Small and Medium Companies (DGPYME)

In 1997 the Agency for Small and Medium Companies (DGPYME) was founded as an office of the Ministry of Industry, Tourism and Trade. The DGPYME has four main subdivisions with a broad set of objectives, from the promotion of a favourable economic environment that facilitates entrepreneurship, to the growth and the competitiveness of companies.

A programme called PROFIT is the main tool for the management of scientific research and technology development policies in SMEs. This programme is part of the Scientific Research, Development and Technology Innovation Plan 2004–7 (Plan de Investigación Científica, Desarrollo e Innovación Tecnológica). Important areas within PROFIT are the support to technology centres offering R&D+I services to SMEs and the development of R&D+I on technology parks. The programme attracted 2,153 SMEs in 2003.

DGPYME is also responsible for the SMEs' Consolidation and Competitiveness Plan 2000–6 (Plan de Consolidación y Competitividad de las PYME) for helping SMEs to improve their competitiveness. The plan's budget for the 2000–6 period is €496 million, aimed at projects on information society, design, quality systems, networking and collabouration among companies, and process innovation. The first four years of the plan saw 12,107 projects approved, mainly in the areas of quality systems and information.

Other areas within DGPYME are (i) prizes to doctoral theses on SMEs and scholarships for studies in this area, (ii) the Sistema Telemático (CIR), aimed at facilitating the constitution of new companies, (iii) the enterprise initiative for the promotion of a positive image of business in society, (iv) sources of funding such as endorsements, loans, microcredits, securitization of assets, or a national network of business angles, (v) a state-owned company for the development and design of innovation (DDI) promoting the design as a source of competitive advantage, (vi) the SME Observer which is a channel for the debate and diffusion of information for SMEs and (vii) the promotion of international cooperation among SMEs.

The Centre for Industrial Technological Development (CDTI)

The CDTI is a state-owned institution under the Ministry of Industry, Tourism and Commerce, that promotes innovation and technological development in Spanish companies through the following initiatives: (i) technical and economic evaluation and funding of R&D+I projects, (ii) participation in international programmes of technological cooperation, (iii) promotion of international knowledge transfers and support services to the technological innovation and (iv) support for the creation and consolidation of companies with a technological base. The CDTI carries out activities for the promotion of national and supra-national programmes, like Eureka,[9] along with initiatives of coordination, evaluation and follow-up of proposals and projects presented by companies in Spain.

The CDTI co-funded 577 projects on industrial research and technology innovation. The total budget assigned to these projects was €519.50 million, and it is important to highlight that 81 per cent of the recipient companies have less than 250 employees. The CDTI, along with the Official Credit Institute (Instituto de Crédito Oficial, ICO) offer loans with preferential conditions for the financing of up to 70 per cent of technology innovation projects with a maximum of €1.5 million per year and beneficiary.

Finally, NEOTEC is an initiative within the CDTI aimed at the creation and consolidation of companies with a technology base. During 2000–3, the programme helped the creation of 200 new companies, working together with risk capital institutions.

Both, DGPYME and CDTI, have proved to be important players in the creation of companies and the enhancement of their technology and competitiveness. For these agencies to have a greater impact in the future, their policies should be more focused on strategic high value-added sectors, chosen considering the Spanish comparative advantages as well as specific international trade opportunities. The OECD (2005) also recognized this challenge by stating that 'Spanish S&T policy is structured by type of recipients of government support rather than around strategic instruments or thematic priorities'. In addition, to reinforce the innovation system and offer better support for technology-based SMEs, these bodies should help in the development of financial markets and the access to risk capital, along with the design of effective fiscal incentives to R&D.

Financing and risk capital for SMEs in Spain

From the government, the Official Credit Institute (ICO) offers access to long-term funding in preferential conditions for the development of investment projects put together by SMEs in Spain. For example, the ICO-SMEs loan gives between 5 and 7 years for repayment, with 1–2 years to make the first payment.

From the private sector, Pellón (2005) found that venture capital companies managed in Spain in 2004 a total of €9.16 billion, four times more than in 2003. Most of the resources came from financial organizations (46 per cent) and these resources were destined to finance consolidated companies (52.5 per cent) and companies in expansion (41 per cent). Only 6.6 per cent were destined to finance small and medium companies in their initial seed stages and at start-up.

These figures show that, in general, Europe lags behind the US in risk capital investment volume. In fact, Moldicz (2004) says that private and risk capital markets in 2001 accounted for 0.32 per cent of the world's GDP, out of which the North American region constituted 62.8 per cent, Europe 21.5 per cent, South East Asia 12 per cent and Latin America, Africa and Asia 1 per cent each. This author also mentioned that low volumes of risk capital are considered to be associated with the technology gap between Europe and the US and Japan and, therefore, the European Union should support investments into the risk capital market for technology-based companies.

Given the great importance that risk capital is called to play in the financing of value-added business activities and the creation of high-quality jobs, European countries urgently need to design and implement policies oriented to stimulate private risk capital markets. In particular, as highlighted by a recent EU report (2005), the public sector should create a supportive regulatory environment, offer fiscal incentives[10] to encourage investments in venture capital, and reduce the obstacles to cross-border investments.

Fiscal incentives for R&D+I in Spain

The Foundation for the Technologic Innovation's 2005 Report (COTEC) found that the Spanish fiscal regime offers more incentives in the area of R&D+I than the OECD countries' average. The report said that this advantage can be seen in both the percentage of tax deductions and the variety of options. In fact, the incentives packages available for SMEs in Spain have been described as attractive in different forums. In this sense, it is worth highlighting that, for example, in 2004, the tax deduction on staff development in the use of new technologies doubled from 10 per cent to 20 per cent, the cap on deductible investments on the acquisition of new technology was raised to €1 million and the limit on deductible expenses on R&D+I was also raised to 50 per cent.

Nevertheless, the COTEC report also mentions that only few companies benefit from these provisions. COTEC conclude that the main factors explaining the poor use of these incentives are (i) the difficulties in identifying and to describing the activities as R&D+I, (ii) the belief that it is necessary to have a R&D department, (iii) the fear of becoming a target for inspections by the revenue agency and (iv) the lack of knowledge on how to submit projects.

The creation of new companies: the role of universities and business schools

Sole Parellada, Ruiz Navarro and Veciana (2004) found that, between 1998 and 2004, more than 450 companies were created in Spanish universities, 60 per cent based in technology and that the current creation rate is 130 companies a year. They compare this rate against other countries and found that it is lower than that in the UK, the Netherlands, the Nordic countries and the US.

These authors also mention that, by the end of 2004, only 37 universities in Spain had programmes in place for the promotion and support for the creation of new companies. Within these institutions, the most important are the INNOVA, at the Universidad Politécnica de Cataluña, the IDEAS programme, set up in 1992 at the Politécnica de Valencia, the UNIEMPRENDE, launched in 2001 by Universidad Santiago de Compostela, and the CIADE, at the Universidad Autónoma de Madrid.

Nevertheless, a study by Fundación Conocimiento y Desarrollo (2005) showed that less than 20 per cent of Spanish companies have contacted universities for the development of research projects, for specific analysis, or for contracting scientific or technical services. This study also showed that more than 60 per cent of the surveyed companies do not identify universities as a development engine.

This gap between companies and universities needs to be reduced, along with the transfer of knowledge and the use of the results from research. In this sense, Spain has developed what is known as the OTRIs (Offices for the Transfer of Research Results) and technology parks, associated to higher education institutions.

The OTRIs were created in the late 1980s to promote the relation between universities and businesses. Their main objective is the use of the R&D capacity available from universities, along with their research activities by the Spanish companies. The OTRIs have been successful in increasing the volume of contracts, from €100 million in 1996 to €282 million in 2004. In 2005, the OTRIs signed 9,447 contracts for consultancies and R&D activities.

Additionally, universities are collabourating with the business sector in the creation of technology-based companies in technology parks. The most important parks in Spain are the Parque Tecnológico de

Andalucía (operating within Universidad de Málaga), the Parques Científicos de Barcelona and the Parque Científico del Mediterráneo (MedPark). These parks work closely with the local universities in the creation of technology-based companies in the fields of biotechnology, environment and information technologies. In addition, the Parque Científico de Madrid (developed by two of the city's universities, Complutense and Autónoma, and private institutions like Grupo Santander and Genetrix – a company born in this park) houses more than 40 companies and carries out research in the areas of biotechnology and food, materials and engineering, information and communication technologies, environment, and renewable energies (PCM, 2006).

Another interesting example is that of business schools, as they seem to be playing an increasingly important role in the field of entrepreneurship. For example, the Madrid-based Instituto de Empresa Business School leads the NETI project, in collabouration with Spanish telecom operator Amena, with the aim of promoting the creation of innovative technology businesses. In recent years, new companies from the project have created 900 direct and indirect jobs and have received over €3 million from private investors. The NETI project also runs a Business Angels School, where private investors offer specific training on funding start-ups and business plan analysis. The Instituto de Empresa also coordinates the ICEVED (International Centre for Entrepreneurship and Ventures Development), a virtual portal serving as an interface for 24 international schools and acting as an intermediary among entrepreneurs and investment funds.

Regional industrialization and clusters formation

The picture described in previous sections shows that Spanish SMEs are relatively small in terms of annual turnover, and that they do not perceive many opportunities in cooperation and R&D-related investments. This situation asks for creativity along with collabourative forms of organization/partnerships to overcome the potential problems posed by these relative weaknesses.

In this context, it is worth mentioning the existence of successful clusters of SMEs in different areas of Spain. These clusters were formed to take advantage of economies of scale and other externalities, and some of them were promoted by the local autonomous governments. It is not a coincidence that these clusters are responsible for the products mentioned previously in this chapter as the most specialized exports from Spain.

Several policies and programmes were designed and implemented to accelerate the creation and the development of these structures.

Governmental agencies, at national and regional level, have been key players in the formation of clusters, offering information on markets and technologies, benchmarking analysis, access to low cost credits and networking.

The following sections will present successful case studies of clusters that grouped SMEs around different industrial projects. These are among the most well known in Spain, the Castellón ceramic cluster, the Mondragón Cooperative Corporation, the Asociación de Investigación y Desarrollo en la Industria del Mueble y Afines, the Consortium for the Commercial Promotion of Catalonia and the Basque Country.

Castellón ceramic cluster

The Castellón cluster is located in the Autonomous Community of Valencia in the east of Spain. It is responsible for 90 per cent of the world production of enamel; in fact, 33 of the 40 existing production facilities in the world are Spanish and 75 per cent of them are located in Castellón. The competitiveness reached by the companies in the clusters is explained mainly by their investments in R&D+I; for example, in 2004 the cluster earmarked 4.27 per cent of its sales to R&D, more than double Spain's and the EU's (15) average (1.1 per cent of the country's GDP and 2 per cent of the union's GDP respectively). This focus on innovation has allowed companies to develop a broad range of products with high added value, to implement automated processes, and to adopt models of production intensive in capital and technology with highly qualified labour.

The cluster has been supported by different agencies from the government, such as the IMPIVA (Valencia Autonomous Community), the MICyT (Ministry of Industry, Commerce and Tourism; Kingdom of Spain), the CDTI and the Ministry of Property of Spain.

The emergence of new competitors, mainly in China, brings new challenges to the companies in the cluster. During the coming years, these companies should specialize in high-range products and, to do so, will need to strengthen even more their innovation and learning capabilities.

Mondragón Cooperative Corporation (MCC)

MCC is a group of companies, SMEs most of them, employing more than 80,000 people with an annual turnover of €11.86 billion. It is organized in 23 subsidiaries, grouped in 23 cooperatives. These companies carry out diverse industrial activities, from the production of appliances to components for the auto industry.

The MCC's success has been based on the group's continuous adaptation to the challenges presented by the environment and the competition. The group's companies continuously innovate in production processes, in organizational forms and in the development of new products oriented mainly to the medium and high markets. For example, the group invests 5.5 per cent of its sales to R&D+I, when the EU's (15) average is close to 2 per cent.

Recent years have seen the internationalization of the group, looking for new growth opportunities. It now has production facilities in NAFTA (Mexico), Brazil and China. Eastern Europe has also been an investment destination for the group, motivated mainly by car manufacturers' demand and low labour costs (Mondragon, 2006).

Consortium for the Commercial Promotion of Catalonia (COPCA)

This consortium, based in the Autonomous Community of Catalonia, is an interesting example of collaboration between the public and private sectors to enhance competitiveness and promote the internationalization of SMEs. It is devoted to promoting the internationalization of SMEs by providing technical assistance and consultancy services. To that end, COPCA assists SMEs in cooperation and development projects financed by multilateral and bilateral organizations. Its main aim is to increase the number of exporting companies and help them to diversify and consolidate their operations into new export markets. COPCA was created with the participation of the Catalan Chambers of Commerce and Industry, the main export and business sector associations, financial institutions, academic centres specialized in international trade and the government of Catalonia. It consists of about 100 members and yearly carries out more than 6,000 projects on training, information and promotion.

Wood Industry's Research and Development Association (AIDIMA)

This association, based in the Valencia Autonomous Community, aims to help SMEs from the furniture and wood industry to improve their competitiveness. It was founded in 1984 by the Wood Business Federation of Valencia (*Federación Empresarial Valenciana de la Madera*) and the Valencia SMEs Institute (*Instituto de la Mediana y Pequeña Empresa Valenciana*), and receives support from the Industry and Energy Ministry (*Ministerio de Industria y Energía*), as well as from other institutions from the autonomous and central governments.

AIDIMA's main initiatives cover a wide range of support activities, from packaging and transportation to environment and human resources development, including innovation and technology development. The association currently has more than 600 member companies.

The Basque Country's case study: business and government working together in the promotion of SMEs

The Basque Country's experience in cluster formation is worth mentioning due to its success in the formation of groups and in the improved competitiveness of their companies. In fact, the joint efforts of local business associations and government agencies in the creation of clusters have been essential to boost new industrial developments and to stimulate cooperation among traditional sectors. There are currently ten clusters in the Basque Country that group SMEs from different economic sectors (Porter, 2005).[11] Mitxeo Grajirena, Idigoras Gamboa and Vicente Molina (2003) highlighted the Basque Country government's role in the creation of these clusters and showed that most of them were based on pre-existing organizations, like the Association of Machine Tool Manufacturers (AFM); the *Asociación de Industrias de las Tecnologías Electrónicas y de la Información del País Vasco* (GAIA); the *Agrupación Cluster de Industrias de Componentes de Automoción de Euskadi* (ACICAE); and the Aeronautics Cluster of the Basque Country (HEGAN).

Asociación de Industrias de las Tecnologías Electrónicas y de la Información del País Vasco (GAIA)

GAIA, the Basque Country's electronic and information technology industries association, founded in 1983, is one of the best examples of the role played by business organizations in the development of SMEs. GAIA's main objective is to help SMEs in the incorporation and efficient use of available technologies to improve their competitive situation and, as a consequence, take advantage of the opportunities posed by globalization, in particular, by the information and knowledge society.

More than 170 companies selling products and services in the electronic and telecommunications markets are members of this association. In order to help them, GAIA has developed an international network along with technical and commercial agreements in different countries that enable its members to participate in multinational projects and improve their access to markets abroad. In addition, GAIA also coordinates the Basque Technological Platforms (*Plataformas Tecnológicas Vascas*), which promote the development of companies in cutting-edge technologies, such as mobile and wireless communications, intelligent transportation systems and nanoelectronics.

In a move to fulfil its objective of helping SMEs to incorporate technology, GAIA is a founding member of the Spanish Confederation of Information Technology, Communications and Electronics Companies (*Confederación Española de Empresas de Tecnologías de la Información, Comunicaciones y Electrónica, CONETIC*). The Confederation is divided in 13 territories, formed by more than 1,700 SMEs, employing around 29,500 employees and with aggregate sales of €4.6 billion a year.

Finally, GAIA also offers services aimed at improving the SMEs' international competitiveness. The most important are the representation of the companies' interests, the creation and coordination of work groups in areas of interest, the development of sectorial studies and the provision of guidance in areas like internationalization, staff development and R&D.

The Auto Industry Components Cluster of the Basque County (ACICAE)

ACICAE, the Auto Industry Components Cluster of the Basque Country, was created in 1993 following recommendations from Harvard Business School professor Michael Porter to improve the competitiveness of the companies in the industry. As part of its activities, the association has developed specialized groups in R&D+I, quality, internationalization and logistics, critical areas for the productivity and international competitiveness of SMEs in the sector. ACICAE has around 280 member SMEs, employing more than 40,000 persons, and represents 16 per cent of the Basque's Country gross regional product (GRP). This cluster is a successful case study of collaboration among SMEs; in fact, the EU recognizes ACICAE as an example of best practice in the field.

The Aeronautics Cluster of the Basque Country (HEGAN)

HEGAN was set up in 1997 following the recommendations of the Basque Country Competitiveness Programme. This association of aeronautics companies promotes the consolidation of the aerospace sector in the Basque Country through activities oriented at strengthening the competitiveness of its associate companies, including training and specialization of human resources, technology transfer, research and development and innovation programmes. By the end of 2005, the cluster had 32 associate companies covering almost all the aerospace sub-sectors, performing diverse activities in the value chain such as services, R&D, design, manufacture, integration, testing, certification and product support. For several years, the Basque Country has consolidated its position as the second largest aerospace centre in Spain after Madrid.

Even though there is no reliable data available to measure the impact of this policy of cluster formation,[12] it is possible to see that a positive dialogue, a relation, has emerged among businesses, universities and public agencies that facilitate the transfer of knowledge and best practices.

These successful stories show the advantages offered by industrial cluster formation policies to improve productivity and international competitiveness in SMEs. Local autonomous governments in other Spanish regions should document and disseminate these best practices in order for their firms to take advantage of economies of scale and other positive externalities.

Spanish SME success stories

Panda Software

Founded in 1990, Panda Software successfully competes internationally in the systems security market. The company creates and develops technologies, products and services aimed at keeping its customers' systems protected from viruses and other threats at the lowest proprietary cost. The company's headquarters is located in Bilbao, the Basque Country's capital, and has offices in more than 50 countries. Panda's products are sold in 230 countries and territories and target corporate clients, SMEs, professionals and final customers.

Grupo Cosentino

Grupo Cosentino became the first Spanish company to advertise in the Superbowl (the NFL final). The company's main product – silestone – is board made from a mixture of marble scrap, silica and quartz. This silestone formula was the result of around two years of in-house research in alternative uses for marble scrap to compete with marble blocks and was carried out with an Italian partner. In 1989 the company registered this product, which currently accounts for 85 per cent of its sales, and added improvements to the patent in 1998 and 2003. Grupo Cosentino's headquarter is located in Macael, Andalucia Autonomous Community, and has set up four subsidiaries in the US, Latin America, Northern Europe and the UK. The company currently operates five manufacturing facilities employing 2,000 people, of which only 850 are located in Spain.

Isofotón

Isofotón was founded in 1991 as a spin-off of Universidad Politécnica de Madrid and has become the first European producer of bifacial photovoltaic cells by volume and the seventh in the world. Bifacial photovoltaic cells were developed in the 1980s by Antonio Luque, the then chairman of the company, and became the foundation of Isofoton's competitive advantage. The company has an annual turnover of around €75 million, from which around 90 per cent comes from international markets (more than 70 countries in the five continents), having achieved important market shares in large countries, such as a 25 per cent share in Germany (the word's second largest market). In 2002 Isofotón received the Prince Felipe Prize for Renewable Energies and Energy Efficiency.

Microelectrónica Española

Founded in 1981, Microelectrónica Española has been a key player in international markets for the development and manufacturing of operative systems for intelligent cards. Currently, around 50 per cent of its sales come from international markets. It received the Prince Felipe Prize for its entrepreneurial spirit, constant technologic advances, personnel policy and success in international markets.

Natura Bissé Internacional

Founded in 1979, Natura Bissé keeps its familiar conception for the production and commercialization of premium cosmetics. More than 50 per cent of the company's sales come from abroad, with subsidiaries in the US and Mexico and distributors in 18 other countries. In Spain, Natura Bissé's products are sold in 90 high street shops and department stores. The company also won the Prince Felipe Prize in recognition for its sustainable development based on constant innovation and its success in international markets, while keeping the family-business structure.

Net Transit and Receive (NTR)

Founded in 2000, NTR is focused on the development and implementation of innovative solutions for companies in need of permanent communication and collaboration without compromising the mobility of their people. The company counts more than 3,000 customers using its technology 'on-demand', giving users remote support, access and control. Among the clients, it is possible to find some of the largest multinational corporations such as Toshiba, ING-Direct, IKEA, Deutsche Bank, Epson, or Honda, among others. NTR's headquarter is located in Barcelona, with subsidiaries in Germany, France, Italy and the US. In addition, it has developed a network of distributors in Scandinavia, the UK, Japan and Chile. In 2005, NTR received the Catalonia Prize for Internationalization for its success in seizing opportunities in markets abroad.

A few caveats

In spite of the many success stories, the situation cited above of SME competitiveness in Spain is far from rosy. For example, 1,000 SMEs in the textile industry have closed their operations in the last four years with a loss of 45,000 jobs, mainly due to the competition from China. This industry has also seen reductions in its output during the same period from €14 billion in 2002 to less than €12 billion in 2005 (De Antonio and Garcia, 2006). This situation contrasts with the success of large companies in the same industry, such as Inditex (owner of high-street brand Zara) and Mango. There is also some question about the efficiency of an independent public spending watchdog in identifying the results achieved by government agencies focused on SMEs.

In order to overcome this problem, a system to evaluate the results of the policies implemented in the area of SMEs and their competitiveness should be put in place. This system could take the form of a scorecard produced by the government agencies working with SMEs.

The scorecard should include indicators such as efficiency and impact of competitiveness policies (R&D+I), number of subsidies offered vs number used, number of SMEs benefiting from tax exemptions, guarantees, loans, etc., number of technology-based start-ups resulting from government programmes, number of exporting technology-based SMEs, number of jobs created by technology-based SMEs, SMEs' access to capital, national and regional innovation systems' efficiency, number of technology-based start-ups originated in universities, number of consortia or alliances/collaborative projects and cluster-creation support.

The system should be audited regularly by an independent body on behalf of, for example, the legislative branch of government. This independent body should be focused on four different aspects, the impact of public regulations and policies: the SMEs' access to funding, the training, knowledge transfer and support initiatives available to SMEs and the effective coordination among government agencies.

Outlook

The internationalization process of the Spanish economy is still in its infancy. In fact, major outward FDI flows took place during the last ten years, mainly to Latin America, taking advantage of the privatization processes that followed the economic reforms of the 1990s. While the first stage of this internationalization process has involved large corporations as the main actors, the next wave of internationalization is expected to come from SMEs. Nevertheless, as illustrated in this chapter, Spanish SMEs are currently facing different barriers that encumber their possibilities to compete successfully in overseas markets.

In this context, the proliferation of clusters across different regions in Spain demonstrates the interest of local governments and SMEs to promote and adopt new industrial arrangements to benefit from economies of scale, improve their access to information, uptake new technologies and diffuse better practices and innovations. Even though there is a multiplicity of recently created clusters, the challenge still remains since the main factors responsible for low competitiveness – low investments in R&D+I; weak linkages with universities, businesses and public entities; and low qualification of human resources – continue to hinder the internationalization of SMEs and may compromise the future success of these initiatives.

Notes

1. It is not the intention of this work to present a detailed macroeconomic analysis, only a framework to introduce an argument about the performance of small business in Spain.
2. Enterprises with between 0 to 249 employees, according to the Spanish government.
3. EU average: average of the available data for the EU-25 member states (composition changes for each activity). Birth data (2002): enterprise births as a proportion of the total number of enterprises. Death data (2001): enterprise deaths as a proportion of the total number of enterprises.
4. Data not available for Spain's death rates in construction and hotels and restaurants.
5. Unfortunately, Eurostat does not provide data for Germany and France.
6. Distributive trades is made up of the motor trades, wholesale trades and retail trades.
7. In this sense, Eurostat (2006) said that the top three Spanish export specialization products in relation with the EU-25 countries are (i) ceramic tiles and flags (CPA 16.3), (ii) monumental or building stone and articles thereof (CPA 26.7) and (iii) animal and vegetable oils and fats (CPA 15.4).
8. The EU's policies act as support and as a complement to the efforts of member states and are concentrated in four policy frameworks along with the development of what is know as the European Database of initiatives in support of SMEs. These instruments have been designed and implemented within the following objectives set by the European Commission: (i) promote enterprise spirit and capacity, (ii) promote enterprise innovation, (iii) improve SMEs'

access to national and international markets, (iv) reduce paperwork and bureaucracy and (v) improve the SMEs' development potential. On the other hand, in 2000, OECD members and other participant countries signed the Bologna Charter on SME Policies, which provides a general framework for the design and evaluation of policies oriented to support the development and competitiveness of SMEs. In 2004, these countries subscribed to the Istanbul declaration on Fostering the Growth of Innovative and Internationally Competitive SMEs, aimed at (i) reducing barriers to SMEs' access to global markets through the promotion of linkages between large enterprises and SMEs, and the reduction of administrative and legal barriers, (ii) improving access to funding for SMEs, (iii) developing an evaluation culture for SMEs policy-makers and (iv) strengthening the policy-making process.
9. Programme Eureka aims to promote the competitiveness of European companies through the promotion of technological projects oriented to the development of products, processes, or services with clear commercial interest in the international market and based on novel technologies.
10. The Kingdom of Spain offers fiscal incentives to promote the risk capital market. Under this new legislation, many private and public institutions have developed, supporting the sector's expansion in the last few years.
11. A list of these clusters includes: machine tools (AFM); cluster grouping of industries and auto industry components of the Basque Country (ACICAE); appliances cluster; ports and logistics cluster (Uniport and Foro Industria Maritima); electronics components, electronics subcontracting, telecommunications, software and multimedia (GAIA): environmental cluster (IHOBE and ACLIMA); knowledge cluster; Basque energy cluster; aeronautical cluster (HEGAN); paper cluster; Basque Foundation for Quality (Euskalit); Euskadi's School of Engineer in Computer Science (COIIE).
12. The design of specific performance indicators and the implementation of an evaluation method is recommended to assess the effectiveness of these initiatives, which have been carried out for more than a decade.

References

Arahuetes, A. and Casilda, R. (2004), 'Spain', in Z. Vodusek (ed.), *Foreign Direct Investment in Latin America. The Role of European Investors: An Update*, Inter-American Development Bank, Paris.

CIA (2005), *The World Factbook*, at http://www.cia.gov/cia/publications/factbook/index.html (accessed 3 April 2006).

De Antonio, A. and Garcia, P. (2006), 'España ha perdido mil empresas textiles y 45000 empleos en cuatro años por la competencia de China', ABC, 24 August.

DGPYME (2005), *Evolucion de las Pymes Españolas 1995-2003*, Ministerio de Industria, Turismo, y Comercio, Reino de España, Madrid.

European Commission (2005), Conference report on the risk capital summit 2005: investing for growth and competitiveness, European Commission, Brussels.

European Commission (2006), *Europa Website*, at www.europa.eu (accessed 17 July 2006).

Eurostat (2006), *European Business Facts and Figures*, European Commission, Brussels.

Fundación Conocimiento y Desarrollo (2005), *La contribución de las universidades españolas al desarrollo*, Madrid.
INE (2003), *Directorio Central de Empresas*, Instituto Nacional de Estadistica. Reino de España, Madrid.
Institut Cerdà (2003), *Estudio de Mercado del Proyecto Pymes Institut Cerdà*, Barcelona.
McRae, H. (2006), 'Higher eurozone rates: Germany is fine but Italy and Spain could be in trouble', *The Independent*, 25 May.
MEPIMED and Institut Cerdà (2004), *Factores Clave de la Competitividad Interna de la Pequeña y Mediana Empresa en España*, at http://www.cein.es/pdf_documentacion/consolidacion/competitividad.pdf (accessed 4 April 2006).
Ministerio de Economía y Hacienda (2006), *Sintesis de Indicadores Economicos*, Reino de España.
Ministerio de Industria, T. y. C. (2006), *La industria ante el nuevo escenario europeo. El papel del Estado*, at http://www.mityc.es/NR/rdonlyres/ (accessed 15 July 2006).
Mitxeo Grajirena, J., Idigoras Gamboa, I. and Vicente Molina, A. (2003), *Los clusters como fuente de competitividad: el caso de la Comunidad Autónoma del País Vasco*, Universidad del Pais Vasco, Pais Vaco.
Moldicz, C. (2004), 'Risk Capital in the European Union', *Development & Finance*, 2, pp. 36-47.
Mondragon (2006), Mondragon Corporación Corporación Cooperativa, company reports, Guipúzcoa, Spain.
Munchau, W. (2006), 'Spain has More Reason to Quit the Euro than Italy', *Financial Times*, 20 February.
OECD (1997), *Globalization and Small and Medium Enterprises*, OECD, Paris.
PCM (2006), *Parque Cientifico de Madrid*, at www.fpcm.es (accessed 10 July 2006).
Pellón J.M. (2005), *Private Equity in Spain 2005*, Asociación Española de Entidades de Capital-Riesgo, Madrid.
Porter, M., Ketels, C. and Miller, K. (2005), 'The Basque Country: Strategy for Economic Development', Harvard Business School Case no. 70611, (published on November 18, 2004) Harvard Business School Publishing, Boston.
Proudfoot Consulting (2005), *An International Study of Company-level Productivity*, Proudfoot Consulting, New York.
Sole Parellada, F., Ruiz Navarro, J. and Veciana, J. (2004), *Creación de empresas y universidad*, Fundación Universidad Empresa de la Provincia de Cadiz, Cadiz.
World Bank (2005), *World Development Indicators*, World Bank, Washington, D.C.

8
Unravelling Informal Entrepreneurship: Small-firm Clusters and Economic Ungovernance in Nigeria

Kate Meagher

Introduction

Small enterprise clusters are viewed as an important means of promoting competitive small-firm development, even in contexts of unstable markets and weak states. Cluster scholars have argued that dense concentrations of small firms give rise to a novel form of economic governance described as 'cooperative competition' (Best, 1990), or 'collective efficiency' (Schmitz, 1992), in which cooperative inter-firm networks, rather than markets or bureaucratic hierarchies, coordinate economic behaviour. The developmental strength of clustered firms lies in 'social ties and socialized production relations that lower transaction costs by providing a basis of trust, social reputation, and reciprocity in interfirm relations' (Nadvi, 1999: 146), enabling clustered firms to out-compete large formal sector enterprises, particularly in times of economic upheaval. In the face of economic restructuring and ongoing market instability, networked small-enterprise clusters have charted a path to economic growth and global integration in a variety of developing economies from Southern Europe to Latin America and East as well as South Asia. Yet they have continued to perform poorly in Africa, despite the apparently conducive environment of strong socio-cultural loyalties and the proliferation of clustered small enterprises (McCormick, 1999; Schmitz and Nadvi, 1999).

Two broad explanations have emerged to account for the developmental failures of African enterprise clusters. The first is that African societies suffer from a *lack* of networks – a handicap attributed to the disruptive impact of colonialism, rapid urbanization and overbearing states (Rasmussen, 1992). Schmitz and Nadvi (1999) find that most African clusters are lacking in both 'strong' ties of trust and social sanctions, and 'weak' ties to link them into wider markets. However, the claim that Africans lack networks seems extraordinary, given the wealth of historical and contemporary literature on African trading, small-scale production and social welfare networks (Meillassoux, 1971; Chazan, 1988).

A second explanation argues that Africans tend to form the *wrong kind* of networks. Abigail Barr (1999) emphasizes the tendency of African producers to form redistributive or 'risk-minimizing' networks rather than 'productivity-enhancing' networks. More provocatively, Bayart (1999) and others argue that African networks are inimical to the development of rational economic institutions owing to embedded cultural logics of clientism, corruption and communal conflict. In either case, cultural embeddedness in African societies is believed to impede rather than foster collective efficiency.

Taken together, these perspectives contend that African clusters suffer from a lack of embeddedness, but that greater embeddedness leads to parochialism or criminality. On the whole, primordialist stereotypes tend to predominate over institutional analysis. What is lacking is a properly institutional and historical treatment of African small-firm organization. How has the institutional history of particular African ethnic groups influenced their ability to form economically dynamic clusters? Is the development of African small-firm networks affected by factors other than ethnic solidarity? Does an environment of state withdrawal and decentralization constitute an opportunity or a liability for the development of economically dynamic African clusters?

With a view to addressing these questions, this chapter will trace the development of three particularly active Nigerian informal manufacturing clusters, focusing on their institutional strengths as well as their weaknesses. The first is a traditional weaving cluster in the Muslim Yoruba town of Ilorin in south-western Nigeria. The second and third are a mechanized garment cluster and an artisanal shoe cluster in the Christian Igbo town of Aba in south-eastern Nigeria. These three clusters each represent different models of cluster development, involving a 'traditional' craft activity (Ilorin), a 'modern' mechanized activity (Aba garments) and a low-capital, low-skill activity associated with poverty. Research on the two Aba clusters was conducted between 1999 and 2000, with subsequent visits in 2001 and 2005, while the Ilorin research was carried out between May 2004 and April 2005. The material presented here is based on a sample of 173 firms distributed across the three clusters, supplemented by in-depth interviews.

Economic dynamism and social disorder

Contrary to prevailing perspectives, all three study clusters show a remarkable level of economic dynamism, particularly since the onset of Nigeria's structural adjustment programme in 1986. In the Ilorin weaving cluster, a census conducted in 2004 indicates that by the mid-1990s as many as 10,000 full-time and part-time weavers were operating in the cluster – more than doubling figures from the late colonial period. Despite its traditional status, levels of global integration in Ilorin weaving are high, with inputs sourced from as far away as China and Japan, and distribution networks extending to Ghana, Sierra Leone, the US and the UK.

In Aba, the informal shoe and garment clusters have shown even more extraordinary levels of dynamism. In 1999, these two informal manufacturing clusters supported a total of 13,910 firms, which generated employment for over 58,000 people, including enterprise heads and workers. More impressive still is their annual turnover, which amounted to roughly US$160 million in the case of shoes and US$12 million for garments. Both clusters are highly globalized, with supply networks extending as far as Asia, and distribution networks extending across Africa (Meagher, 2006).

More remarkable still, the spectacular growth of these three clusters has taken place without the assistance of the state. The majority of these firms are informal, meaning they are unregistered, do not pay many of their taxes and operate in violation of basic labour, factory and zoning regulations. A handful of formal sector firms operating in and around these clusters had comparatively little interaction with the bulk of clustered firms. The pervasive informality of the economic environment tends to be viewed in the cluster literature as a conducive environment for the development of innovative small-firm clusters (Sabel, 1986:48).

Despite dynamic growth in the 1980s and 1990s, all three clusters were in a state of precipitous decline by the early years of the new millennium. Mounting economic pressure, collapsing businesses and rising social tensions have created an increasingly volatile social milieu, leading in the Aba shoe cluster to the rise of the infamous Bakassi Boys vigilante group (Human Rights Watch/CLEEN 2002). What underlies this remarkable combination of economic dynamism and social dysfunction? Is it a problem of too little embeddedness or too much, of culturally perverse strong ties or insufficiently globalized weak ties? Did the state play a role, either by smothering local institutional initiatives or by failing to support them?

African enterprise clusters and informal institutions

Owing to their marginalization from the formal economy, these informal enterprise clusters have drawn on culturally embedded institutions to provide an organizational infrastructure for the coordination of training and access to capital, labour and markets. Far from promoting parochialism and stagnation, however, these indigenous institutional arrangements have facilitated the development of market-oriented rather than redistributive institutions, inter-ethnic cooperation rather than conflict, and innovation rather than timeless traditional practice.

The Ilorin weaving cluster

The Ilorin weaving cluster developed over a century before colonialism in the context of the decline of the Oyo Empire in the Yoruba ethnic sphere of what is now south-western Nigeria. Specialized craftsmen from Oyo weaving towns migrated to Ilorin, the rising Yoruba power at the time (Lloyd, 1953; O'Hear, 1987). Over the ensuing 200 years, weavers from a variety of Yoruba as well as non-Yoruba communities have been integrated into the cluster, and have gradually been assimilated under a common Yoruba Muslim identity. Despite origins spreading across several very different ethnic groups – my research encountered weavers of Yoruba, Hausa, Nupe, Fulani and Igbirra origins – all of the enterprise heads in the cluster were Ilorin indigenes, and all regarded themselves as Yoruba.

The key product of the Ilorin weaving cluster is a local strip cloth known as *aso-oke*, a local luxury cloth. *Aso-oke* weaving is an unmechanized activity, carried out on a narrow loom that produces strips of cloth conventionally four to six inches wide, which are sewn together into garments. In Ilorin, *aso-oke* weaving is a male activity. While women traditionally engaged in broad-loom weaving, their role in narrow-loom weaving was only at the level of the spinning and dyeing of cotton yarns, activities which have almost completely died out with the introduction of factory-made yarns.

The traditional organization of Yoruba weaving involves apprentices and weavers who work for master weavers of the same lineage (Lloyd, 1953; Bray, 1968: 273). Only master weavers – trained weavers with the capital to supply yarn to workers – can market finished cloth at the main *aso-oke* markets in Ibadan, Ede and Lagos, and only masters can join the weavers' guild. Conventionally, no weaver can work for more than one master, though this restriction is often relaxed when business is slow. A lineage-based master-weavers' guild, which is part of the pre-colonial structure of Yoruba weaving, regulates the activity in each weaving town, and is still the main weavers' association in Ilorin. The Ilorin weavers' guild regulates prices and disputes among weavers, controls access to the status of master weaver, organizes collective celebrations and mediates between weavers and the state.

By the 1950s, the lineage-based organization of production was beginning to loosen (Bray, 1968; Lloyd, 1953). It has become increasingly common for apprentices to be trained by masters to whom they are not related by blood. Increased demand for labour, particularly since the 1980s, has encouraged the incorporation of non-Ilorin, non-Muslim and even non-Yoruba groups into weaving – as workers, but not as masters. There was also a limited penetration of women from outside Ilorin into narrow-loom weaving. Among master weavers interviewed, more than two-thirds had trained or employed non-Ilorin weavers, 40 per cent had trained or employed non-Muslims, and a number of masters had trained women, though only one had employed them as weavers. The traditional character of the activity and the centrality of Islam in Ilorin society initially made weaving resistant to the penetration of Western (perceived as Christian) education, but the rising importance of English for establishing wider trading contacts, and the entry of young men into weaving to sponsor further education, has led to rising levels of education among weavers since the 1970s.

Labour arrangements involve a dispersed homeworker system, rather than centralized workshops. Embedded in strong communal structures of regulation, weavers working under a given master often work in their own compounds rather than in the master's weaving shed, and may be distributed across the town, and even in outlying villages or in weaving towns in neighbouring states. Labour discipline is maintained by a combination of supervisory visits, paternalistic ties and strict norms of trustworthy behaviour backed up with severe sanctions. Payment of workers is by piece-rate, based on the quality and complexity of the work, supplemented with patrimonial assistance from the master in times of ceremonies or financial difficulty. Theft of materials or funds provided for weaving is punished with dismissal and a reputation for dishonesty. Persistent offenders are forced to leave town or enter another activity outside the traditional quarters of Ilorin, challenging claims that African community-based networks suffer from a lack of sanctioning capacity (Fafchamps and Minten, 1999).

The Aba shoe and garment clusters

Aba's shoe and garment clusters have a much more recent history. Aba itself was founded during the early colonial period, and both clusters developed in the town during the 1950s. Despite their comparatively recent origins, the organization and cohesion of these clusters is based on much older social institutions. Although the Igbo, unlike the Yoruba, had no centralized state systems in pre-colonial times, the lack of political centralization co-existed with a range of pan-Igbo social and economic institutions that have contributed importantly to the legendary commercial dynamism of the Igbo (Dike and Ekejiuba, 1990). Pre-colonial Igbo society was made up of independent hometown communities embedded in a wider network of shared religious and economic institutions. These include systems of hometown-based occupational specialization, the remarkably effective Igbo apprenticeship system and pan-Igbo credit systems and trading networks, backed by communal and religious systems of economic sanctions (Isichei, 1976).

Informal garment production is the specialization of migrants from the relatively prosperous farming and trading communities of the former colonial district of Bende, in north-eastern Abia state. The Aba garment cluster developed in the part of town settled by migrants from the 'Old Bende' area. Bende indigenes had no pre-colonial specialization in weaving or tailoring, but during the colonial period became involved in cotton production and in itinerant tailoring, bringing them into contact with the colonial garment industry (Meagher, forthcoming). The comparative prosperity of Bende indigenes facilitated their entry into small-scale garment production, a mechanized activity with comparatively high capital costs. Membership in a prosperous community and a strong pre-colonial involvement in long-distance trade meant that indigenes of Old Bende played a dominant role in trading as well as producing garments, leading to advantaged access to markets and credit among Bende producers.

While the Igbo apprenticeship system is conventionally confined to relatives or townsmen, the expansion of informal garment production from the 1970s brought the penetration of a wider range of Igbo communities as garment producers turned to other Igbo groups in their search for apprentices and workers. Despite more diverse patterns of entry, however, Bende tailors and garment producers have retained their dominance in the activity owing to a reputation for superior skills, and advantaged access to training and credit networks. The garment cluster includes a high percentage of women producers, owing to a conventional division of labour in which women produce women's clothes. However, the tendency of men to dominate the high-capital, mass-production end of the activity, and to penetrate into the production of women's clothes at the high-fashion end, has meant that women were heavily concentrated at the low-income end of the informal garment cluster. The mechanized character of small-scale garment production, and its comparative respectability, was compatible with relatively high levels of education despite the pervasive informality of the garment cluster.

Informal shoe manufacturing developed in Aba as the specialization of migrants from the former colonial district of Mbaise, a poor, particularly land-scarce area located in nearby Imo state. Mbaise migrants turned to informal shoe production owing to its extremely low capital and skill threshold. The activity initially involved the use of simple hand tools for the production of crude sandals. Mbaise shoe producers had no artisanal history of shoe production or leather working; in fact the sandals they produced were initially made of used tyres rather than leather. Over time, however, skills, equipment and materials became more sophisticated, leading to the production of contemporary 'fashion shoes'. The development of input and output trading networks was dominated by other, more prosperous Igbo communities with whom the Mbaise producers developed credit relations that fuelled the rapid growth of the activity from the 1970s.

As in the case of the garment cluster, the expansion of the informal shoe cluster from the late 1970s led to the entry of other Igbo and even non-Igbo communities from southern minority groups. One shoe producer even trained a Yoruba apprentice. However, the status of informal shoe production as a 'poor man's business', and the comparatively low skill levels of the original Mbaise producers, led to a different pattern of social restructuring from that observed in the garment cluster. Seen as a low-status group among the Igbo, with a reputation for low-quality production, Mbaise producers were easily out-competed by new entrants. Despite being the founding artisanal group, Mbaise producers rapidly dwindled to a small proportion of informal producers as the cluster grew. Moreover, the low status of informal shoe production tended to attract a very different class of entrants, predominantly those who lacked the capital to enter something better. This led to significantly lower levels of education than are observed in the garment cluster. Informal shoe production has also remained an almost exclusively male activity. No female enterprise heads were found, owing to the low status and physically arduous character of the work. However, there was limited evidence of women entering as workers, or as shoe tailors.

Restructuring social networks

While socio-cultural factors have played an important role in the organization of all three clusters, economic expansion has led to varying degrees of social restructuring within the clusters. Figure 8.1 summarizes

Cluster	% from original artisanal community	% Local indigenes	% from other ethnic groups	% women	No. of generations in the activity
Ilorin weaving	13.5*	100.0	(7.6)**	0.0	3.4
Aba garments	44.3	8.2	0.0	44.3	<1
Aba shoes	14.1	23.9	5.6	0.0	<1

Figure 8.1 Socio-cultural and gender composition of enterprise heads
Source: Fieldwork
* Migrants from Oyo weaving towns.
** 33 percent of weavers were no longer aware of their origins.

the current socio-cultural and gender composition of enterprise heads in the three activities. The activities show very different levels of communal control. While all three clusters were founded by migrant communities, Ilorin master weavers have all been incorporated over time into the indigenous socio-cultural identity. In the Aba garment cluster, the migrant community maintained a distinctive identity as well as a reputation for superior skills, leading to the continued prominence of this group in the garment cluster. In the shoe cluster, by contrast, the founding 'artisanal' group, known for their poor skills and low levels of capital, has been overwhelmed by entrants from other Igbo as well as non-Igbo communities.

As Figure 8.1 indicates, the informal gender division of labour has prevented women from entering into the Ilorin weaving cluster and the Aba shoe cluster as enterprise heads, though they have entered to a limited extent as workers. By contrast, these same factors have supported the strong presence of women as heads of informal garment firms, though their advancement within the activity is constrained. In Ilorin, weaving is deeply embedded in the community, with master weavers averaging more than three generations in the activity. In the two Aba clusters, the majority of producers are the first in their families to be involved in the activity, leading to a shallower degree of occupational embeddedness.

In addition to varying levels of communal homogeneity in the three clusters, occupational and skill indicators challenge many stereotypes about African informal enterprise, as indicated in Figure 8.2. While African informal operators are associated with a propensity to diversify into a range of income-generating activities in the face of poverty and economic instability (Berry, 1993; Pedersen, 1996), producers in these clusters show a startling level of occupational specialization, meaning that

Cluster	Occupational specialization	Primary education only	Secondary education only	Some post-secondary education	Share from advantaged class backgrounds
Ilorin weaving	69.2	17.3	25.0	13.4	30.8
Aba garments	72.9	27.9	59.0	6.5	26.3
Aba shoes	85.5	80.3	12.7	0.0	18.5

Figure 8.2 Occupational specialization and education (percent of enterprise heads)
Source: Fieldwork

they continue to earn their living from only one activity. Approximately 70 per cent of producers in the two textile clusters practice no other income-generating activity, rising as high as 86 per cent in the shoe cluster. Levels of education are also comparatively high, especially in the two textile clusters. Challenging the association between informality and low levels of education, nearly 60 per cent of garment producers had completed secondary school, and a significant proportion of garment producers and weavers had some form of post-secondary education. The unmechanized, low-status character of informal shoe production shows up in significantly lower levels of education. While 80 per cent had primary education, only 13 per cent had completed secondary school, and post-secondary education was extremely rare. Surprisingly, the traditional Muslim weaving cluster had higher levels of secondary and post-secondary education than the much more Westernized Igbo shoe cluster.

Patterns of social change have also led to a penetration of producers from advantaged class backgrounds – defined here to mean self or parents in formal sector employment or middle-level business activities (large-scale trade, capital-intensive small enterprises). Middle-class penetration occurred particularly in the first decade of structural adjustment when informal manufacturing activities were booming, and alternative jobs were scarce. By early 2000, producers with advantaged class backgrounds made up over 25 per cent of enterprise heads in the weaving and garment clusters, and just under 20 per cent in the shoe cluster.

Network governance

Significant variations in the social organization of the three clusters have been accompanied by distinctive but remarkably dynamic forms of economic organization. Contrary to the assertions of many cluster scholars, all three of these African clusters show a strong presence of inter-firm networks, voluntary associations and cluster-based producers' associations, as well as participation in subcontracting relations with the formal sector and national as well as international supply and distribution networks.

Production networks

Firms in all three clusters are very small, ranging from an average of one to two workers or apprentices in the Aba shoe cluster to seven workers in the Ilorin weaving cluster, where the status of independent producer is hedged by more exacting social and occupational standards (Figure 8.3). Labour forces in the three clusters are supplemented with the hiring of one or two temporary workers in periods of high demand. Up to one-fifth of firms in the Aba clusters have no workers at all. Despite the small size of firms, these clusters have enhanced their productive capacity through the development of a division of labour and well-developed cooperative and subcontracting networks that coordinate productive activities among firms.

The Aba shoe cluster most closely resembles the conventional cluster model of cooperating small firms specializing in different aspects of the production process. Owing to the poorer backgrounds of most shoe producers, there is a sharp inter-firm division of labour centred on the type of equipment needed. The two mechanized areas of shoe production – the sewing of uppers and the smoothing of soles – constitute distinct activities with separate apprenticeships. Those who produce the finished shoe are largely dependent on hand tools, and specialize in the production of men's, ladies', or children's shoes. Production is

Cluster	% of firms with no workers	Avg. no. of regular workers (excluding temporary workers)	Avg. no. of apprentices	Avg. no. of employees	Avg. no. of temporary workers	Avg. no. of unpaid family workers	Own specialized machinery
Ilorin weaving	0.1	7.0	0.2	4.8	2.0	2.0	0.0
Aba garments	20.3	3.6	1.4	1.9	0.9	0.3	57.6
Aba shoes	16.1	1.4	1.1	0.2	1.7	0.1	16.1

Figure 8.3 Firm size and types of labor used
Source: Fieldwork.

structurally dependent on subcontracting among firms specialized in various processes, and regular informal borrowing of equipment and inputs. Within the firm, however, there is no fixed division of labour. Owing to lack of capital among most shoe producers, apprenticeship and temporary employment represent the main sources of labour. The allocation of tasks within the firm depends on the level of training of workers and the conjunctural needs of the enterprise.

In the two textile clusters, the division of labour between firms is less clearly institutionalized. In the Ilorin weaving cluster, all of the processes involved in producing the finished cloth have traditionally been carried out within the firm, with weavers being trained in every aspect of the production process. As business expanded, particularly during the early years of structural adjustment, a greater division of labour has emerged in which masters hire less-skilled weavers to perform the preparatory tasks, which attract a lower wage, and deliver bundles of prepared thread to the weavers who will produce the finished cloth. Such practices have developed as a means of speeding up the production process, and also to minimize cheating on the quality or amount of yarn used at a time when high demand forced masters to employ weavers they did not regard as completely trustworthy.

Borrowing of equipment between firms is comparatively rare in the Ilorin cluster, since most workers as well as masters have their own looms. However, increased demand for workers during 1980s and 1990s has led some weavers to develop into free agents, working for a number of different masters. The more recent decline in the weaving business has increased the circulation of workers, as masters have been forced by lack of orders to release their regular weavers to work for other masters. The subcontracting of large orders among masters is also common practice. The result is a dense network of subcontracts and circulating workers. In contrast to the shoe cluster, waged workers and unpaid family workers remained a significant source of labour among weavers, while the use of apprentices has all but withered away.

In the Aba garment cluster, a greater tendency to internalize operations within the firm has not precluded the emergence of dense subcontracting networks. Subcontracting has arisen from the inability of many firms to afford the full range of required sewing and embroidery machinery. Those unable to afford the more costly machines subcontract these processes to better-endowed fellow producers. As in the Ilorin weaving cluster, Aba garment firms show a greater dependence on employees relative to apprentices, although apprentices and family workers remain a significant part of the labour force among struggling garment producers and tailors.

Supply and marketing networks

In contrast to the prevailing assumption that African clusters lack well-developed trading networks (Pedersen and McCormick, 1999; Schmitz and Nadvi, 1999), the three study clusters have wide-ranging supply and marketing networks, extending across Nigeria, and as far as Asia, Europe and North America. These far-flung networks not only draw on long-distance Yoruba or Igbo trading systems, which date from pre-colonial times, but involve integration into the trading networks of other ethnic groups, both Nigerian and foreign. The expansion of all three clusters during the 1980s and 1990s has depended on the penetration of Yoruba and Igbo traders into new territories in Africa, Asia, Europe and North America, as well as the development of new links with traders from other ethnic groups. Producers court linkages with buyers from across Africa and beyond, often specializing in styles appropriate to a particular ethnic group or country. Francophone African traders – known locally as 'ça va' – are common in the Aba shoe cluster, and knowledge of French is considered an asset among shoe producers.

As Figure 8.4 indicates, nearly all of the firms in the Ilorin weaving and Aba shoe clusters have their main source of demand outside the town in which the cluster is located, and the vast majority participate in distribution circuits to other African countries. This wide market reach is less pronounced in the Aba garment cluster, owing to the more localized logic of 'tailor-made' clothes. That said, nearly 40 per cent of garment producers have their main market outside Aba, and a significant proportion have some distribution to other African countries. In all three clusters, marketing circuits extend to other continents, though only Ilorin weavers, the least Westernized of the three clusters, participate extensively in overseas markets. Weavers have benefited from a demand for indigenous luxury garments generated by the growing

Cluster	Main market outside town	Distribution to other African countries	Distribution to Europe/North America	Subcontract to formal sector	Use business cards
Ilorin weaving	98.1	86.5	63.5	84.6	80.8
Aba garments	39.0	16.4	1.6	36.1	49.2
Aba shoes	98.0	74.6	2.8	25.4	26.8

Figure 8.4 Supply Networks
Source: Fieldwork

Nigerian and West African diaspora, largely in the UK and the US, as well as by a rising demand for African fashions among other Africans and Afro-Americans. 'European' buyers used to frequent the main *aso-oke* market in Ibadan, buying for trendy African boutiques in the US – one can even buy *aso-oke* on the Internet!

In addition to global distribution networks, all three clusters are involved in significant subcontracting to the formal sector. This largely involves orders for boutiques, production of uniforms and footwear for companies, schools and occasionally parastatals, and, in the case of Ilorin weavers, the production of ceremonial headwear (*aso-ebi*) or banners for special events in companies, churches, or political parties. Once again, it is in the Ilorin weaving cluster that the largest proportion of firms, over 80 per cent, have received contracts from the formal sector. During the early 1990s, however, the Aba shoe cluster was receiving orders from the multinational shoe firm, Bata, and agents from Italian shoe companies circulated in the cluster. In all three clusters, however, it is important to note that such subcontracts are relatively infrequent, most firms having received only a few such orders in their entire history.

Growing dependence on distribution linkages with the formal sector and ethnic trading networks from other parts of Nigeria and West Africa has encouraged the use of more 'modern' forms of business networking. Use of business cards is widespread, involving the majority of Ilorin weavers and nearly half of Aba garment producers. Mobile phones, introduced in Nigeria in 2002, have become even more widespread, and mobile phone numbers are rapidly replacing business cards a means of establishing business contact.

The role of associations

African clusters are reputed to have weak or non-existent occupational associations, and an absence of anything other than ethnic forms of solidarity (Haan, 1999). The three clusters examined here reveal a very different picture. Producers in all three clusters participate in a wider range of cross-cutting voluntary associations, including hometown or ward associations, religious groups, social clubs and producers' associations. Total associational participation rates are highest in the Aba shoe cluster, where producers were each found to participate in an average of four associations, and lowest in the Ilorin weaving cluster, where producers averaged just over two associations. Well-established producers' associations existed in all three clusters. In Ilorin, the main producers' association has developed from the pre-colonial guild system, enjoying deep social roots and continuing influence in the spheres of entry, marketing and prices, as well as by far the highest rates of participation (90 per cent) of any voluntary organization in the cluster. While membership is only open to Ilorin indigenes, this does not preclude congenial relations between masters and weavers of other origins, though it does force non-Ilorin weavers to return to their hometowns to set up as masters.

In Aba, producers' associations have much more recent origins. They arose in the shoe and garment cluster during the late 1970s and early 1980s. In the shoe cluster, there are six different associations governing different parts of the cluster, with a strong membership base involving over 80 per cent of enterprise heads in the cluster, including non-Igbos. The functions of the associations involve social welfare assistance and market regulation in the areas of security, dispute settlement, marketing practices and, in some cases, quality control. In the garment cluster, the main producers' association developed to protect the interests of mass-producers rather than tailors, resulting in low levels of participation, involving less than 7 per cent of firms in the cluster. Although it has been the most effective producers' association in terms of services to members and negotiations with government, the garment association is confronted by the need to widen its base to accommodate tailors and weaker garment producers within the cluster.

All of these producers' associations date back at least 20 years, have a recognized basis of authority within the cluster and in local government circles, and a primary commitment to local occupational rather than communal interests. However, they also suffer from serious organizational problems owing to weak internal structures, lack of resources, low social status and the pervasive informality of their members. This has resulted in poor institutional links with the formal sector and an inability to offer, or lobby for, many basic business services.

Capacity for innovation

Whatever their weaknesses, the complex web of production, supply and marketing networks in these three clusters has gone hand in hand with high levels of innovation. In the shoe and garment clusters, expansion of markets has required constant innovation in styles, materials and equipment to maintain access to markets. In the garment cluster, those with adequate resources have adopted new types of buttonholing and embroidery machines, though cost constraints have restricted the majority to cheap or obsolete machinery. Deficiencies in machinery have been compensated for by rapid changes in styles and the use of foreign as well as local brand names. Aba's garment cluster produces St Michael's and Fruit of the Loom underwear, Lee jeans, and Gap shirts. In the shoe cluster, rising costs and poor facilities have led to democratization of production, but innovation in styles has been so rapid that a large-scale Chinese-owned shoe factory in the northern Nigerian city of Kano has stopped producing women's shoes because it feels it cannot compete with the Aba cluster (Meagher, 2006).

In the Ilorin weaving cluster, demand for the 'traditional' cloth has been sustained, not by conservative local tastes, but by ongoing process and product innovation. Ilorin has distinguished itself from other Yoruba weaving towns by the introduction in the early twentieth century of more complex patterns rather than the traditional stripes and checks associated with Yoruba cloth – an innovation that appears to have come from early contacts with Ghanaian weavers. The adoption of factory-made yarns in the early colonial period facilitated increased production speed, greater innovations in design and the development of mechanized yarn production, with factories springing up across Nigeria. Synthetic yarns imported from Asia were introduced in the 1980s and 1990s, along with constant changes in designs and colour to attract demand in the face of changing local tastes (O'Hear, 1987: 515). These forms of product innovation have been accompanied by a range of process innovations during the 1980s and 1990s, including the 'iron loom' – made from cannibalizing industrial looms and fitting them into the frame of a local loom, which increases production speed and the smoothness of the finished cloth – and the widening of the loom from four inches to six and then eight inches in order to accommodate more complex patterns.

The challenges of liberalization and globalization

Despite an impressive informal institutional infrastructure, the 'twin challenges' of liberalization and globalization have pushed these Nigerian clusters to the brink of collapse. Why have these dynamic enterprise clusters failed to cope with rapid economic reform when other Third World clusters have succeeded in upgrading and increasing productivity. The answer lies not in the cultural or cooperative incapacities of African clusters, but in the organizational limitations of informality, and in the failure of the formal institutional environment to provide even the most basic forms of institutional support for local restructuring and technical upgrading.

Coping with a disabling environment

In the three study clusters, structural adjustment reforms have created an economic environment that has been more daunting than enabling, involving rapid devaluation, skyrocketing inflation and rampant unemployment. Between 1985 and 1999, the Nigerian currency lost 99 per cent of its value, and urban dwellers faced an average annual inflation rate of more than 200 per cent (Meagher, forthcoming). Massive public and private sector retrenchment generated serious unemployment, leading to a flood of entrants into all manner of informal activities. In Ilorin, more than half of firm heads have become masters since the onset of structural adjustment, while in the two Aba clusters, the overwhelming majority of producers have entered under structural adjustment – with the result that more than half of them are 30 or under. The extreme competitive pressures unleashed by this flood of young, undercapitalized and increasingly under-trained producers has overwhelmed the regulatory capacity of cluster institutions, including apprenticeship and credit systems, and informal conventions governing quality, price and ownership of designs. All three clusters are suffering from problems of declining quality and increased copying and undercutting as producers resort to increasingly cut-throat strategies in their struggle for markets.

In addition to intense internal competitive pressures, producers have to grapple with depressed consumer incomes and an influx of cheap Asian manufactures. These factors reached crisis proportions in the Ilorin weaving cluster in 1998, triggered by the liberalization of textile imports and changes in local fashion. A widespread shift to imported 'damask' and 'lace' fabrics from Asia and Europe in place of the local luxury cloth has devastated the Ilorin weaving cluster. Efforts are being made by better-off masters to create new designs that imitate the more elegant patterns of damask and lace, but the bulk of weavers simply cut costs to attract customers. Demand stands at barely a tenth of its level in the late 1980s, and masters and weavers alike are haemorrhaging out of the business.

In the Aba garment cluster, the removal of textile import bans in 1997, and subsequent tariff reductions, have precipitated a flood of Asian competition in finished garments. Faced with rising costs of domestic and industrial sewing machinery post-devaluation, informal producers have been unable to compete with the superior finishing and low cost of Asian imports. Pressures of Asian competition hit the shoe cluster in late 2000, when ongoing trade liberalization flooded the market with cheap Chinese shoes. Once again, the low price and superior finishing of the Chinese imports has left Aba producers unable to compete except by further squeezing profits and reducing quality.

In all three clusters, efforts to reduce costs have led to an increasing reliance on substandard and smuggled inputs – inferior dyes and smuggled thread in the weaving cluster, fabric seconds and elastic off-cuts in the garment cluster, and cardboard insoles and adulterated adhesives in the shoe cluster. This represents a reversal of trends towards technical innovation and quality improvements in the period before structural adjustment. Instead, mounting competition from within and without has produced an intensification of low-road strategies of copying, undercutting, sweated labour and declining quality. The result has been a breakdown of trust and cooperation within and between firms, undermining credit, supply and marketing networks.

Unable to clear global quality standards, the output of these clusters is drawn into smuggling networks that fan out across Africa. Smuggling networks for inputs as well as finished goods have arisen from a combination of state incapacity, economic imbalances and the marginalization of the active indigenous private sector. Particularly in West Africa, long-distance ethnic and religious trading networks have existed since pre-colonial times, involving specialized trading groups, credit arrangements, and far-flung informal marketing systems (Austen, 1987). This has provided an institutional infrastructure for circumventing new economic obstacles, such as colonial borders, protectionist policies, shortages and foreign exchange controls. Economic restructuring policies have triggered the dramatic expansion of African smuggling networks, often with the collusion of state officials, providing an expanding infrastructure for various forms of informal and illicit trade, including the export of substandard Nigerian goods. Unable to link into global export markets, low-quality Nigerian clusters have become nodes in a growing system of parallel global commodity chains operating under the radar of the global trading system.

These involutionary cluster dynamics have given rise to even more disruptive *social* dynamics. Intensifying competitive pressures and collapsing networks of credit and trust within these Nigerian clusters have triggered a massive collapse of clustered firms. In Ilorin, an estimated 80 per cent of weavers have left the business since the mid-1990s. In Aba, perhaps a third of firms in the garment cluster have gone under or changed line, and there has been a severe contraction in the shoe cluster. Across the three clusters, firms that have not gone under have taken up additional activities to make ends meet, reversing processes of occupational specialization. Struggling weavers, garment producers and shoemakers are heavily represented in such petty activities as casual labour, motorcycle taxis and mobile phone card kiosks. This has generated an increasingly volatile segment of semi-skilled and frustrated youth forced into activities that have no future prospects and bear the stamp of failure.

Among those firms that have managed to stay in business, difficult economic conditions have triggered increased ethnic and religious polarization in informal economic networks. The traditional avoidance of politics among Ilorin weavers has been replaced by a tendency among weavers to join political associations in the effort to integrate themselves into local cliental networks, for access to business or assistance. More educated weavers, seeking to disembed themselves from the gerontocratic and cliental networks of the weaving leadership, have gravitated towards more fundamentalist Islamic brotherhoods and societies, such as Tijjaniyya and Nasfat, which encourage an ethic of frugality, piety and education. In Aba, shoe producers have tended to integrate into local cliental networks, while garment producers have tended to pursue a strategy of disembedding themselves from hometown unions and local political networks through conversion to Pentecostal Christianity (Meagher, forthcoming). Both Islamic and Christian religious networks provide alternative support linkages offering contacts, resources, and an ethic of occupational advancement and anti-corruption, with networks stretching as far as Senegal and Saudi Arabia in the case of Islam, and to England and the United States in the case of Pentecostal Christianity. This economic and social fragmentation of informal manufacturing networks is reflected in the fragmentation of producers' associations. In Ilorin, the weavers' association split in 1992 into two acrimonious groups, while efforts among the Aba shoe associations in the late 1990s to come together into a single umbrella association have fractured under mounting competitive pressures.

The collapse of firms and the recourse of surviving firms to political and religious networks of assistance have increased the vulnerability of small enterprise clusters to political manipulation in the game of identity politics. The expansion of volatile groups of angry youth, and the increased ethnic and religious polarization of contemporary small firm networks represent a social tinderbox in an increasingly unstable economic and political climate. The case of the Bakassi Boys vigilante group illustrates the potential of this situation to spiral into social disorder and communal violence. Formed in 1998 by the Aba shoe producers to protect property rights in a town overridden by criminal gangs, the Bakassi Boys not only restored law and order for a time, but became a welcome source of employment for struggling shoe producers. By 2000, however, the vigilante group was taken over by state governors in the Igbo areas, and had degenerated into a source of violence, ethnic conflict and political thuggery in the run-up to the 2003 elections (Human Rights Watch/CLEEN, 2002; Ukiwo, 2002).

The role of the state

A closer look at the processes at work reveals that the inability of the Ilorin and Aba clusters to rise to the enormous challenge of liberalization and globalization has had more to do with state neglect and informality than with culture. Scholars of European clusters and industrial districts have noted that state support is critical to cluster survival, particularly in periods of rapid economic change (Best, 1990). As Whitford (2001: 59) explains, enterprise clusters require more than a 'conducive' culture; 'their continued viability is dependent on sustaining formal institutions that can ensure co-ordination, ... and, importantly, guarantee the reproduction of the norms and values underlying the system'.

Studies of Third World clusters that have coped more successfully with contemporary economic restructuring invariably show evidence of the active state involvement, although this is often downplayed for ideological reasons. Nadvi's (1999) research on a Pakistani surgical instruments cluster, and studies of Indian (Knorringa, 1999) and Mexican footwear clusters (Rabellotti, 1999), reveal that the successful restructuring of these clusters had a great deal to do with the active role of the state in providing infrastructure and technical services and, in the Mexican case, allowing a return to protectionism to give clusters time to reorganize.

In Nigeria, by contrast, the state is conspicuous in its absence. Even at the local level, relations between clustered firms and state officials were characterized by a combination of neglect and predation rather than by solidarity and support. Significant economic liberalization and political decentralization tended to disrupt rather than promote local relations of solidarity. Devolution of powers to local and regional government (Wunsch and Olowu, 1997) has been rapidly implemented and weakly institutionalized, often leaving new local structures less rather than more able to support local economic initiatives. Moreover, decentralization has been accompanied by an enormous increase in revenue allocation from the federal government, which by the late 1990s accounted for over 90 per cent of local government finances. With the bulk of local revenue coming from the federal purse, local officials have little incentive to promote the development of small-firm clusters, especially in Aba where clusters are dominated by migrants rather than indigenes.

To make matters worse, the pervasive informality of small firms in all three clusters puts the vast majority of them and their associations on the wrong side of the law in their relations with devolved local government structures. The increased authority of local governments has not served to support small-firm clusters so much as to increase their vulnerability to taxation demands, arbitrary enforcement of the dizzying regulatory shifts of the restructuring process and harassment owing to their general inability to comply. Informality has also denied the vast majority of firms access to the local chamber of commerce or the local branch of the manufacturers' association, both of which demand that members be formally registered. The lack of access to local government or to institutions of the formal private sector has left Nigerian informal manufacturing clusters and their associations institutionally marooned and unable to lobby effectively for basic facilities or support, except through cliental ties with traditional rulers and local government or state officials.

Support at the state and federal government levels is even farther beyond the reach of clustered firms. Despite the emphasis on the importance of local rather than central governments as agents of cluster development, the collapse of regional and federal government services has been a major obstacle to cluster development in Nigeria. Rapid reform and privatization, combined with severe cutbacks in state expenditure, have led to a massive deterioration in federally and regionally controlled public services, including education, policing, roads and electricity. Instead of institutional support, producers were forced to contend with poorly educated apprentices, rampant crime and police corruption, roads that are impassible during the rainy season and unreliable electricity supplies. Despite the existence of a number of microenterprise assistance programmes, less than 5 per cent of producers interviewed had ever had any contact with them, and none had ever received any training or funds as a result.

Conclusion

In Nigerian enterprise clusters, the development of globalized enterprise networks has not fostered novel forms of economic governance, but has given rise to increasingly volatile processes of ungovernance. Indeed, the pressures of liberalization, globalization and state neglect have produced a parody of the conventional cluster model. Instead of collective efficiency, global value chains and rising productivity, the Nigerian clusters have succumbed to a dynamic of 'collective inefficiencies', clandestine global value chains and social disorder. The argument put forward here is that the processes of economic ungovernance unleashed by these Nigerian clusters are not a product of cultural inadequacies. On the contrary, the clusters examined here display a rich tapestry of production and trading networks operating across ethnic and religious divides, which have underpinned the development of market-oriented institutions and increasingly globalized operations. Although embedded in ties of ethnicity and religion, these African clusters have provided an institutional framework for change and innovation, for ethnic incorporation and the rationalization of production and labour relations.

As shown here, economic ungovernance in African clusters derives less from cultural failures, than from the hostile economic and political environment created and reinforced by ruthless liberalization and state neglect. The prevailing tendency to use the cluster model to promote a DIY approach to industrial development fails to reflect the actual processes underpinning the growth of more successful Third World clusters, in which the state plays an extensive role in the provision of infrastructure and institutional support. While vibrant informal institutions and global linkages constitute valuable resources for cluster development, they cannot 'substitute for the state', as so many cluster analysts seem to believe. Efforts to make them do so are squandering rather than promoting the institutional dynamism of African small enterprise.

References

Austen, R.A. (1987), *African Economic History: Iinternal Development and External Dependency*, James Currey/Heinemann, London/Portsmouth, NH.

Barr, A. (1999), 'Do SMEs network for growth?', in K. King and S. McGrath (eds), *Enterprise in Africa: Between Poverty and Growth*, Intermediate Technology Publications, London, pp. 121–31.

Bayart, J.-F. (1999), 'The "Social Capital" of the Felonious State', in J.-F. Bayart, S. Ellis and B. Hibou (eds), *The Criminalization of the State in Africa*, International African Institute, in association with James Currey; Indiana University Press, Oxford; Bloomington and Indianapolis.

Berry, S. (1993), 'Coping with Confusion: African Farmers' Responses to Economic Instability in the 1970s and 1980s', in T.M. Callaghy and J. Ravenhill (eds), *Hemmed In. Responses to Africa's Economic Decline*, Columbia University Press, New York, pp. 248–78.

Best, M.H. (1990), *The New Competition: Institutions of Industrial Reconstruction*, Polity Press, Cambridge, MA.

Bray, J.M. (1968), 'The Organization of Traditional Weaving in Iseyin, Nigeria', *Africa*, 38(3), pp. 270–80.

Chazan, N. (1988), 'Patterns of State-Society Incorporation and Disengagement in Africa', in D. Rothchild and N. Chazan (eds), *The Precarious Balance. State and Society in Africa*, Westview, Boulder, CO, and London, pp. 121–48.

Dike, K.O., and Ekejiuba, F.I. (1990), *The Aro of South-eastern Nigeria, 1650–1980: A Study of Socio-economic Formation and Transformation in Nigeria*, University Press, Ibadan.

Fafchamps, M. and Minten, B. (1999), *Property Rights in a Flea Market Economy*, Centre for the Study of African Economies Institute of Economics and Statistics University of Oxford, Oxford.

Haan, H.C. (1999), 'MSE Association and Enterprise Promotion in Africa', in K. King and S. McGrath (eds), *Enterprise in Africa. Between Poverty and Growth*, Intermediate Technology Publications, London, pp. 156–68.

Human Rights Watch/CLEEN (2002), 'The Bakassi Boys: The Legitimation of Murder and Torture', *Human Rights Watch Reports*, 14(5)A 1-45.
Isichei, E.A. (1976), *A History of the Igbo People*, Macmillan, London.
Knorringa, P. (1999), 'Agra: An Old Cluster Facing New Competition', *World Development*, 27(9), pp. 1587–604.
Lloyd, P. (1953), 'Craft Organization in Yoruba Towns', *Africa*, 23, pp. 30–44.
McCormick, D. (1999), 'Enterprise Clusters in Africa: Linkages for Growth and Development', in K. King and S. McGrath (eds), *Enterprise in Africa: Between Poverty and Growth*, Intermediate Technology Publications, London, pp. 132–43.
Meagher, K. (2006), 'Social Capital, Social Liabilities, and Political Capital: Social Networks and Informal Manufacturing in Nigeria', *African Affairs*, 105(421), pp. 553–82.
Meagher, K. (forthcoming), *Identity Economics: Social Networks and the Informal Economy in Africa*, James Currey/University of Indiana Press, Oxford/Bloomington.
Meillassoux, C. (1971), *The Development of Indigenous Trade and Markets in West Africa*, Oxford University Press, London.
Nadvi, K. (1999), 'Collective Efficiency and Collective Failure: The Response of the Sialkot Surgical Instrument Cluster to Global Quality Pressures', *World Development*, 27(9), pp. 1605–26.
O'Hear, A. (1987), 'Craft Industries in Ilorin: Dependency or Independence?', *African Affairs*, 86(345), pp. 505–21.
Pedersen, P.O. (1996), 'Flexibility and Networking: European and African Context', in D. McCormick and P.O. Pedersen (eds), *Small Enterprises: Flexibility and Networking in an African Context*, Longhorn Kenya, Nairobi, pp. 3–17.
Pedersen, P.O. and McCormick, D. (1999), 'African Business Systems in a Globalising World', *Journal of Modern African Studies*, 37(1), pp. 109–35.
Rabellotti, R. (1999), 'Recovery of a Mexican Cluster: Devaluation Bonanza or Collective Efficiency?', *World Development*, 27(9), pp. 1571–85.
Rasmussen, J. (1992), 'The Small Enterprise Environment in Zimbabwe: Growing in the Shadow of Large Enterprises', *IDS Bulletin*, 23(3), pp. 21–7.
Sabel, C.F. (1986), 'Changing Models of Economic Efficiency and Their Implications for Industrialization in the Third World', in A. Foxley, M.S. McPherson and G. O'Donnell (eds), *Development, Democracy and the Art of Trespassing: Essays in Honor of Albert O. Hirschman*, University of Notre Dame Press, South Bend, Indiana, pp. 27–55.
Schmitz, H. (1992), 'On the Clustering of Small Firms', *IDS Bulletin*, 23(3), pp. 64–8.
Schmitz, H. and Nadvi, K. (1999), 'Clustering and Industrialization: Introduction', *World Development*, 27(9), pp. 1503–14.
Ukiwo, U. (2002), 'Deus ex Machina or Frankenstein Monster? The Changing Roles of Bakassi Boys in Eastern Nigeria', *Democracy and Development*, 3(1), pp. 39–51.
Whitford, J. (2001), 'The Decline of a Model? Challenge and Response in the Italian Industrial Districts', *Economy and Society*, 30(1), pp. 38–65.
Wunsch, J.S. and Olowu, D. (1997), 'Regime Transformation from Below: Decentralization, Local Governance, and Democratic Reform in Nigeria', *Studies in Comparative International Development*, 31(4), pp. 66–82.

9
Indian Small Firms under Globalization: Has Policy Helped?
Keshab Das

The elephantine presence and distinctive functioning of India's small firms, often complex to comprehend, arguably promise to contribute much to the economic progress of the nation. With an impressive history of small-firm development policy dating back to the early 1950s, post-Independence India has a rich repertoire of experiences and experiments in making this vital sector perform and grow. It is important to acknowledge at the outset that small firms in India, through numerous policy pronouncements, have been looked up to historically as a vital mechanism for generating large-scale employment, and, in the process, for helping to reduce regional disparities in growth. The underlying assumption has been that these forms of productive activity would have adequate flexibility to accommodate a great variety of skill and educational levels, including the unskilled and illiterate, even in the countryside, which would effectively limit huge rural–urban migration driven by desperation rather than the potential of a reasonable job in the milling cities. The employment dimension needs underscoring because, as will be seen, the post-reform small-firm policies have diverted attention from this basic objective of small-firm promotion in India.

Imperatives of globalization and the outward orientation of small firms

Until the early 1980s, if not later, the macroeconomic framework nurtured a dedicated import-substitution regime whereby small firms would have to be protected through, *inter alia*, hiked import tariffs, product reservations, capacity restrictions, duty concessions and targeted credit. Over the years, a host of policy measures, mostly fiscal, controlled and influenced small-firm production as well as its spatial spread. These included provision of government purchases, tax concessions and easy availability of land and machinery for the small-scale-industry (SSI) sector.

Never before had small and medium enterprises (SMEs) or micro and small enterprises (MSEs) occupied such a vital space, both in the global policy sphere and in academic discourse, as they have since the mid 1980s or so – as an effective instrument of addressing economic revival through (1) ensuring the creation of massive employment opportunities, (2) regenerating depressed regions, and (3) enhancing factor incomes, especially in the developing economies. The mantra, as hyped by the recently emboldened neoliberal school, lay in the proposal that SMEs/MSEs could enhance competitiveness, market share and factor productivity by being linked to global business. This assertion, that local growth is possible by participating in the global market, has been the basic tenet of neolocalism, the vital component of the process of globalization.

Although in certain SSI sub-sectors strong external orientation could be observed even by the early 1980s, it is since 1991 that the small-firm policy in India has been openly and keenly pursuing approaches which emphasize the importance of internationalization, trade, and interdependence in the spheres of innovation, learning, and market and business strategies.

Despite an elaborate and dynamic policy framework, the progress of Indian small enterprises has continued to be hindered by some persisting roadblocks such as poor credit availability, low levels of technology (hence, low product quality and limited exportability) and inadequate or no basic infrastructure, physical or economic. The complexity in intervening effectively in this sector has often arisen from the manner the small enterprises have been defined officially, organized (being dominated by 'tiny' units and informality) and impinged upon by changing policies – macro, sectoral or locational – both at the national and regional levels. The frequent revision in the definition of small firms based solely on the investment-value criterion (discussed).

Shifting definitional ceilings: bigger units as favourites

An indication of the impact of the advent of globalization on the small-enterprise sphere in India is given by the way small enterprises have been defined formally, time and again. Unlike in many countries and despite the emphasis on job generation through this sector, the defining criterion for an SSI unit makes no reference whatever to numbers employed. What continues to classify a firm as small is the historical/original value of investment in plant and machinery. Although estimating this value needs to follow a given procedure, the pursuance of the investment limit criterion has been been criticized as an inadequate/ impractical approach. Whereas often the valuation is based on unverifiable data, it has also been noted that even when an SSI unit has progressed far beyond the prescribed limit there is no need/intent to reregister it as a medium or large unit (Das, 2006: 1). Notwithstanding the anomalies in the registration/deregistration of SSI units, the ceiling of investment provides a reference to the size of the small firm in India. A striking dimension of the definitional changes, certainly since 1980, has been a series of rises in the ceiling that could easily be linked to the need for the external orientation of firms and a strong bias towards the larger of the SSI units.

As may be seen in Figure 9.1, the ceiling was raised from Rs. 2 million in 1980 to Rs. 3.5 million in 1985 and then to Rs. 6 million by 1991, the year economic reforms were formally initiated. The next time it was sought to raise the ceiling was in 1997, when the first major committee on small enterprises since the reforms (GoI, 1997) recommended a huge jump, to Rs. 30 million, five times the previous limit; this was applicable for the 'Ancillary' units as well. An ancillary unit is an industrial undertaking which is engaged or is proposed to be engaged in the manufacture or production of parts, components, sub-assemblies, tooling or intermediates, or the rendering of services and the undertaking supplies or renders or proposes to supply or render not less than 50 per cent of its production or services, as the case may be, to one or more other industrial undertakings.

In a similar move, the investment limit defining 'tiny' units was also upped from Rs. 0.5 million in 1991 to Rs. 2.5 million in 1997.

Further, by 1991 a new category of small unit was introduced, namely, the export-oriented unit (EOU). Its investment limit had also been greatly hiked from Rs. 7.5 million to Rs. 30 million. That the committee was strongly biased towards promotion of the larger 'small' units (which are still in the minority numerically) and those engaged solely in export activities was quite obvious. Even though two years later, in 1999 the Rs. 30 million limit was brought down to Rs. 10 million, the latest policy pronouncement, namely, the Micro, Small and Medium Enterprises Development Act 2006 (the MSMED Act) has defined a small enterprise as having an upper investment limit of Rs. 50 million. The post-reform period has, hence, witnessed a significant policy shift that emphasizes the

Year	Upper limit of the historical/original value of plant and machinery				
	(Rs Million)				
	SSI	Ancillary	Tiny*	EOU**	SSSE/ SSSBE***
1980	2.0	2.5	0.2	–	–
1985	3.5	4.5	0.2	–	0.2
1991	6.0	7.5	0.5	7.5	0.5
1997	30.0	30.0	2.5	30.0	0.5
1999	10.0	10.0	2.5	10.0	0.5
2001	10.0****	10.0	2.5	10.0	1.0
2006	10.0/ 50.0*****	10.0	2.5	10.0	1.0/ 20.0*****

Figure 9.1 Definitional investment ceilings criteria for SSI India, 1980-2006

Notes:
* In 1980, these referred to the units located in rural areas or towns having a maximum population of 50,000, as per *Census of India 1971*. By 1985, the population limit increased to 0.5 million, as per *Census of India 1981*. However, by 1991, the locational-conditions had been dropped.
** EOU – export oriented unit; this category was introduced in 1991.
*** SSSE – small-scale service establishment; introduced in 1985. SSSBE – small-scale service and business enterprise; this category replaced SSSE in 1991.
**** Since October 2001, for 41 items of hosiery and hand tools; since June 2003, for 23 more items of stationery and drugs and pharmaceutical industry and since October 2004 for seven more items of sports goods the upper limit of investment had been raised to Rs 50 million.
***** Since February 2006, the investment limit for 69 new items of food and allied, plastic, chemicals, glass and ceramic and auto parts industries was raised to Rs 50 million. Also for all items in the drugs and pharmaceuticals sector (whether reserved or not) the investment ceiling has been raised to Rs 50 million. However, the Micro, Small and Medium Enterprises Development Act, 2006, being operational from 2 October 2006, fixed the ceiling for all small enterprises at Rs 50 million and for SSSBEs at Rs 20 million.

Source: Up to 1999, SIDBI (2000: 28); after 1999, http://www.laghu-udyog.com/ssiindia/definition.htm<?xml:namespace prefix = o ns = "urn:schemas-microsoft-com:office:office" />

predominance of larger, modern SSI units and those geared towards the export market as well as service (as different from manufacturing) units.

Such a policy move has been justified on the grounds that it would result in the decline of the dependence by small enterprises on state subsidies and other concessions by the state. The fact remains however that small firms are still almost entirely characterized by very low levels of investment, far lower than the latest limit prescribed. Figure 9.2 shows that a staggering 99.5 per cent of the so-called SSI units are, in fact, tiny units. The prevailing scenario of a capital-constrained and labor-surplus

Type of units	Registered	Unregistered
Size of the sector	1,374,974	9,146,216
SSI Units	901,291	3,544,577
Tiny Units within SSI	882,496 (97.9 %)	3,543,091 (99.9 %)

Figure 9.2 Distribution of units in the SSI and tiny sector, 2001–02
Source: GoI (2004: 1).

small-firm regime has not, in fact, been transformed; the definitional changes have hardly done the trick.

Size and contribution of small firms: ambivalent?

The official statistics/documents on the contribution of the SSI sector provide at first sight an impressive picture of performance. The typical data on this sector, as exemplified through what is available on the departmental website, would indicate that small firms contribute about 40 per cent of industrial production and 35 per cent of direct exports, and that the growth rate of the sector has been higher than that of the industrial sector as a whole. The website shows also that small enterprises produce over 8000 items and have provided employment to about 20 million workers. However, scholars have expressed reservations over these figures on various counts, including non-comparability between sources of data, incorrect and unreliable records of the registration of small firms, underestimation of employment and value addition figures (for a discussion, see Das, 2003; Morris and Basant, 2005: 4–6). An example of erroneous data is shown in Figure 9.3, where basic information about SSI status and performance purports to reveal that the number of units has been increasing year on year, every year for 15 years, at the *exact* rate of 4.07 per annum – a figure not only most unlikely but also 'grossly inflated'. Similarly, the production figures of SSIs provided by the apex body, the Small Industries Development Organisation (SIDO), show gross overstatement when compared with those provided by the National Accounts Statistics (NAS).

Such inadequacies and lack of clarity of official data have prevented any meaningful and realistic analysis of this vast and diverse sector. In fact, pointing to the deficient methodology followed by SIDO, Mohan (2003: 241) observes that

Year	Total SSI units (in million)	Fixed investment (Rs million)	Production (Rs million)		Employment (in million)
			Current prices	Constant prices (1993–4)	
1990–1	6.79	935,550	635,180	682950	15.83
1991–2	7.06 (4.07)	1,003,510 (7.26)	730,720 (15.04)	791,800 (15.94)	16.60 (4.83)
1992–3	7.35 (4.07)	1,096,230 (9.24)	855,810 (17.12)	935,230 (18.11)	17.48 (5.33)
1993–4	7.65 (4.07)	1,157,950 (5.63)	988,040 (15.45)	988,040 (5.65)	18.26 (4.46)
1994–5	7.96 (4.07)	1,237,900 (6.90)	1,222,100 (23.69)	1,091,160 (10.44)	19.14 (4.79)
1995–6	8.28 (4.07)	1,257,500 (1.58)	1,482,900 (21.34)	1,216,490 (11.49)	19.79 (3.42)
1996–7	8.62 (4.07)	1,305,600 (3.82)	1,684,130 (13.57)	1,353,800 (11.29)	20.59 (4.00)
1997–8	8.97 (4.07)	1,332,420 (2.05)	1,891,780 (12.33)	1,478,240 (9.19)	21.32 (3.55)
1998–9	9.34 (4.07)	1,354,820 (1.68)	2,129,010 (12.54)	1,594,070 (7.84)	22.06 (3.46)
1999–2000	9.72 (4.07)	1,399,820 (3.32)	2,342,550 (10.03)	1,707,090 (7.09)	22.91 (3.88)
2000–1	10.11 (4.07)	1,473,480 (5.26)	2,612,890 (11.54)	1,844,280 (8.04)	23.91 (4.36)
2001–2	10.52 (4.07)	1,543,490 (4.75)	2,822,700 (8.03)	1,956,130 (6.06)	24.91 (4.18)
2002–3	10.95 (4.07)	1,625,330 (5.30)	3,119,930 (10.53)	2,106,360 (7.68)	26.01 (4.43)
2003–4	11.40 (4.07)	1,707,260 (5.04)	3,577,330 (14.66)	2,287,300 (8.59)	27.14 (4.32)
2004–5	11.86 (4.07)	NA	4,182,630 (16.92)	2,515,110 (9.96)	28.29 (4.26)

Figure 9.3 Aspects of growth of SSI in India, 1990–2005

Notes:
(1) Figures in brackets show the percentage growth over the previous year.
(2) The production, at constant prices for the year 2003–4, is based on the growth rate achieved in the first three-quarters of 2003–4 (i.e. April–December, 2003).
(3) The production at current prices is compiled on the basis of average Wholesale Price Index (April–December, 2003) of manufactured products.

Source: GoI (2005), Annual Report 2004–05, Ministry of Small Scale Industries, New Delhi at http://www.ssi.gov.in/ssi-eng-2004-05.pdf

220 *Small Firms, Global Markets*

It appears that SIDO arrives at its figures on a gross basis from an estimated number of SSI units without allowing for mortality of previously counted units...Because SIDO is a government agency, the data they publish must be repeated by all government and government-associated agencies, including the Planning Commission. Thus a distorted picture on the progress of SSI has been consistently provided to policy makers and observers alike. It is possible that, had the correct picture been available to policy makers, there might have been less complacency with regard to SSI policy.

Hence, often mistakenly, these data strengthen the 'common erroneous perception' that SSIs have been performing 'extremely well'.

Unimpressive exports

With an explicit emphasis on the internationalization of Indian small firms holding the key to prosperity, export figures have often been highlighted as a measure of success of the sector in an era of globalization. In extolling the competitiveness of small firms, it has been pointed out that at least since 1992–93 the share of SSI exports has remained as high as over one-third of total exports. In fact, within the SSI sector, the

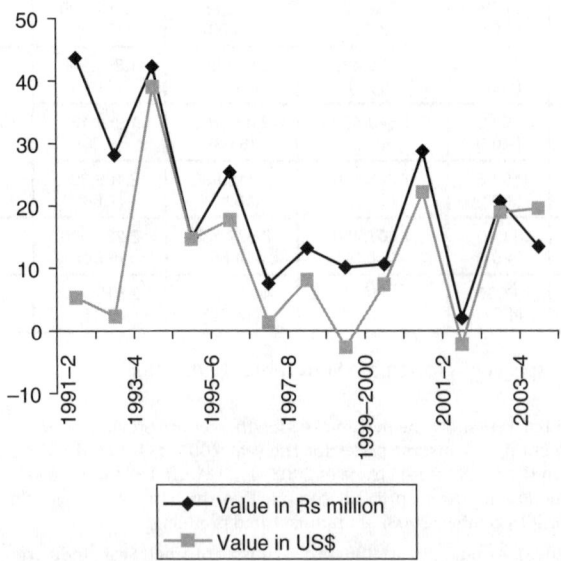

Figure 9.4 Rate of growth of SSI exports in India, 1990–2004

proportion of exports to the value of production has risen sharply from about 5.8 per cent to 26.5 per cent, if one compares a representative pre-reform (1988–91) period with a post-reform one (2000–03).

It is important, however, to examine in some detail the export euphoria. In order to obtain a realistic and useful picture of exports, the relevant dollar values of the same need to be observed. In Figure 9.4, a

Sl. no	Product group	1988–91		2000–03	
		Value	%	Value	%
1	Readymade garments	31,029	40.9	249,751	33.0
2	Engineering goods	6,573	8.7	94,780	12.5
3	Basic chemicals, pharmaceuticals and cosmetics	10,467	13.8	84,642	11.2
4	Processed goods	3,090	4.1	75,970	10.0
5	Electronic and computer software	–	–	63,850	8.4
6	Finished leather and leather products	15,528	20.5	55,025	7.3
7	Marine products	2,681	3.5	28,570	3.8
8	Woolen garments and knitwear	845	1.1	20,886	2.8
9	Plastic products	477	0.6	18,149	2.4
10	Cashew kernel, cashew nut shell liquid*	3,166	4.2	18,398	2.4
11	Chemicals and allied products	905	1.2	14,371	1.9
12	Synthetic and rayon textiles	114	0.2	13,503	1.8
13	Spices, spice oil oleoresins*	196	0.3	8,657	1.1
14	Processed tobacco, snuff and *bidis*	165	0.2	6,239	0.8
15	Sports goods	532	0.7	2,812	0.4
16	Lac*	165	0.2	1,242	0.2
	Total	75,932	100.0	756,843	100.0

Figure 9.5 Export of major product groups from the Indian SSI sector, 1988–2003 (Value in Rs million)

Note: * Classified as 'traditional' products, the rest being 'non-traditional'.

Sources: For the period 1988–91, estimated from Table 97, GoI (1994: 189); and for the period 2000–03, estimated from Table 7.16, GoI (2005: 183).

comparison of annual growth rates of the rupee value and dollar value of SSI exports is presented for the period 1990–2004. This reveals not only massive year-to-year fluctuations but, at times, very low and even negative annual growth rates – a discomforting situation.

Further, as one looks into the composition of SSI exports, it is striking that even between the pre-reform (1988–91) and post-reform (2000–03) period, practically no diversification of products exported has taken place (Figure 9.5). What is interesting is that just about six product groups continue to account for over 80 per cent of total SSI exports, and there has hardly been any change during the phase of globalization, except for the appearance of electronic and computer software products in the list.

During the period of reforms, macroeconomic policy distortions have also been cited as major constraints to export growth. As Morris *et al.* (2001: 199–204) argue, 'monetary conservatism' failed to target the interest rate regime and to support fiscal expenditure to boost the well-directed infrastructure spending after the mid 1990s. Drastic reductions in export-related credit and difficulties experienced by firms in obtaining it have been cited as poor marketing support by the government. Non-availability of adequate working capital has been a major stumbling block for most exporting firms. Also, the pursuit of an inverted tariff structure – which protected inefficient bulk producers of such materials as plastics, rubber, steel, basic chemicals, non-ferrous metals, etc. through high import tariffs, but infused a negative effective protection rate for many a manufactured tradable – hit the small exporting firms which were more labour-using, depended on these raw materials as inputs and had high material-output ratios. These policy instruments adversely affected the costs of, and hence the demand for, exportable goods produced by small enterprises.

The study group report (GoI, 2004: 153), after a decade of reforms, has expressed regret at the unimpressive performance of the exports and has offered some of the standard recommendations, as follows:

- A well-planned strategy at national level for developing exports from the small-scale industries sector, including the identification of subsectors with high export potential.
- Greater coordination between the various ministries, departments and organizations of the government looking after production by the small-scale industries sector and those providing export-marketing services.
- Close linkages between small exporters and merchant export houses, export development organizations, joint marketing arrangements, export consortia and so on.

- Comprehension of the issues of concern at macro level and their relevance to small exporters, including the difficulties faced by them in the export endeavour.
- Infrastructural support.

As may be observed, these suggestions had often been made even before the economic reforms began in 1991. Export promotion efforts have contributed precious little to include various traditional products (which account for the paltry figure of less than 4 per cent of total SSI exports in recent years) and, especially, products from the rural regions.

Credit: the crunch and the bias

Access to adequate and timely credit has been the most important issue of perpetual concern for small firms, who, unlike their large counterparts, depend heavily upon 'intermediated' banks – that is public development banks – for finance. Although several policy efforts have been made to address this foremost problem facing the small-scale sector, the credit crunch never seems to have faded, not even during the last decade and a half of globalization and economic reforms. Indeed, as may be observed from Figure 9.6, there has been a drop in the share of bank lending to SSIs (from about 16 percent to 11 percent between 1990–91 and 2002–03). It is interesting to note here that the sudden jump in the figures showing credit provided to the tiny sector in 1999–2000 onwards reflects the effect of raising the investment limit from Rs. 0.5 to 2.5 million, in a move to include relatively larger units in that category.

A major cause of the credit problem has been a typically high rate of interest pursued by the Reserve Bank of India (RBI), often as a precautionary step to avoid potential balance of payments difficulties. Further, with more avenues to invest in, schemes other than direct savings (the rate of interest offered in the former being much greater than in the latter), and the requirement of banks to maintain a high deposit ratio, little in the way of bank funds has been available for intermediation, and small firms' access to bank loans has been therefore reduced. As Morris and Basant (2005: 19) put it,

> Since small and medium firms have a comparative advantage to access bank funds (while large firms could go on to markets) there is an implicit discrimination in these distortionary policies. The distortions have not reduced with 'reform' of the financial sector, nor have the banks' 'need' for large spreads come down.

Year (as on end March)	Net bank credit	Credit to		Proportion of credit of		
		SSI	tiny sector	SSI to net bank	Tiny to net bank	Tiny to SSI
1990–1	1,056,320	167,830	–	15.89	–	–
1991–2	1,121,600	173,980	–	15.51	–	–
1992–3	1,327,820	193,880	–	14.60	–	–
1993–4	1,409,140	215,610	–	15.30	–	–
1994–5	1,690,380	258,430	77,340	15.29	4.58	29.93
1995–6	1,843,810	294,850	81,830	15.99	4.44	27.76
1996–7	1,896,840	315,420	95,150	16.63	5.02	30.20
1997–8	2,182,190	381,090	102,730	17.46	4.71	27.00
1998–9	2,462,030	426,740	88,370	17.33	3.59	20.70
1999–2000	2,929,430	457,880	227,420	15.63	7.76	54.03
2000–1	3,408,880	484,450	260,190	14.21	7.63	53.70
2001–2	3,969,540	497,430	270,300	12.53	6.81	54.34
2002–3	4,778,990	529,880	269,370	11.09	5.64	50.84

Figure 9.6 Bank credit to SSI and tiny sector (Rs Million)
Source: http://www.laghu-udyog.com/thrustareas/CREDIT.htm

An additional policy area not receiving adequate attention in this context relates to the absence of incentive provision for bankers assessing loan eligibility for small entrepreneurs. While in case of a default the risk involved (for the banker) is quite high, the absence of a built-in reward mechanism for a good loan has generated an ambience of indifference towards the sanctioning of loans (Morris *et al.*, 2001: 269).

Of the various constraints in the problem of credit, failure to pledge collateral by the borrower has been an important one. Quite in violation of the RBI guidelines, which unequivocally state that assets created by utilizing loans should be treated as security, there have been instances of banks not extending loans to small firms on the ground of collateral/ security. Even if banks are warned against insisting upon any collateral guarantee for a loan to a small enterprise, the old biases have continued. In a strongly worded view on such objectionable practices, the parliamentary Estimates Committee held that it considered this

> a serious divergence from the guidelines/instructions of the Ministry/RBI. They, therefore, desire that appropriate action should be taken against such banks which are flouting the guidelines... The Committee also desires that banks should not be allowed as a rule to reject an application merely on the ground that the borrower is not in a position to offer any collateral security. (Quoted in Goyal *et al.*, 2004: 36)

Even within the priority sector, data for lending by the public sector banks between 1998 and 2005 suggest that despite an increase in the advances made to SSIs, the SSIs' annual growth rate has been the lowest of any sector. The recent RBI *Report on Trend and Progress of Banking in India 2004–05* (p. 70) noted that the public sector banks have 'failed' to achieve the sub-target for the 'tiny' sector within the SSI sector. Increasing the investment limit criterion for tiny units seems to have adversely affected the flow of bank credit.

Modern and basic infrastructure: inadequacy and uneven spread

In research into infrastructural facilities, based on a massive field survey covering some 12 states and over 1000 units – probably the largest in terms of the coverage of units and states in any single research study so far – deficiencies were clearly shown up in several vital areas (Morris *et al.*, 2001: 205–27). Figure 9.7 gives an idea of the regional distribution of infrastructure problems facing small firms. As we might expect, poor provisioning of infrastructure impedes the growth of firms striving to enhance the geographical limits of their markets, whether domestic or foreign.

The study brought out a series of issues concerning inadequate infrastructure faced by small enterprises in India. Clearly, power is the single most important constraint faced across the states. An improvement in its availability will ensure positive gains in terms of both locational spread and industrial output and productivity. Poor access to physical infrastructure such as transportation and communications is also identified by small firms across the country as a major restriction. Improvements here would surely bring great long-term benefits by helping to increase sales, efficiency and market integration. For

States	No. of firms	All infra-structure	Power	Transportation	Port facilities	Industrial estate facilities	Communication facilities	Pollution locally	Water supply	Congestion in nearby city	Lack of CETP	Industrial security and safety	Other
Assam	45	57.7	8.7	6.9	2.4	6.9	7.4	3.0	6.0	4.0	4.1	7.2	1.2
Bihar	40	47.3	8.0	4.8	1.1	5.2	6.1	4.1	4.5	3.6	3.2	5.8	0.8
Gujarat	70	39.1	9.2	5.2	1.5	3.3	4.6	3.1	5.8	1.2	2.3	2.7	0.2
Karnataka	56	52.8	9.8	5.4	1.7	5.2	7.7	4.1	5.8	3.1	3.7	5.9	0.4
Kerala	167	48.8	9.7	5.9	2.9	5.0	6.0	3.3	5.6	2.4	3.1	4.5	0.4
Maharashtra	231	51.0	8.4	5.3	1.8	6.1	6.5	3.9	5.4	3.2	3.0	6.7	0.5
Orissa	135	54.9	9.1	7.1	2.4	6.7	6.9	3.5	5.7	3.1	4.1	5.9	0.5
Punjab	42	60.8	8.7	6.7	3.2	5.8	7.7	5.3	7.1	4.8	4.1	6.6	0.7
Tamil Nadu	118	49.4	9.0	6.9	1.9	4.7	7.4	3.0	5.0	2.7	2.4	6.4	0.0
Uttar Pradesh	102	29.3	8.2	5.1	0.7	1.2	3.5	3.0	3.5	1.9	1.0	1.1	0.1
West Bengal	180	36.1	6.6	4.9	1.2	2.9	4.4	2.6	3.7	3.0	1.8	4.0	1.2
All States	1186	46.7	8.5	5.8	1.9	4.7	6.0	3.4	5.1	2.9	2.8	5.1	0.5

Figure 9.7 Status of infrastructure for SSI in Indian states

Notes: Estimated on the basis of simple average of firms' responses to a scale: 10 – very important; 5 – important; and 0 – unimportant. For all infrastructure, the score is the aggregate of the scores of each of the infrastructural areas.

Source: Based on Table 6.6 of Morris et al. (2001: 226).

fast-growing industrial clusters especially, promoting connections with urban areas, railheads and ports and improving municipal functions would have substantive positive gains. For exporting firms, port performance actually determines the progress of their business.

While not often highlighted in the literature, facilities such as industrial estates, and their location, design, and quality of construction, have nevertheless been seen as important for small firms, who have expressed concern over industrial security and safety. A number of entrepreneurs have also suggested a review favouring relaxation of land use legislation that would facilitate convenient location with stronger connectivity. The provision of water supply and CETPs (Common effluent treatment plants?) is also listed as an area where restriction imposes significant limits on the ability of modern small firms to prosper.

Persisting sickness: tough to tackle

A large number of Indian small enterprises are often listed as 'sick', that is in debt arrears. The perpetuating and widespread sickness has resulted in the 'locking up of resources, wastage of capital assets, loss of production and increase in unemployment. In addition, the incidence of sickness leads to reduction of loanable funds of the financial institutions' (GoI, 2005: 163).

A close look at sickness prevailing in the SSI sector is essential to appreciate the impact of policy intervention. As shown in Figure 9.8, the number of sick units has risen significantly within a decade, from 221,471 in 1991 to 304,235 by 2000. This has occurred as their outstanding loan amount with the scheduled commercial banks also has grown massively. The loan amount has continued to rise over recent years, until 2004, when one notices a dramatic drop in the number of these units, clearly since 2000. In fact, by 2004, the figure for the number of sick units (138,811) was almost half of that in 2004 (304,235).

This recent fast decline in the sick units is, essentially, illusory. This has been mainly a result of a change in the definition of sick units in 2001 by a Working Group constituted by the RBI. This panel recommended 'writing off' of large amounts of bad loans as a strategy to address the ticklish problem of growing non-performing assets (NPAs) in banks. The revised definition, it was held, would enable banks to take action at an early stage for the revival of the sick units. Drawing upon the Working Group recommendations, the *Revised Guidelines for Rehabilitation of Sick SSI Units* were circulated to all scheduled commercial banks in early 2002. What is not clear, however, is if, in the process, the

Year	Sick/ weak units (number)	Outstanding amount (Rs million)
1991	221,471 (98.96)	27,920 (25.93)
1996	262,376 (99.10)	37,220 (27.07)
2000	304,235 (98.97)	46,080 (19.78)
2001	249,630 (98.69)	45,060 (17.48)
2002	177,336 (98.19)	48,190 (18.49)
2003	167,980 (98.02)	57,060 (16.39)
2004 (P)	138,811 (*)	52,850 (*)

Figure 9.8 Sickness in small-scale industries, 1991–2004

Notes: Figures in brackets are percentages of respective 'totals' of sick/ weak units from both SSI and non-SSI categories.
P – Provisional
* As data on 'total' sick/ weak units are not available, percentage shares could not be worked out.

Sources: Reserve Bank of India, Report on Trend and Progress of Banking in India and Handbook of Statistics on Indian Economy, RBI, various issues.

'delisted units are functioning better, worse, have wound up or have been taken over' (Das, 2006: 8). The concern is real, as the halving of units (between 2000 and 2004) has actually resulted in an increasing figure for outstanding amount for these units.

Beyond the maze of numbers, what are important are the major causes of sickness. Some of these are listed in Government of India (2005: 163): a) inadequacy of working capital, delay in sanction of working capital and time gap between sanction of term loan and working capital; b) poor and obsolete technology; c) problems related to availability of raw material; d) inadequate demand and other marketing problems; e) erratic power supply; f) labour problems; g) infrastructural constraints; h) poor management; i) inadequate attention to research and development; j) diversion of resources; and, interestingly, k) inability of the units to face growing competition due to liberalization and globalization.

The reasons for sickness, we would suggest, all point to basic structural constraints plaguing the small firms. That sickness persists during the reform era is in itself a commentary on the role of policy interventions. One and a half decades of reforms do not seem to have made much impact on the health of small enterprises as yet.

Policy of reservation: amiss?

An area of much debate in the SSI policy sphere has been the reservation of products for manufacture exclusively by small firms. In existence for about four decades now, the primary objectives of the reservation policy are: a) to ensure increased production of consumer goods in the small-scale sector and b) to expand employment opportunities through setting up of SSIs. Although no unequivocal view exists on the merit of this longstanding policy, scholars have raised the issue of technical inefficiency of products manufactured under reserved category (Sandesara, 1993; Balasubrahmanya, 1995; and Morris *et al.*, 2001). Time and again, studies have highlighted the impracticality and even irrelevance of the policy of reservation.

Some of the standard issues raised relate to the following: a) frequent changes (adding/deleting) in the products listed were not always justified and supposed to have been influenced by political vested interests; b) a lackadaisical approach to the policy marked its broad-basing, as surveys found that producers engaged in manufacturing 'reserved' items had no clue about the policy; c) certain items continued to be produced by the medium and large scale firms as they had been doing so prior to the specific products were reserved; and d) the quality of reserved products was often not satisfactory (Das, 2006: 10).

During recent years, however, there have been notable changes towards promoting the 'export obligation' of the reserved products. The Ministry of Commerce has been encouraging larger units to produce reserved items provided such units accept an export obligation of 50 per cent.

This would enable India to cater more efficiently to the large volume orders which are placed for reserved items such as garments, footwear, plastic items in the chemical sector etc. which cannot be met from many separate units in the SSI sector with the same standard or uniformity and quality assurance. (http://web5.laghu-udyog.com/publications/comitterep/ abid.htm#_Toc518334232)

This has led to a number of reserved items with high export potential being earmarked as 'extreme focus products', with a high export potential. Moreover, between 1998 and 2002, as part of its pursuance of a liberal trade regime, the Exim Policy systematically removed quantitative restrictions (QRs) on imports of all reserved items. These items have since been included under the Open General Licence (OGL) category (Figure 9.9). Implications of removal of QRs on small firms unprepared for WTO strictures and indiscriminate dumping have been discussed in Das (2001).

Year	Items reserved for SSI	Items on OGL	Remaining reserved items
1998–9	821	478	343
1999–2000	812	576	236
2000–1	812	643	169
2001–2	799	799	Nil

Figure 9.9 Reserved items put on OGL
Source: http://www.laghu-udyog.com/policies/preserve.htm

It needs to be mentioned, nevertheless, that a large proportion of these 'reserved' products is manufactured in units based in villages and small towns providing local job opportunities. Given the lack of business promotion measures for these products, neglect of provisioning basic physical and economic infrastructure, exposing the products to cheap imports and inviting large firms to produce to export may have defeated the basic objectives for which this rather unique policy stood.

Fostering clusters: issues for policy

Over two decades now, there has been immense interest in the role of small firms in job creation and regional economic regeneration; this has often been attributed to a certain form of industrial organization – industrial clustering. Clustering as a phenomenon has been inspired by the 'achieving' small-firm clusters in Third Italy and other industrialized nations in the Occident. Worldwide the subject has generated much interest, mainly due to the potential of clusters to be resilient, self-sustaining and technologically dynamic even in a tough competitive environment. This has prompted hectic efforts at both global and national levels to promote clusters through policy initiatives, now, with a greater focus on the developing nations. India has been one country that has not fallen behind in this race to emulate the West; although, in the hurry, little effort has gone into *understanding* the functional dynamics of Indian clusters and the socio-economic and legal contexts, which strongly impact their business (for detailed arguments, see, Das, 2005a).

Launched in late 1998 in India, UNIDO's cluster development programme has largely influenced other similar efforts at the local, state and central government levels. Driven purely by a neoliberal framework, the central purpose of cluster development initiatives in India has been to link up with a wider market, importantly, the external/ global market. All that these programmes have managed to highlight is the role of certain business development services, cluster development agents and, of late, a nonchalant approach to linking cluster development with poverty reduction.

The other mechanisms of provisioning of credit and creation of a technology development fund are essentially old instruments. In fact, there remains much to be learnt from and critiqued about India's own long and unmatched experience in formulating policies for SMEs/MSEs; how these efforts can be made more responsive and broad-based is the important issue to be reviewed.

Anyone concerned with cluster development must appreciate the diversity and complex nature of clustering in India; that first step would help one judge the relevance of a *pre-given* approach developed in a different context. Available estimates suggest the existence of about 2,400 clusters, including nearly 2,000 rural and artisan-based ones, spread across the country. Industrial clusters, including numerous artisanal/ traditional ones, present a host of local strategies for their survival and growth, conditioned by heightened competition or a calibrated (or even shrinking) market. Whereas successful European clusters have focused on technological dynamism, business networking and provision of real services and improved working environment, in India the general lack of technological dynamism, claimed to transform 'production' clusters into 'innovation' clusters, has often been rooted in the regional constraints, including that of basic infrastructure. Further, the overwhelmingly informalnature of the production sphere, the lack of collective vigilance, both from the local state and industry bodies, and the existence of surplus labour have contributed to price competition, unfair business practices and pathetic working conditions, including a high incidence of child labour.

Nevertheless, there are statistics to suggest that they contribute about 60 per cent of manufactured exports. This is a contestable claim, as cluster-level export figures are just not available and no reliable information exists on the contribution of the informal sector units that often dominate clusters, even in the so-called regulated industries.

In the Indian context, industrial clusters cannot be viewed only from a sub-sectoral market expansion point (for details, see, Das, 2005b). In fact, the *spatiality* of clustering has remained a grossly neglected dimension in the sphere of intervention strategies in India. An industrial cluster, intrinsically, is a dual entity, encompassing both the sectoral *and* spatial. The spatiality is not merely the place, that is, say, rural or urban, but has a strong reference to the level of regional development that determines the cluster's access to both social and economic infrastructure.

Poor basic infrastructure can stifle the growth and diversification of these clusters. It is essential that the technology of traditional industries be modernized to meet new demands. Policy must aim at enhancing business capabilities, especially in rural areas and small and medium towns, through finance and training. In addition to such standard interventions as improving access to credit, providing tax incentives and supporting local innovative activities, a key area concerns provision of electricity for rural enterprises; this would, in a substantive sense, 'empower' clusters in neglected regions.

Rural industries and employment

While the current initiatives emphasize the aspect of catering to and competing in the global market, the reality on the ground has more to do with the larger issues of regional underdevelopment and massive unemployment, especially in rural, semi-urban and peri-urban regions. What has happened to the rural areas? What impact has policy had in terms of developing industries in rural India?

Has the labour dimension received the highest attention through the myriad programmes of rural industrialization? As shown in Figure 9.10, over 70 per cent of units are based in rural locations and over 90 per cent of these units are Own Account Manufacturing Enterprises (OAMEs); essentially, these are self-employed, family-labour based and using no hired worker. Although it appears that the employment situation improved during the post-reform period, the rural OAMEs have suffered the most. Between 1984 and 1995, the rural OAMEs (the most predominant segment of the rural unorganized manufacturing sector) lost 3.7 million full-time jobs; between 1994 and 2001 1.4 million part-time jobswere created but a further 0.1 million full-time jobs were lost, even during that period (Sahu, 2005: 134).

Concluding observations

Beyond the hype of neolocalism, strategies for promoting small firms, whether in clusters or not, must encompass a regional development perspective, wherein addressing issues of structural infirmities, especially basic infrastructure and job creation, assume critical importance.

A mechanistic and essentially *ad hoc* approach to small-firm and/or cluster development that is oblivious to the structural factors – inadequate

Period	Rural			Urban			All unorganized		
	OAMEs	NDMEs	DMEs	OAMEs	NDMEs	DMEs	Rural	Urban	Total
Number of units									
1984–5	13.4	1.0	0.2	3.7	1.1	0.3	14.6	5.18	19.7
1994–5	9.5	0.7	0.3	2.7	0.9	0.4	10.5	4.0	14.5
2000–1	11.1	0.6	0.3	3.6	1.1	0.4	11.9	5.1	17.0
Increment/decrement									
1994–5/1984–5	−3.9	−0.4	0.1	−0.9	−0.2	0.1	−4.2	−10.7	−5.2
2000–1/1994–5	1.5	−0.04	−0.1	0.9	0.2	0.04	1.4	10.8	2.5
2000–1/1984–5	−2.4	−0.4	0.1	−0.04	−0.1	0.1	−2.7	0.1	−2.7
Composition of workers									
1984–5 Full time	18.7	2.2	1.9	4.8	2.5	2.6	22.8	9.9	32.7
1984–5 Part time	3.3	0.2	0.1	0.6	0.1	0.1	3.5	0.8	4.3
1984–5 Total	21.9	2.4	2.0	5.3	2.7	2.7	26.3	10.7	37.0
1994–5 Full time	15.0	1.7	2.4	4.5	2.9	3.1	19.0	10.6	29.6
1994–5 Part time	2.9	0.1	0.1	0.30	0.1	0.1	3.1	0.5	3.6
1994–5 Total	17.8	1.8	2.5	4.8	3.1	3.2	22.1	11.1	33.2
2000–1 Full time	14.7	1.8	2.8	4.9	3.5	3.5	19.4	11.8	31.3
2000–1 Part time	4.3	0.2	0.1	1.0	0.2	0.1	4.6	1.3	5.8
2000–1 Total	19.2	1.9	2.9	5.9	3.6	3.6	24.0	13.1	37.1
Increment/decrement									
1994–5/1984–5 Full time	−3.7	−0.5	0.4	−0.3	0.4	0.5	−3.8	0.7	−3.1
1994–5/1984–5 Part time	−0.4	−0.1	0.01	−0.3	−0.02	0.0	−0.4	−0.3	−0.7
1994–5/1984–5 Total	−4.1	−0.5	0.5	−0.5	0.4	0.5	−4.1	0.4	−3.8
2000–1/1994–5 Full time	−0.1	0.1	0.4	0.4	0.5	0.3	0.4	1.3	1.7
2000–1/1994–5 Part time	1.4	0.04	0.1	0.7	0.04	0.01	1.5	0.7	2.2
2000–1/1994–5 Total	1.3	0.1	0.5	1.1	0.6	0.4	1.9	2.0	3.9
2000–1/1984–5 Full time	−3.8	−0.4	0.9	0.2	1.0	0.8	−3.4	2.0	−1.4
2000–1/1984–5 Part time	1.0	−0.01	0.1	0.4	0.02	0.01	1.1	0.5	1.6
2000–1/1984–5 Total	−2.8	−0.4	0.9	0.6	1.0	0.9	−2.3	2.4	0.1

Figure 9.10 Units and workers in unorganized manufacturing, 1984–2001 (in million)

Notes: OAMEs – Own account manufacturing enterprises (no hired workers).

NDMEs – Non-directory manufacturing enterprises (hiring 1–5 workers).

DMEs – Directory manufacturing enterprises (hiring 6–10 workers).

Source: Sahu (2005: 148).

infrastructure being a key constraint – facing the Indian economy would most certainly falter in generating employment opportunities and also in creating a competitive and sustainable regional industrial base, especially in the rural areas and small and medium towns.

In an era of economic reforms and globalization, the plethora of novel strategies to bring SMEs/MSEs centre stage with an avid goal of building up a world-class reputation is not uncommon; however, it is worrying that some age-old concerns that adversely affect the otherwise vibrant and broad-based small enterprises have been pushed to the margins. What must not be forgotten is that even today, as over two decades ago, the unorganized sector accounts for more than 99 per cent of all manufacturing enterprises and over 86 per cent of employment; the overwhelming presence of this sector is seen in both rural and urban areas.

While certain types of industries, especially the much-mentioned high-tech and knowledge-based industries such as pharmaceuticals, IT or IT-enabled service-related, clothing and a very marginal section of handicrafts might be privileged due to the process of reforms and globalization, it would be potentially dangerous to continue to neglect the vast number of ailing small and tiny enterprises in underdeveloped regions. A close look at the performance of the small enterprises, as attempted here, clearly points to many policy lapses of the past that continue to this day. A reorientation in policy approach that ensures credit availability, provision of basic physical and economic infrastructure and enhances labour productivity is what is needed now. That the tiniest units, in the unorganized sector particularly, in rural areas have been worst hit in terms of decline in factor productivity, dwindling demand, poor-quality products and insecure nature of jobs calls for a different set of strategies to promote enterprises in India. For a start, any policy effort to promote the enormous small-scale industrial sector in India needs to critically examine its own relationship with various interventions and also to address various longstanding constraints if future initiatives are to be inclusive and relevant in the local context. There lies the challenge to policy.

References

Balasubrahmanya, M.H. (1995), 'Reservation Policy for Small-Scale Industry: Has It Delivered the Goods?', *Economic and Political Weekly*, 30(21).

Das, K. (2006), 'Micro and Small Enterprises during Reforms: Policy and Concerns', Working Paper No. 171, Gujarat Institute of Development Research, Ahmedabad.

Das, K. (2005a), 'Industrial Clustering in India: Local Dynamics and the Global Debate', in K. Das (ed.), *Indian Industrial Clusters*, Ashgate, Aldershot.

Das, K. (2005b), 'Can Firm Clusters Foster Non-farm Jobs? Policy Issues for Rural India', in R. Nayyar and A.N. Sharma (eds), *Rural Transformation in India: The Role of Non-farm Sector*, Institute for Human Development, New Delhi.

Das, K. (2003), 'Income and Employment in Informal Manufacturing: A Case Study', in R. Jhabvala, R. Sudarshan and J. Unni (eds), *Informal Economy Centrestage: New Structures of Employment*, Sage, New Delhi.

Das, K. (2001), 'Small Enterprises and Trade Policy', in Alternative Survey Group, *Alternative Economic Survey 2000–2001, Second Generation Reforms: Delusion of Development*, Rainbow, New Delhi.

Government of India (GoI) (2005), *Handbook of Industrial Policy and Statistics 2003–2005*, Ministry of Industry, New Delhi.

Government of India (2004), *Final Results: Third All India Census of Small Scale Industries 2001–2002*, Development Commissioner (SSI), Ministry of Small Scale Industries, New Delhi.

Government of India (2001), *Report of the Study Group on Development of Small Scale Enterprises* (Chairman: S.P. Gupta), Planning Commission, New Delhi.

Government of India (1997), *Report of the Expert Committee on Small Enterprises* (Chairman: Abid Hussain), National Council of Applied Economic Research, New Delhi.

Government of India (1994), *Handbook of Industrial Statistics 1993*, Ministry of Industry, New Delhi.

Goyal, S.K., K.S.C. Rao, M.R. Murthy and K.V.K. Ranganathan (2004), *Review of Existing Policies and Legislations of MSEs in India and Uttar Pradesh*, Institute for Studies in Industrial Development, New Delhi (Mimeo).

Mohan, R. (2003), 'Small-Scale Industry Policy in India: A Critical Evaluation', in A.O. Krueger (ed.), *Economic Policy Reforms and the Indian Economy*, Oxford University Press, New Delhi.

Morris, S. and R. Basant (2005), 'Role of Small Scale Industries in the Age of Liberalisation', at http://www.adb.org/Documents/Reports/Consultant/TAR-IND-4066/Trade/morris-basant.pdf

Morris, S., R. Basant, K. Das, K. Ramachandran and A. Koshy (2001), *The Growth and Transformation of Small Firms in India*, Oxford University Press, New Delhi.

Reserve Bank of India, *Report on Trend and Progress of Banking in India*, Reserve Bank of India, Mumbai. (Various issues).

Reserve Bank of India, *Handbook of Statistics on Indian Economy*, Reserve Bank of India, Mumbai. (Various issues).

Sahu, P.P. (2005), 'Employment in Small and Tiny Enterprises in India: Post-Reform Trends and Dimensions', in S.K. Thorat, J.P. Pradhan and V. Abraham (eds), *Industrialization, Economic Reforms and Regional Development*, Shipra, New Delhi.

Sandesara, J.C. (1993), 'Modern Small Industry, 1972 and 1987–88: Aspects of Growth and Structural Change', *Economic and Political Weekly*, 28(6).

Small Industries Development Bank of India (SIDBI) (2000), *SIDBI Report on Small Scale Industries Sector 2000*, SIDBI, Lucknow. <?xml:namespace prefix = st1 ns = "urn:schemas-microsoft-com:office:smarttags"/>

Conclusion: Between a Rock and a Hard Place: The Harsh Reality of SMEs in the New Global Economy

Jerry Haar and Jörg Meyer-Stamer

The new economy poses daunting challenges for SMEs. Whether based in developing or industrialized nations, these enterprises must rapidly adapt to survive, let alone thrive, as globalization – including trade, investment and financial liberalization – bring relentless pressure upon them.

Traditionally, protectionist policies, including those aimed at fostering infant industries in a cloistered environment, insulated SMEs from free market competitiveness threats. However, WTO regulations, free-trade agreements and – more importantly – domestic policy reforms aiming at deregulation, liberalization and decentralization have altered the playing field in favour of the market rather than government fiat. As trade and investment barriers have been lowered, large firms from both developing and industrialized nations are entering foreign markets and (if present already) expanding their business operations. In a great many instances the suppliers (both large firms and SMEs) follow their customers into foreign markets. The electronics/IT cluster in Guadalajara, Mexico, is a typical example where contract manufacturers have co-located to serve their multinational customers. The consolidation of global value chains creates relentless pressure on SME suppliers in particular. In addition to the costs and learning-curve challenges associated with following prime customers into foreign markets, compliance with rigorous international standards (ISO certification, HACCP and EUREPGAP standards, etc.) is for many an impediment to entry into value chains. This is especially true for SMEs from developing nations.

Nevertheless, smallness can also be a virtue, and the new global economy also presents notable opportunities for SMEs. To begin with, technology is the great 'leveler' – accessible and generally affordable to firms of all sizes across a wide spectrum of industries. Consequently, technology-based systems for market intelligence, production, information systems, control, financial management and customer relations help level the playing field for SMEs vis-à-vis large firms. In addition, smallness allows SMEs greater flexibility, latitude and speed in responding to both threats and opportunities. For *entrepreneurial* SMEs from developing or industrialized nations, a globalizing business environment and the continuation of market liberalizing and reform measures aimed at their domestic business environment will provide more benefits than costs. For example, while tariff reductions may pose threats to domestic SMEs whose pricing, quality levels, and production volumes cannot match those of foreign exporters, domestic SMEs can benefit from foreign investors who wish to source from local suppliers as well as from large domestic firms that need to outsource to local SME suppliers to compete in both domestic and global markets.

As amply illustrated in the international literature on small firms and business development, government programmes to support small business, whether for domestic-oriented or international-oriented, are widespread and varied and take place largely at the federal level, although state/province and local governments have taken a more active role in assisting SMEs. Whether based on the 'business development services' (BDS) model or some other framework for supporting SMEs, one inalienable truth is that off-the-shelf approaches to assisting SMEs are not the most effective. As we asserted in the introductory chapter: 'Lumping all sorts of micro, small and medium-sized businesses together and addressing them under headers such as "promoting competitiveness" does not give justice to the diverse realities that underlie the SME sector and the diversified policy responses that are needed.'

Recognizably, government-supported SME promotion programmes, particularly those that are export-oriented, can produce results (for example, U.S., Italy, Colombia, Chile and South Korea). In addition to basic information to help SMEs, critically important knowledge on market intelligence/ opportunities, import regulations and procedures, market entry strategies and access to financing go far in assisting SMEs. How to maximize the benefits from attending international trade fairs is another area where government SME promotion programmes can yield results. Nevertheless, SME promotion programmes do not focus on the bottlenecks of business competitiveness that SMEs – and large firms for that matter – face. Namely, *government* itself. If a Eurobarometer survey found that 50 per cent of SMEs are constrained by governmental dysfunctionality, one can easily imagine how SMEs respond to similar surveys in developing nations. The World

Bank's annual *Doing Business* report catalogues the tax, regulatory and administrative barriers that businesses face.[1] One can readily surmise that without the immediate removal of these barriers and implementation of business-friendly reforms, governmental SME promotion programmes will come up short in achieving their intended results.

Both the generic issues addressed and country case studies analysed in the volume provide insights and conclusions about the present state and outlook for small firms and the challenges they face in global markets.

The principal lessons learned and summaries of chapter findings are as follows:

Local economic development matters greatly. Peter Knorringa and Jörg Meyer-Stamer find that local economic development (LED) can make some difference by turning a given location into a place where it is easier to do business. For SMEs especially, LED can streamline government procedures, improve infrastructure and address skills bottlenecks. But these are tactical, not strategic, issues. The writers note: 'Latecomer countries need strategic interventions to build competitive sectors with a strong growth effect. This implies defining a new role for local government. Strategic upgrading efforts are not an alternative to LED and to localized efforts to integrate producers into value chains. All these approaches have important roles to play, and ultimately they complement each other.'

Financial access remains a major challenge for SMEs, especially in developing countries. New programmes to increase financing must consider the institutional and business environment in which the SMEs operate and respond accordingly. The Mexican experience, analysed by Deborah Riner, has demonstrated that there is an impressive capacity for creating financing channels when the standard ones are not active. In economies with well developed, smoothly functioning legal systems and a financial infrastructure, banks are a logical choice for SMEs. In countries in which a large share of economic activity takes place outside the formal economy, banks are not a likely financing source for companies operating informally, and neither are banks the place to which SMEs should turn if the banking system makes its money by financing the government.

SMEs can facilitate but not solve the development problems of low income sectors. Integrating Low Income Sectors (LIS) into the global economy and contributing to economic and social development is not an easy task and cannot be done by just one type of organization. The centrality of LIS markets for some SMEs, their flexibility and capacity to innovate, their proximity to LIS and the ability to become 'socially embedded' with them, coupled with their low-opportunity costs, make SMEs a very apt tool in the integration of LIS to economically vibrant value chains. Patricia Marquez and Ezequiel Reficco draw upon the case of a joint venture Peruvian company to illustrate that SMEs can provide some but not all of the innovative solutions that are needed. In other words, there is a role to be played in market initiatives targeting LIS by SMEs, but they are not a panacea.

Innovativeness and entrepreneurial orientation are necessary for success. There are few small firms today that are not affected by the globalization of competition. Renko and Haar look at the innovativeness and entrepreneurial orientation of international new ventures and global start-ups. They claim that both innovativeness and entrepreneurial orientation are necessary characteristics for small firms to succeed in global competition. They discuss four key characteristics that are typical in these types of firms: people, markets, technology and networks. The authors also suggest that the more successful international small ventures operate in growth markets, and adopt a proactive approach to marketing and sales. It is these types of firms that act as the engine of the growth of economies and expand technologies into new frontiers.

The lack of policy clarity and SMEs' lack of knowledge of government assistance programmes remain impediments. Jaime Alonzo Gomez's analysis of competitive business practices in Mexico hold true for other countries and regions, as well. He finds the main challenges to SMEs are lack of clear industrial policy, labour policy and fiscal policy, insufficient financial support and/or non-competitive interest rates, scale factors related to size of domestic markets in the presence of competition from USA, Asia and European companies, lack of quality and prices on public services and infrastructure. While there are programmes established and run by the government, a majority of SMEs do not even know of them. Therefore, additional efforts need to be undertaken for SMEs to use these support packages, incentives and special funds. On the positive side, new emerging trends based on innovation and value-added processes and production are increasingly growing through new alliances. Through current and expected reforms, the use of assistance programmes, the new emerging trends involving government agencies, universities and business schools, and in particular with the new younger generations, economic growth will allow Mexico to enjoy the same levels of SME productivity and GDP/capita that the other OECD countries have.

As clusters are becoming more diversified, medium size firms are increasing their competitiveness. Carabelli, Hirsch and Rabellotti note that recent data on exports and sales have been interpreted as the first positive signs of a recovery in Italy's manufacturing sector, but it is not clear whether these improvements are due to a more favourable international economic environment or whether something is really changing in the Italian manufacturing system. Industrial districts that rely primarily on small enterprise are under duress, since they battle to keep the pace of innovation going and to internationalize their operations in the manner that is required by the realities of globalized markets. The main drivers of structural change in industrial districts are medium sized companies. Medium sized companies are the most dynamic and economic actors currently in the Italian manufacturing industry. The growing importance of medium sized firms can be interpreted as a positive sign of increasing potential in the Italian manufacturing system to undertake new efforts in terms of more innovation and internationalization.

SMES are increasingly globalizing but it is unclear that government assistance agencies are effective. Cardoza and Fornes predict the next wave of internationalization to come from SMEs. The growth of clusters in different regions in Spain demonstrates the interest of local governments and SMEs to promote and adopt new industrial arrangements to benefit from economies of scale, improve their access to information, uptake new technologies, and diffuse better practices and innovations. However, Spanish SMEs are currently facing barriers to compete successfully in international markets. There is also question about the efficiency in identifying the results achieved by government agencies focused on SMEs. In order to overcome this problem, a system to evaluate the results of the policies implemented in the area of SMEs should be put in place through use of a scorecard produced by those agencies working with SMEs.

Public support of SMEs is not only helpful but often indispensable, especially in poorer economies In unravelling informal entrepreneurship, Kate Meagher establishes that the three examples in her case study all show a good level of dynamism and all three have developed as informal clusters without assistance from the state. Although they are globalized enterprise networks, Nigerian clusters did not foster novel forms of economic governance but rather un-governance. All suffer from collective inefficiencies that are not due to cultural inadequacies but rather from hostile economic and political environment. Also, Meagher emphasizes that global linkages cannot substitute for state intervention and that the African small enterprise clusters suffer from the absence of an effective, never mind supportive, state.

Addressing infrastructure needs is a pre-requisite for success. Strategies for promoting small firms must encompass a regional development perspective that addresses and assigns importance to the key issues of basic infrastructure and job creation. Keshab Das examines the Indian small business sector and concludes that a different set of strategies is needed to promote enterprises in India. He asserts: 'A reorientation in policy approach that ensures credit availability, provision of basic physical and economic infrastructure and enhances labour productivity is the need of the hour.'

SMEs face many competitive challenges in the new economy, and they will continue to do so. There are increasing opportunities before them as well, in both their home markets and foreign ones. Although SMEs are not a panacea for economic growth, increased incomes and poverty reduction, they nonetheless play a vital role in developing and industrialized economies and in fostering private enterprise. There is not one single high-income economy that does not have a competitive SME sector. If these entities are to flourish in the twenty-first century economy, they must design, plan and implement firm-level changes to enhance and sustain their competitiveness; and the enabling institutions and structures at the federal, state/provincial and local levels must institute major changes to strip away administrative and regulatory barriers and work closely with private enterprise organizations to unleash entrepreneurship, innovation and the spirit of enterprise among SMEs.

Note

1. This includes starting a business, dealing with licenses, employing workers, registering property, obtaining credit, paying taxes, protecting investors, trading across borders, enforcing contracts, and closing a business.

Index

(Please note that page numbers in *italics* indicate end notes.)

ABN Amro, 70
Accel Partners, 98
ACCION International, 70
Acer, 87
Aje Group, 63, 66–67
Alexa.com, 95
Altenburg, Tillman, 8
Añaños, Jorge and Javier, 63
Arrospides, Hernan, *83*

Banco de México, 58, *60*
Basque Country, 184–186
  ACICAE and, 185
  GAIA and, 184–185
  HEGAN and, 185–186
Beck, Thorsten, 3, *58*
Bell, J., 94
Benchmark Capital, 98
Best, Michael H., 4
Bolivia, 19, 69, *83*
Bollinger. L., 89
Brazil
  ACCION and, 70
  A/Rs and, 49
  competitive business practices and, 110, 119, 120
  international growth and, 87, 139, 173, 183
  macroeconomic shock, 6
  production and, 31
Brennan, M.J., *59*
Brinckerhorff, Joris, 73
business development services (BDS), 8–9, 29–30, 237

Cadenas Productivas, 51, *60*, 114
Caniels, Marjolein, 8
Carabelli, Anna, xiii, 14, 131–157, 240
Cardoza, Guillermo, xiii, 15, 166–189, 240
Carree, Martin, 4
casas de bolsa, 55–56

Cavusgil, S.T., 88
Chandler, G.N., xi, 4, 20
changarros, *60*
Chase, Robin, 91
Chile, 19, *82*, 119, 124, 188, 237
China, *16*, 35
  China-plus region, 32, 34
  competitive business practices and, 119, 120
  entrepreneurship and, 194, 206, 207
  FDI and, 12
  globalization and, 31
  Italy and, 132, 139, 141, 149
  Spain and, 171, 173, 182–183, 188
CIPI, 113, 116, 117, 127
clusters
  diversification and, 240
  India and, 227
  innovation and, 87
  Italy and, 132, 151, 153, 156, *159*
  LED and, 20–22, 26–27, 32, 34
  Mexico and, 236
  Nigeria and, 15, 192–212
  policy and, 230–232
  SMEs and, 108, 110, 112, 114, 117, 124, 127, 240–241
  Spain and, 15, 167, 176–177, 181–182, 184–189, *190*
  value chain promotion and, 13
Committee of Donor Agencies for Small Enterprise Development, 26
competitiveness, social policy compared to, 23–24
CONACYT, 117, 120–121, 128
Costa Rica, 73–75, 78–79, 81, *84*
  assessing economic and social value, 74–75
  overcoming barriers faced by LIS suppliers, 74
  See also CRES (Costa Rica Entomological Supplies)

Covin, J.G., 88
credit bureaus, 53–55
CRES (Costa Rica Entomological Supplies), 73–75
Creswin, 121–122
Cruzsalud, 71, 72–73, 78, 81, *83*
Cuba, 72, *83*

D'Andrea, G., 66
Danielson, Antje, 91
Das, Keshab, xiii, 15, 214–234, 241
Daveri, F., 131
Demirgüc-Kunt, Asli, 21, *58*
Digg.com, 95
downsizing, 3, 26
Dryclean USA, 86

Eisenhardt, K.M., 94
entrepreneurship, 86–98
  international growth and, 87–89
  markets and, 90–92
  networks and, 94–96
  people and, 89–90
  technology and, 92–94
Ese'eja de Infierno, 75–78, 81, *84*
Esser, Klaus, 34
Estonia, 93

FACOE, 114
FAMPYME, 114
FIDECAP, 114
Fierro, Edgar, 110
Finland, 14, 92–94
Flores, Juliano, *83*
FOAFI, 114
Fobaproa, 57, *60*
FON, 98
foreign direct investment (FDI)
  China and, 12
  globalization and, 11–12
  Italy and, 133, 143, 146–147, 148, 157, *159*
  Spain and, 188–189
Fornes, Gastón, xiv, 15, 240
Fortune at the Bottom of the Pyramid (Prahalad), 64
Fox, Vicente, 39, 45
Fox News, 95
FPC (Peru-Canada Fund), 75–76, *83*

Fraunhofer Society, 95–96
free trade agreements (FTAs), 44, 52, 112, 117, 124, 128, *129*, 183
  See also NAFTA

G3 group, 124
Germany, xvi, 3, 10, 24
  economy, 176
  innovation and entrepreneurship, 93, 95
  Isofoton and, 187
  Italy and, 149
  NTR and, 188
  SMEs and, 133–135
  Spain and, 167
Global Entrepreneurship Monitor, The, 5
global value chains (GVCs), 20, 33, 34
Goldsmith, Stephen, 22
Gómez, Jaime Alonso, xiv, 14, 105–129, 239
Gonzalez, Rosa Amelia, *83*
Google Inc., 95
GTZ, 7

Haar, Jerry, xiv, 3–16, 86–98, 239
Hausmann, Ricardo, 25
Heller Financial, 50
Hennes+Mauritz, 11
Herrera, Patricia, *84*
Herrero, G., 66
Hirsch, Giovanna, xiv–xv, 14, 131–157, 240
Hope, K., 89

Ickis, Catalina, *83*
Ickis, John, *83*
Ikea, 11
ILO, 7, 8
India, xv, 14, 210, 214–234, 241
  clustering, 230–232
  credit and, 223–225
  EU and, 132, 171
  exports, 220–223
  globalization and, 139, 214–215
  infrastructure, 225–227
  innovation and entrepreneurship, 87
  Mexico and, 119

India – *continued*
  reservation policy, 229–230
  rural industries and employment, 232
  shifting definitional ceilings, 215–218
  size and contribution of small firms, 218–220
  SMEs and, 15
  software development, 12
  Spain and, 173
  SSI sickness, 227–228
Indianapolis, 22
Italy, 131–157
  China and, 132, 139, 141, 149
  Germany and, 149
  manufacturing system, 133–142
    industrial districts, 136–138
    international pattern of specialization, 138–142
    predominance of SMEs, 133–135
    specialization pattern, 135–136
  new challenges for SMEs, 142–156
    globalization, 145–150
    IDs and innovation capacity, 150–154
    medium firms and business groups in IDs, 154–156
    new specializations of districts, 143–145
  OECD and, 135, 141

Japan, xiii, 18, 112, 149, 179, 188, 194
Jona-Lasinio, C., 131

Kaplinsky, R., 32–33
Knight, G.A., 88
Knorringa, Peter, xv, 13, 18–35, 31, 238
Kola Real, 63

Last.fm, 98
Lee, Y.W., 59
Levine, Ross, 21
local economic development (LED), 20–28
  downside of, 21–22
  focus on an enabling environment and, 24–25
  locational policy paradox and, 25–27
  planning instead of, 22–23
  SMEs and, 27–28
  social policy and, 23–24
  upside of, 20–21
Lonely Planet, 83
López Portillo, Jose, 55
low-income sectors (LIS), 63–81
  as customers, 71–73
    assessing social and economic value, 73
    market access and social inclusion, 71–73
  ecotourism and, 75–78
    assessing economic and social value, 76–78
    market access and social inclusion, 75–76
  SMEs and, 65–70, 78–81
    flexibility and innovation, 67–70
    lower opportunity costs, 70
    mission centrality, 65–66
    proximity, 66–67
  as suppliers, 73–75
    assessing economic and social value, 74–75
    barriers faced by, 74

Maksimovic, V., 59
Malaysia, 19
Mangrove Capital partners, 98
maquiladoras, 119
Márquez, Patricia, xv, 13, 63–81, 239
McDougall, P.P., 86, 94, 97
McKinsey Global Institute, 7
Meagher, Kate, xv, 15, 192–212, 240
Metro, 11
Mexico, 38–58, 59, 60, 105–129, 238, 239
  banks and, 39–51
    alternatives to financing with, 43–51
    bankruptcies, 52–53
    concentration, 40–41
    factoring, 50–51
    ownership, 41–43
    retained earnings, 44–45
    trade credit, 45–50

Mexico – *continued*
  biotechnology and, 122–123
  Cadenas Productivas, 51, 60, 114
  classification of companies in, 106–108
  clusters and, 210, 236
  CNBV, 52
  competition with Asia, x
  CONACYT, 117, 120–121, 128
  economic growth, 117–118
  FACOE, 114
  FAMPYME, 114
  FIDECAP, 114
  FOAFI, 114
  Fobaproa, 57, *60*
  globalization and, 139
  Kola Real and, 63
  maquiladoras, 119
  MCC and, 183
  Nafinsa, 126–127
  Natura Bissé, 187
  OECD and, 117–118, 129, 239
  Plan Nacional de Desarrollo Empresarial, 115
  policy recommendations, 51–56
    credit bureau information, 53–55
    informal economy, 55
    non-bank financing entities, 55–56
    regulation and "rule of law", 52–53
  pymes and, 43, 51, *60*
  SMEs and, 14, 105–129
    business orientation and, 108–111
    current status and challenges, 111–113
    emerging/innovative business practices, 118–119
    financing, 13
    FTA and, 124
    government policy for, 113–118
    innovation-driven positioning and differentiation, 120
    remittances, 124–127
    technology-based new venture creation, 120–124
    trends in, 119
  Sofoles, 44, 56

Wal-Mart and, 50, *60*
Meyer-Stamer, Jörg, xvi, 3–16, 18–35, 153, 238
Miller, D., 88
Minuteman Press, 86
Morris, M., 32
MyQSL, 98

Nadvi, K., 192
Nafin, 43, 51, *60*
NAFTA, 44, 52, 112, 117, 183
Negrín, Jose Luis, *60*
NGOs (nongovernmental organizations), 65, 81, *82*
Nigeria, 192–212
  challenges of liberalization and globalization, 206–211
    coping with disabling environment, 206–209
    role of the state, 210–211
  economic dynamism and social disorder, 194
  enterprise clusters and informal institutions, 195–200
    Aba shoe and garment clusters, 196–198
    Ilorin weaving cluster, 195–196
    reconstructing social networks, 198–200
  network governance, 200–206
    capacity for innovation, 205–206
    production networks, 201–202
    role of associations, 204–205
    supply and marketing networks, 203–204
Nike, 12, 153
Norway, 94

Obrador, Andres Manuel López, *60*
Ofoto, 98
Organization of Economic Cooperation and Development (OECD)
  high-tech industries and, *158*
  Italy and, 135, 141
  Mexico and, 117–118, 129, 239
  SMEs and, 3, 9–10, 38
  Spain and, 173, 175, 176, 178, 179, *190*

outsourcing, 3, 5, 50, 65, 133, 143–144, 147–149, 157, *159*, 237
Oviatt, B.M., 86, 94, 97

Pageflakes, 98
Peru, 63, 66, 69, 75, 77, 239
 Ese'eja de Infierno, 75–78, 81, *84*
 Posada Amazonas, 75, 77–78, 81, *83*, *84*
 Rainforest Expeditions (RFE), 75–77, 79, 81, *83*, *84*
Pesha, Juan, *83*
Petersen, Mitchell A., *59*
Piore, Michael J., 4
planning, LED compared to, 22–23
Porter, Michael, 24, 185
Posada Amazonas, 75, 77–78, 81, *83*, *84*
Prahalad, C.K., 64, 78, *82*, 119
proximity, LIS markets and, 66–67
pymes, 43, 51, *60*

Rabellotti, Roberta, xvi, 14, 131–157, 147, 153, 240
Rainforest Expeditions (RFE), 75–77, 79, 81, *83*, *84*
Rajan, Raghuram G., *59*
Ramos, Gabriela, 118
Readman, J., 32
Reficco, Ezequiel, xvi, 13, 63–81, 239
remittances, 119, 124–127, 128
Renko, Maija, xvi–xvii, 14, 86–98, 239
Riner, Deborah, xvii, 13, 38–58, 238
Rodrik, Dani, 25
Romijn, Henny, 8

Sabel, Charles F., 4
Salinas, Carlos, 43
Sarbanes-Oxley Act, *60*
Schmitz, Hubert, 31, 192
Schoonhoven, C.B., 94
Shane, S., 94
Skype, 98
Slevin, D.P., 88
small and medium-sized enterprises. *See* SMEs
SMEs
 entrepreneurship and, 3–4
 evolution and promotion, 9–11
 financing of, 38–42, 45, 47, 50–53, 55, 56–58, *59*
 Germany and, 133–135
 globalization and, 11–13
 importance of, 3–13
 India and, 15, 215, 231, 234
 Italy and, 131–157
 large corporations and, 6–7
 LED and, 18, 20–21, 23–24, 26–28, 34
 limits to growth, 5–6
 local economic development (LED) and, 27–28
 low-income sectors (LIS) and, 63, 65–70, 65–71, 74, 78–81
 Mexico and, 105–129
 MSMED Act and, 216
 new global economy and, 236–241
 OECD and, 3, 9–10, 38
 promotion in developing countries, 7–9
 Spain and, 166–189
 United Kingdom (UK) and, 39
Smith, Janet K., *59*
Social Enterprise Knowledge Network (SEKN), xv, *82*, *83*
social policy, competitiveness compared to, 23–24
Sofoles, 44, 56
Soto, Hernando de, 4
South Africa, xv, 19, 24
South Korea, x, 19, 112, 237
Spain
 Basque Country and, 184–186
  ACICAE and, 185
  GAIA and, 184–185
  HEGAN and, 185–186
 China and, 171, 173, 182–183, 188
 economic outlook, 188–189
 economy, 167–169
 Germany and, 167
 OECD and, 173, 175, 176, 178, 179, *190*
 regional industrialization and clusters formation, 181–184
  Castellon ceramic cluster, 182
  Consortium for the Commercial Promotion of Catalonia (COPCA), 183

Spain – *continued*
  Mondragon Cooperative
    Corporation (MCC), 182–183
  Wood Industry's Research and
    Development Association
    (AIDIMA), 183–184
  SMEs and, 166–188
    CDTI, 177–178
    DGPYME, 177
    financing and risk capital for,
      178–179
    fiscal incentives for RD + I, 179–180
    globalization and, 171–176
    overview of, 169–170
    policies and incentives for,
      176–188
    success stories, 186–188
    universities and business schools,
      180–181
Springfield Centre, 8
Stamm, Andreas, 8
Starbucks, 86, 90
Stel, André van, 4
Stowe, J.D., *59*
Sweden, 93–94, 149
systemic competitiveness, 34

Taiwan, x, 19, 87, 112
Tesco, 11
Thurik, Roy, 4
total factor productivity (TFP), 131

UN Habitat, 22
United Kingdom (UK)
  economic dynamism, 194
  internationalization and, 93
  Italy and, 134–135
  Nigeria and, 204
  SMEs and, 39
  Spain and, 167, 170, 173, 180, 186,
    188
USAID, 7, 22
Utterback, J.M., 89

value added tax, 55, *60*
value chain promotion, 28–34
  downside of, 30–34
  types, 30
  upside of, 28–30
variability, LIS markets and, 67
Velasco, Andrés, 25
Venezuela, xv, 63, *83*, 124
  healthcare and, 71–73
Viana, Horacio, *83*
Vietnam, xv, 31, 56

Wal-Mart, 50, *60*
Wendy's, 86
World Bank, 3, 5, 7, 22

Zechner, J., *59*
Zimbabwe, 56
Zipcar, 91